James Wayland Joyce

Acts of the Church, 1531-1885

The Church of England her Own Reformer, as Testified by the Records...

James Wayland Joyce

Acts of the Church, 1531-1885
The Church of England her Own Reformer, as Testified by the Records...

ISBN/EAN: 9783337000769

Printed in Europe, USA, Canada, Australia, Japan

Cover: Foto ©Lupo / pixelio.de

More available books at **www.hansebooks.com**

ACTS OF THE CHURCH
1531—1885

LIST OF SUBSCRIBERS.

St. Alban's, The Right Rev. the Lord Bishop of (two copies).
Ainger, The Rev. Canon G. H., D.D., Rothbury.
Ainslie, The Rev. Prebendary, M.A., Langport, Taunton.
Allen, The Very Rev. James, M.A., Dean of St. David's.
Argles, The Rev. Canon Marsham, M.A., Barnack, Stamford.
Ashley, The Rev. G. E., M.A., Stretton, Hereford.
Atkinson, Ven. P. R., M.A., Archdeacon of Surrey.

Bangor, The Right Rev. the Lord Bishop of.
Baldwyn-Childe, The Rev. Prebendary, M.A., Kyre Park, Tenbury.
Balston, The Ven. Archdeacon, D.D., Bakewell.
Pardsley, The Ven. John W., M.A., Archdeacon of Warrington.
Bevan, The Rev. Canon W. L., M.A., Hay.
Bickersteth, The Very Rev. E., D.D., Dean of Lichfield.
Blenkinsopp, The Rev. E. C. L., M.A., Springthorpe, Gainsborough.
Blew, The Rev. W. J., M.A., Warwick Street, Pall Mall.
Bonnor, The Very Rev. R. B. M., M.A., Dean of St. Asaph.
Boyd, The Ven. Archdeacon, M.A., Arncliffe, Skipton.
Boyle, The Very Rev. G. D., M.A., Dean of Salisbury.
Bree, The Rev. Canon William, M.A., Allesley, Coventry.
Brewster, The Rev. Waldegrave, B.A., Middleton-in-Chirbury, Salop.
Bright, The Rev. Canon William, D.D., Ch. Ch., Oxford.
Bromfield, The Rev. George H. W., M.A., St. Mary-the-Less, Lambeth.

LIST OF SUBSCRIBERS.

Buchanan, The Ven. T. B., M.A., Archdeacon of Wilts.
Burgon, The Very Rev. J. W., B.D., Dean of Chichester.
Burrough, The Rev. Chas., M.A., Eaton Bishop, Hereford.
Burrows, The Rev. Canon H. W., B.D., Rochester.
Burton, The Rev. J. R., Woodfield, Kidderminster.
Butler, The Very Rev. W. John, D.D., Dean of Lincoln.

Canterbury, The Most Rev. the Lord Archbishop of.
Chichester, The Right Rev. the Lord Bishop of.
Carr, The Rev. Canon, LL.D., St. Helen's, Lancashire.
Chatfield, The Rev. A. W., M.A., Much Marcle.
Church, The Very Rev. R. W., D.C.L., Dean of St. Paul's.
Clay, The Rev. G. Hollis, M.A., Aston Rectory, Ludlow.
Clayton, The Rev. Prebendary, M.A., Rectory, Ludlow.
Clements, The Rev. J., M.A., Sub-Dean of Lincoln.
Cobbold, The Rev. Prebendary R. H., M.A., Rectory, Ross.
Cook, The Rev. Canon F. C., M.A., Exeter (two copies).
Cooke, The Rev. Canon William, M.A., F.S.A., Clifton Place, Sussex Gardens.
Cowie, The Very Rev. B. M., D.D., Dean of Exeter.
Cranbrook, Lord, 17, Grosvenor Crescent.
Crawley, The Ven. Archdeacon Wm., M.A., Bryngwyn.
Cundill, The Rev. Canon, D.D., St. Margaret's, Durham.

Darwall, The Rev. L., M.A., Criggion, Shrewsbury.
Davis, The Rev. Edmund, M.A., Longtown, Abergavenny.
Day, The Rev. T. T., LL.D., Benthall, Broseley.
Douglas, The Rev. Canon W. W., M.A., Salwarpe.

Ely, The Right Rev. the Lord Bishop of (two copies).
Echalaz, The Rev. T. S., Surbiton (two copies).
Edmondes, The Ven. Charles Gresford, M.A., Archdeacon of St. David's.
Ellis, The Rev. P. C., M.A., Llanfairfechan.
Ellis, W. H. M., Esq., M.A., Monkstown, Dublin.
Ellison, The Rev. Canon H., M.A., Melsonby, Darlington.
English Church Union (ten copies).
Evans, The Rev. Canon T. S., M.A., Durham.

Ffoulkes, The Ven. Henry Powell, B.D., Archdeacon of Montgomery.

LIST OF SUBSCRIBERS.

Fletcher, The Rev. E. S. B., M.A., Tenbury.
Fuller, The Rev. Morris, M.A., Ryburgh, Fakenham.

Gibbs, Henry Hucks, Esq., St. Dunstan's, Regent's Park.
Gifford, The Ven. E. H., D.D., Archdeacon of London.
Gladstone, Rev. Stephen E., M.A., Hawarden.
Green, The Rev. C. E. Maddison, M.A., Lyonshall, Hereford.
Gregory, The Rev. Canon Robert, M.A., St. Paul's.
Gresley, Charles, Esq., The Close, Lichfield (for Cathedral Library).
Grey, The Hon. and Rev. Francis R., M.A., Morpeth (two copies).
Gurney, The Rev. Augustus W., M.A., Little Hereford, Tenbury.

Hereford, The Right Rev. the Lord Bishop of.
Halifax, The Right Hon. Viscount, 88, Eaton Square.
Hampton, The Rev. J., M.A., Tenbury.
Hannah, The Ven. John, D.C.L., Archdeacon of Lewes.
Hawkins, The Rev. Canon Edw., M.A., Newport, Mon.
Hayman, The Rev. Canon, D.D., Aldingham, Ulverston.
Hayward, The Ven. Henry R., M.A., Archdeacon of Cirencester.
Hessey, The Ven. J. A., D.C.L., D.D., Archdeacon of Middlesex.
Hewitt, The Rev. T. Swinton, M.A., Leysters, Tenbury.
Hill, The Rev. W. Wilmot, M.A., Ocle Pychard, Hereford.
Hobhouse, The Ven. Reginald, M.A., Archdeacon of Bodmin.
Hockin, The Rev. Canon, M.A., Phillack, Hayle.
Hodson, The Rev. Prebendary Geo. H., M.A., Enfield.
Holbech, The Ven. C. W., M.A., Archdeacon of Coventry.
Holland, The Rev. Canon F. J., M.A., Canterbury.
Holloway, The Rev. E. J., M.A., Clehonger, Hereford.
Hopkins, The Rev. Canon, B.D., Littleport, Ely.
Hornby, The Rev. Canon Edw. J., M.A., Bury, Lanc.
Howell, The Rev. Canon Hinds, M.A., Drayton, Norwich.
Hubbard, Right Hon. J. G., M.P., 24, Princes' Gate (two copies).

LIST OF SUBSCRIBERS.

Iles, The Ven. J. H., M.A., Archdeacon of Stafford.
Ince, The Rev. Canon William, D.D., Ch. Ch., Oxford.

Jellicorse, The Rev. W., B.A., Clunbury, Aston-on-Clun.
Joyce, The Rev. F. Hayward, M.A., Rural Dean, Harrow (three copies).
Joyce, The Rev. James B., B.A., Coreley, Tenbury.

Kelly, The Rev. Canon James Davenport, M.A., Old Trafford, Manchester.
Kempe, The Rev. Prebendary J. C., M.A., Merton, Beaford.
Knight, The Rev. Charles R., M.A., Tythegston Court, Bridgend.
Knowles, The Rev. Canon, M.A., St. Bees (three copies).

Lichfield, The Right Rev. the Lord Bishop of.
Liverpool, The Right Rev. the Lord Bishop of.
Lake, The Very Rev. W. C., D.D., Dean of Durham.
Lambert, The Rev. W. H., M.A., Stoke Edith, Hereford.
Lewis, The Very Rev. Evan, M.A., Dean of Bangor.
Lewis, The Rev. Canon D., M.A., St. David's.
Lightfoot, The Ven. R. P., M.A., Archdeacon of Oakham.
Lloyd, The Rev. Prebendary T. B., M.A., Shrewsbury.
Lonsdale, The Rev. Canon J. G., M.A., Lichfield.
Lowe, The Rev. Canon E. C., D.D., Uttoxeter.
Lowndes, The Rev. E. Spencer, M.A., Little Comberton, Pershore.

McDougall, The Right Rev. Bishop, Archdeacon of the Isle of Wight.
McLaughlin, Colonel, The Crescent, Plymouth.
Maddison, The Ven. G., M.A., Archdeacon of Ludlow.
Male, The Rev. Arthur S., M.A., More, Bishopscastle.
Maltby, The Ven. Brough, M.A., Archdeacon of Nottingham.
Marshall, The Rev. H. B. Derham, M.A., Norton Canon, Weobley.
Mather, The Rev. Canon F. V., M.A., Clifton.
Medd, The Rev. Canon P. G., M.A., North Cerney, Cirencester.
Mence, The Rev. Richard, M.A., Bockleton, Tenbury.
Miller, The Rev. Edward, M.A., Bucknell, Bicester.
Mills, The Rev. H. Holroyd, B.A., Burford, Tenbury.

Mitchell, The Rev. Jos., M.A., Alberbury, Shrewsbury.
More, R. Jasper, Esq., M.P., Linley, Bishopscastle.
Mount-Edgcumbe, The Right Hon. the Earl of, Devonport.
Musgrave, The Rev. Canon, M.A., Hereford.

Newcastle, The Right Rev. the Lord Bishop of.
Nevill, The Ven. H. R., M.A., Archdeacon of Norfolk.
North, The Rev. Henry, B.A., Wentnor, Bishopscastle.

Oldham, The Rev. A. L., M.A., Bridgnorth.
Ouseley, The Rev. Sir F. A. G., Bart., LL.D., Tenbury.
Owen, The Rev. Canon R. D., M.A., Boroughbridge.

Palin, The Rev. E., B.D., Linton, Ross.
Palmer, The Rev. C. S., M.A., Eardisley, Hereford.
Palmer, The Ven. Edwin, D.D., Archdeacon of Oxford.
Palmes, The Rev. J., M.A., Escrick Rectory, York.
Pardoe, Mrs., The Priory, Cheltenham.
Parker, James, & Co., Oxford.
Perry, The Rev. Canon Thomas W., Ardleigh.
Phelps, The Rev. Thomas P., B.A., Ridley, Wrotham.
Phillips, The Rev. W. D., B.A., Crunwere, Byelley.
Phillott, The Rev. Prebendary H. W., M.A., Staunton-on-Wye.
Pott, The Ven. Alfred, B.D., Archdeacon of Berks.
Powis, Earl of, Powis Castle, Welshpool.
Pownall, The Ven. A., M.A., Archdeacon of Leicester.
Puckle, The Rev. Canon John, M.A., Dover (two copies).

Randall, The Ven. J. L., M.A., Archdeacon of Buckingham.
Rawlinson, The Rev. Canon, M.A., Precincts, Canterbury.
Rayson, The Rev. W., M.A., Lindridge, Tenbury.

Salisbury, The Right Rev. the Lord Bishop of.
Southwell, The Right Rev. the Lord Bishop of.
Salmon, The Rev. Prebendary E. A., M.A., Martock.
Salt, Thomas, Esq., Weeping Cross, Stafford.
Savory, The Rev. Canon E., M.A., Binfield, Bracknell.
Scott, The Very Rev. Robert, D.D., Dean of Rochester.
Sheringham, The Ven. John William, M.A., Archdeacon of Gloucester.
Sidebotham, The Rev. J. S., M.A., Kingsland, Hereford.
Smart, The Ven. Edward, M.A., Archdeacon and Canon Resident of St. Asaph.

Smith, The Rev. T. Ayscough, M.A., Tenbury.
Smith, The Very Rev. R. Payne, D.D., Dean of Canterbury.
Stamer, The Ven. Sir Lovelace T., M.A., Archdeacon of Stoke.
Stanhope, The Right Hon. the Earl, 20, Grosvenor Place.
Stooke-Vaughan, The Rev. F. S., M.A., Wellington Heath, Ledbury.
Sumner, The Ven. Geo. H., M.A., Archdeacon of Winchester.
Swayne, The Rev. Canon R. G., M.A., Salisbury.

Talbot, John G., Esq., M.P., Falconhurst, Edenbridge.
Talbot, The Rev. E. S., M.A., Warden of Keble College, Oxford.
Thicknesse, The Ven. F. H., D.D., Archdeacon of Peterborough.
Thomas, The Rev. Canon D. R., M.A., F.S.A., Meifod, Welshpool.
Twells, The Rev. Canon H., M.A., Waltham, Melton Mowbray.

Vere-Bayne, The Rev. Thomas, M.A., Ch. Ch., Oxford.

Walker, The Ven. J. Russell, M.A., Archdeacon of Chichester.
Walters, The Rev. Thomas, D.D., Llansamlet, Glamorgan.
Ware, The Rev. Canon Henry, M.A., Kirkby Lonsdale.
Warner, The Rev. Prebendary C., M.A., Clun (two copies).
Weyman, H. T., Esq., Ludlow, Salop.
Whitefoord, The Rev. B., M.A., Principal of Theological College, Salisbury.
Whitefoord, The Rev. Caleb, M.A., Whitton, Tenbury.
Wight, The Rev. Alfred, M.A., Ludlow.
Williams, The Rev. Canon D., B.D., Llanelly.
Williams, The Rev. J. D., B.A., Farlow, Cleobury Mortimer.
Wilton, The Rev. Charles Turner, M.A., Foy, Ross.
Winton, The Ven. Henry de, M.A., Archdeacon of Brecon (two copies).
Wintour, The Rev. G., Ironbridge.

Acts of the Church
1531—1885

THE CHURCH OF ENGLAND
HER OWN REFORMER

AS TESTIFIED BY THE RECORDS OF HER CONVOCATIONS

WITH APPENDIX CONTAINING LEGAL INSTRUMENTS ANCIENT
AND MODERN CONNECTED WITH THOSE ASSEMBLIES
AND COMMENTS THEREON

BY

JAMES WAYLAND JOYCE M.A.

LATE STUDENT OF CH. CH. RECTOR OF BURFORD [THIRD PORTION] CO. SALOP PREBENDARY OF HEREFORD
AND FORMERLY A PROCTOR IN CONVOCATION FOR THE CLERGY OF THAT DIOCESE

Author of *"England's Sacred Synods"* *"Ecclesia Vindicata"* *"The Sword and the Keys"*
"The Latin Sermon" preached before the Provincial Synod of Canterbury Feb. 2, 1866
in St. Paul's Cathedral London &c. &c. &c.

London
J. WHITAKER 12 WARWICK LANE PATERNOSTER ROW

1886

Oxford
PRINTED BY HORACE HART, PRINTER TO THE UNIVERSITY.

TO THE RIGHT REVEREND

JAMES LORD BISHOP OF HEREFORD,

WITH A DEEP SENSE OF HIS FATHERLY CARE

FOR THAT ANCIENT DIOCESE, AND AN

ABIDING REMEMBRANCE OF MUCH PERSONAL KINDNESS

RECEIVED AT HIS HANDS,

THIS VOLUME IS RESPECTFULLY DEDICATED

BY ONE WHO WHEN IN HEALTH WAS HIS

EXAMINING CHAPLAIN

THE AUTHOR.

BURFORD RECTORY, TENBURY,
October, 1885.

CONTENTS.

INTRODUCTION.

PART I.

THE ORIGIN, CONSTITUTION, AND PROPER FUNCTIONS OF THE CHURCH'S REPRESENTATIVE ASSEMBLIES.

I.

PAGE

ANCIENT TERRITORIAL DIVISIONS FOR CHURCH GOVERNMENT 5

II.

DIOCESAN SYNODS.

Constitution of a Diocesan Synod	6
Ancient Form of holding an English Diocesan Synod . .	7
Benedictions and Duration	8
Borromeo's Address to his Eleventh Diocesan Synod . .	8
Objects of a Diocesan Synod	10
English Diocesan Synods	10
Diocesan Conferences	11
Bishop C. Wordsworth's Letter	12

III.

PROVINCIAL SYNODS.

Primitive Provincial Organization	12
Ancient Form of holding a Provincial Synod	14
British Provincial Organization	16
Mission of Augustine	17
Independence of British Church on Rome	18
Locality of Interview between British Bishops and Augustine	19
Metropolitan Jurisdiction finally confined to Canterbury and York	22

	PAGE
Error touching the Origin of Convocations	23
Constitution of the Provincial Synods or Convocations of Canterbury and York	29
Proper Functions and Duties of Provincial Synods or Convocations	31
Prescription of the Canon of Scripture	31
Promulgation of Symbols of Faith	31
Condemnation of False Doctrine	32
Enactment of Canons	32
Authorization of Liturgical Formularies	33
Statutable Jurisdiction of Convocations over "Kings' Causes"	35

IV.

SYNODS OF THE EXARCHATE.

English Synods of the Exarchate	37
Authority to Convene a Synod of the English Exarchate	38
Subordination of York to Canterbury	39
Resistance of York to Jurisdiction of Canterbury	41
Present State of the Case	45
Forms of Proceeding in a Synod of the English Exarchate	47
Various Methods for Securing the Authority of a Synod of the English Exarchate	48

PART II.

THE INAUGURATION, PROMOTION, AND COMPLETION OF THE REFORMATION IN DOCTRINE, RITUAL, AND DISCIPLINE BY THE CONVOCATIONS OF THE CHURCH OF ENGLAND. 1531—1562-3.

I.

THE REFORMATION INAUGURATED BY CONVOCATIONAL ACTION.

King Henry VIII., his Courtiers and Favourites, unpromising as Reformers	50
Royal Title—"So far as the Law of Christ permits, even Supreme Head"	53

CONTENTS. vii

	PAGE
Continual Resistance of the Church of England to the Encroachments of Rome	55
Convocation invokes aid of the Civil power for repressing Roman exactions	68
"Submission of the Clergy"	70
Parliamentary Legislation	71
Convocational Jurisdiction in Causes "touching the King"	72
Queen Catharine of Arragon's Divorce	73
Queen Anne Boleyn's Divorce	74
Nullification of the Marriage of Anne of Cleves	75
Odd Announcements in the Courts of Common Pleas and Exchequer	76
Formal Rejection of the Papal Supremacy by the Convocations of Canterbury and York the chief corner-stone of the Reformation	77
Rejection of Papal Supremacy warranted by the Jus Cyprium	79

II.

THE REFORMATION PROMOTED BY CONVOCATIONAL ACTION.

Ecclesiastical corroborated by Civil Authority in early times	82
Summary of Synodical Acts promoting and completing the Reformation	85
Comparison of the Dates of Synodical Acts and Civil Ratifications	86

III.

THE REFORMATION COMPLETED BY CONVOCATIONAL ACTION.

Seven events which completed the Reformation	103
(1) Restoration of the Cup to the Laity	104
(2) Compilation of the first English "Communion Office"	105
(3) Abrogation of the Cœlibacy of the Clergy	110
(4) First English "Book of Common Prayer"	113
(5) Second English "Book of Common Prayer"	122
(6) Forty-two "Articles of Religion"	127
(7) Thirty-nine "Articles of Religion"	132
York Assent to the Thirty-nine "Articles of Religion"	134

PART III.

SURVEY OF SOME MEMORABLE ACTS OF THE CONVOCATIONS FROM THE DATE OF THE COMPLETION OF THE REFORMATION TO THE SUSPENSION OF SYNODICAL ACTION. 1562-3—1718.

I.

GENERAL REVIEW OF SYNODICAL ACTS AFTER THE COMPLETION OF THE REFORMATION.

	PAGE
Review of some Synodical Events in Queen Elizabeth's reign	136
Ecclesiastical Essays in Parliament	138
Summary of Synodical Acts from the Accession of King James I. to the Suspension of Synodical Action	141

II.

ENACTMENT OF THE 141 CANONS OF 1603-4.

Review of some Synodical Events in King James I.'s reign	143
Canons of 1603-4	145
Constructions of Law to the Disadvantage of the Church by the Learned Profession	146
York Synod enacts the 141 Canons	149
An odd Announcement in the House of Lords	151
Legal Obligation of Canons	152
Contradictory Decisions of the learned Judges	152

III.

ENACTMENT OF THE SEVENTEEN CANONS OF 1640.

An evil Augury	158
Three more evil Omens	159
Sessions at Oxford	161
Ecclesiastical Aspirations in the House of Commons	162
Assembly of the Canterbury Synod	165
Subsidies voted to the Crown	167
Controversy as to whether Convocations are necessarily Dissolved by a Dissolution of Parliament	167
Riots in London	169
A Pontifical for the Church of England contemplated	171
Enactment of the Seventeen Canons of 1640	171
The " &c." Oath	172
York Convocation enacts the Seventeen Canons and votes Subsidies	175

CONTENTS. ix

	PAGE
Parliamentary Flowers of Rhetoric	177
Parliamentary Precautions against Subsidies being voted by the Convocations	181
Monetary Transactions between Parliament and the Scotch for the Purchase of the King's Person	184
Nemesis of Fate overtakes this House of Commons	187

IV.

COMPILATION AND SYNODICAL AUTHORIZATION OF THE PRESENT "BOOK OF COMMON PRAYER."

Authority of the present "Book of Common Prayer"	189
Republican tender Mercies	190
Schemes for Restoring a "Book of Common Prayer"	192
First Essay at Liturgical Revision, Savoy Conference	193
Second Essay at Liturgical Revision, by Parliament	194
Parliamentary Prayer Book	195
Capacity of "Members of the Long Robe" for Theological engagements. A Digression	198
A Lord Chancellor	203
Other Lord Chancellors	205
Justices of the Court of Queen's Bench	206
Justices of the Court of Common Pleas	207
Barons of the Court of Exchequer	208
Judicial Committee of Privy Council	209
Dr. Peter Heylin's Letter	217
Canterbury Convocation, May, 1661	220
York Convocation, May, 1661	221
The Canterbury and York Convocations, Nov. 1661	222
York Convocation, Nov. 1661	222
Appointment of Proxies by York to appear in the Canterbury Synod	223
Canterbury Convocation, Nov. 1661	227
Methods adopted in compiling the present "Book of Common Prayer"	227
Instruments of Ratification, Canterbury and York	231
Civil Sanction accorded to the "Book of Common Prayer"	240

V.

REJECTION OF THE "COMPREHENSION" LITURGY.

A "Comprehension" Liturgy proposed	243
Canterbury Convocation meets, Nov. 1689	245
Court Intrigues to secure a pliant Prolocutor	246
Vain attempt to impose the title "Protestant" on the Church of England	248
"Comprehension" Liturgy abandoned	249
Synodical Action suspended	250

b

CONTENTS.

VI.

SUSPENSION OF SYNODICAL ACTION IN THE CHURCH OF ENGLAND.

	PAGE
Suspension of Synodical Action not justly chargeable on the Civil Power	253
Real Causes of the Suspension of Synodical Action	255
Lack of Harmony between Bishops and Presbyters	256
General Lethargy in the Church	259
Unreasonable Exaltation of Personal Authority	260

PART IV.

SURVEY OF THE HISTORY OF THE CONVOCATIONS AFTER THE REVIVAL OF SYNODICAL ACTION.
1852—1885.

I.

REVIVAL OF SYNODICAL ACTION.

Measures taken for the Revival of Synodical Action	264
Resistance of the two Metropolitans	265

II.

SUMMARY OF THE MOST MEMORABLE ACTS OF THE CONVOCATIONS SINCE THE REVIVAL OF SYNODICAL ACTION.

Summary of Acts	266

III.

CONVOCATIONS CONVENED 1852, DISSOLVED 1857.

Canterbury	268
York	269

IV.

CONVOCATIONS CONVENED 1857, DISSOLVED 1859.

Canterbury	271
York	271

V.

CONVOCATIONS CONVENED 1859, DISSOLVED 1865.

Canterbury	272

CONTENTS.

xi

	PAGE
Harvest Thanksgiving Service	274
Synodical Condemnation of Dr. Colenso's Volume	274
Synodical Condemnation of "Essays and Reviews"	276
Clerical Lawbreaking	278
New Canons enacted	279
Excursion of the "Crown Office"	280
York	281
Accession of Dr. C. T. Longley to the See of Canterbury	281

VI.
CONVOCATIONS CONVENED 1866, DISSOLVED 1868.

Canterbury	282
Dr. Colenso not in Communion with the Church of England	283
York	284

VII.
CONVOCATIONS CONVENED 1868, DISSOLVED 1874.

Canterbury	284
Summary of Acts	286
Decrees on Vatican Council	286
Canterbury Decrees on Vatican Council transmitted to other Churches	289
Revision of "the Authorized Translation" of Holy Scripture	290
The Revised Lectionary	290
A Lord Chancellor's exposition of Law	291
Shortened Services authorized	293
Act of Supererogation in Crown Office	294
Revision of Rubrics	296
York	298
New Lectionary	298
Rubrical Revision	298
Revised New Testament	299

VIII.
CONVOCATIONS CONVENED 1874, DISSOLVED 1880.

Canterbury	303
Manuals of Private Prayer	305
Summary of Debates	306
Public Worship Regulation Act	307
A Crown Office Excursion	310
Revision of Rubrics	310
Important Revision of a Rubric in the Communion Service	312
Measure suggested for obtaining Ecclesiastical Legislation in Parliament	313
York	314

xii   CONTENTS.

IX.
CONVOCATIONS CONVENED 1880.

	PAGE
Canterbury	315
Accession of Dr. Benson to the See of Canterbury . . .	316
Amazing Announcement made by the Judicial Committee of Privy Council	317
Ecclesiastical Courts Commissioners' Report	318
Manuals of Private Prayer	318
York	320
Summary of Proceedings	320

PART V.

PRESENT REGULATIONS AND METHODS OF PROCEEDING IN THE CONVOCATIONS OF CANTERBURY AND YORK, THE PROVINCIAL SYNODS OF THE CHURCH OF ENGLAND.

I.
CONVOCATIONS IN CONNEXION WITH THE CROWN.

Royal Writ for Convention	321
Letter of Business	322
Licence to enact Canons	322
Writ of Prorogation	322
Writ of Dissolution	323

II.
PROCEEDINGS BEFORE ASSEMBLY.

A peculiarity of English Provincial Synods	324
Privilege of Freedom from Arrest pertaining to Members of the Convocations	325

III.
PROCEEDINGS ON ASSEMBLY 329

IV.
PROCEEDINGS IN SESSION.

Separation into two Houses	332
Proceedings in Upper House	333
Proceedings in Lower House	333
CONCLUSION	336

APPENDIX.

A.

ROYAL WRIT FOR CONVENTION.

	PAGE
Writ of King Edward III.	342
Writ of King Henry VIII.	342
Writ of Queen Victoria	343

B.

METROPOLITAN'S MANDATE AND OTHER INSTRUMENTS FOR CONVENTION.

Mandate of Archbishop Kilwarby	343
Mandate of Archbishop Howley	344
Citation issued by the Provincial Dean of the Canterbury Province	346
Citation directed by a Diocesan Bishop to a Dean and Chapter	347
Citation directed by a Diocesan Bishop to Archdeacons	347
Citation directed by an Archdeacon to the Clergy	348
Citation sent by the Archdeacon's Apparitor to each Beneficed Clergyman	349
Return of the Provincial Dean of the Canterbury Province	350
Return of a Suffragan Bishop	351
Return of a Dean and Chapter	352
Return of an Archdeacon certifying the Election of Proctors	352
Comments on a proposed Method for Reforming a Convocation	354

C.

ROYAL LETTER OF BUSINESS.

Letter of Business of King Edward I.	355
Letter of Business of King William III.	356
Letter of Business of Queen Victoria	356
Comments on a Letter of Business	357

D.

ROYAL ASSENT AND LICENCE TO ENACT, PROMULGE, AND EXECUTE CANONS.

Explanation of the Instrument	359

xiv   CONTENTS.

	PAGE
Synodical Request to Queen Elizabeth for Royal Assent and Licence	360
Royal Assent and Licence of Queen Elizabeth's Reign	361
Unstatutable Excursions of Judges and Legal Officers	363
Precautions taken in this generation against those Aggressions	365
Synodical Request to Queen Victoria for a Royal Licence	366
Royal Licence of Queen Victoria's Reign	367
Comments on the Excursions of Legal Officials in this generation	370

E.

ROYAL WRIT AND METROPOLITAN'S MANDATE FOR PROROGATION.

Writ of Queen Victoria for Prorogation	373
Mandate of Metropolitan for Prorogation	374

F.

ROYAL WRIT FOR DISSOLUTION.

Writ of King Henry VIII. for Dissolution	375
Writ of Queen Victoria for Dissolution	375
Dissolution by Commission from Metropolitan	376

G.

"SUBMISSION OF THE CLERGY," AND EXTRACTS FROM "CLERGY SUBMISSION ACT."

Form of Submission	376
Comments thereon	377
Clergy Submission Act	378
Comments thereon	379

H.

ROYAL WRIT SUMMONING CLERGY TO PARLIAMENT.

Writ of King Edward I. for Summoning Parliament	380
Writ of Queen Victoria for Summoning Parliament	381
Comments on the above	382

ALPHABETICAL LIST OF
SOME WORKS AND AUTHORITIES
REFERRED TO IN THE FOLLOWING PAGES.

ATTERBURY.—Rights, Powers, and Privileges of an English Convocation.
AYLIFFE.—Parergon.
BACON.—Works.
BARROW.—Works.
BELLARMINE.—De Conciliis.
BENNETT.—Essay on XXXIX. Articles.
BILSON.—Perpetual Government of Christ's Church.
BINGHAM.—Antiquities of the Christian Church.
BLACKSTONE.—Commentaries.
BRETT.—Account of Church Government.
BRODRICK AND FREMANTLE.—Ecclesiastical Judgments of the Privy Council.
BULLEY.—Variations of Liturgies.
BURN.—Ecclesiastical Law.
BURNET.—History of the Reformation.
CANONS.—Canons of Œcumenical Councils.
CARDWELL.—Synodalia—Two Liturgies.
CHRONICLE.—Chronicle of Convocation.
CHRYSOSTOM.—De Sacerdotio—Homilies.
CHURTON.—Early English Church.
CLARENDON.—History of the Rebellion.
COKE.—Institutes—Reports.
COLENSO.—Pentateuch and Book of Joshua.
COLLIER.—Ecclesiastical History.
COMYN—Digest.
Concilia Magnæ Britanniæ, *passim.*
CYPRIAN.—Epistles.
D'EWES.—Journal.
ECCLESIASTICAL COURTS' COMMISSIONERS.—Report.
ECHARD.—History of England.
Essays and Reviews.
EUSEBIUS.—Ecclesiastical History.
FIELD.—Of the Church.
FOXE.—Acts and Monuments.
FROUDE.—History of England.
FULLER.—Church History.
GIBSON.—Codex—Synodus Anglicana.
GLADSTONE.—Church in its Relations to the State.
GODWIN.—De Præsulibus.
HANSARD.—Parliamentary Debates.
HEYLIN.—Ecclesia Vindicata—Examen—Help to English History—History of the Reformation—Life of Laud—Miscellaneous Tracts.
History of Later Puritans.
HODY.—History of English Councils.
HOOK.—Church Dictionary.
HOOKER.—Ecclesiastical Polity.

HUME.—History of England.
HUSSEY.—Church from the Beginning until Now.
IGNATIUS.—Epistles.
INETT.—Origines Anglicanæ.
IRENÆUS.—Adv. Hæreses.
JOHNSON.—Canons—Vade Mecum.
KEELING.—Liturgies.
KENNETT.—Ecclesiastical Synods—Complete History of England.
KING.—Primitive Church.
LABBE and COSSART.—Councils.
LANDON.—Manual of Councils.
LATHBURY.—History of Convocation.
LYNDWOOD.—Provinciale.
MATTHEW PARIS.
MOSHEIM.—Ecclesiastical History.
MSS. AND COLLECTIONS.—In British Museum (inspected).—In State Paper Office, now Rolls (inspected).—Private Collections since revival of Convocation.
NALSON.—Collections.
NEANDER, ed. BRUNS.—Canons.
NICHOLLS.—History of Common Prayer.
ORIGEN.—Contra Celsum.
PALGRAVE.—History of Anglo-Saxons.
Pamphlets, Collection of 18th Century.
PARRY.—Parliaments and Councils of England.
PEARCE.—Law of Convocation.
POTTER.—Church Government.
Reformatio Legum.
RITUAL COMMISSIONERS.—Report.
ROSE.—Biographical Dictionary.
SHARON TURNER.—History of Anglo-Saxons.
SOUTHEY.—Book of the Church.
SOZOMEN.—Ecclesiastical History.
SPARROW.—Collections—Rationale.
SPELMAN.—Concilia—Glossary.
Statutes at Large, *passim*.
STILLINGFLEET.—Irenicon—Origines Britannicæ.
STRYPE.—Life of Cranmer—Life of Parker—Life of Whitgift—Memorials—Annals.
Student's Hume.
TAYLOR, JEREMY.—Works.
THEODORET.
THIERRY.—Norman Conquest.
TREVOR.—The Two Convocations.
VATICAN COUNCIL.—Decrees.
WAKE.—Authority of Christian Princes—Present State.
WALKER.—Sufferings of the Clergy.
WARNER.—Ecclesiastical History.
WHEATLEY.—On the Common Prayer.
WILKINS.—Epistolaris Dissertatio.
WOODESON.—Lectures.
WORDSWORTH.—Greek Testament—Theophilus Anglicanus.

THE CHURCH OF ENGLAND HER OWN REFORMER.

INTRODUCTION.

THE history of the Church of England, more especially as it relates to times since the Reformation, has been for the most part represented exclusively from two points of view: the first a secular one, discovering legal enactments and civil ordinances; the second a personal one, unveiling biographical details of individual character. In the first case Statutes of the Realm, Proclamations, Royal Injunctions and Advertisements, and the political Acts of Sovereigns and Statesmen have been the principal objects submitted to notice. In the second case the virtues or vices, the wisdom or folly of those who have taken prominent parts in public affairs have been specially commended to the reader's attention.

But there is a third point of view from which the history of the Church of England, and especially the later part of it, may be more reasonably regarded. And that is the one which opens out the prospect of the records of her own Acts and of her own Decrees as ratified in her own proper representative assemblies. This is a position of outlook which, if discovered, has certainly not been usually adopted, but, on the other hand, almost wholly deserted.

Acts of Parliament and State papers have been most sedulously studied and reproduced by historians; the records of the Church's Synods have either not been seen or have been cast aside as uninstructive. The pages of Atterbury, Brett, Hody, Kennett, King, Potter, and such like writers; the folios of Lyndwood, Spelman, and Wake; and the elephantine tomes of the "Concilia Magnæ Britanniæ," have been sadly disregarded. But if it should appear, as most surely hereafter will be shewn, that the Acts and Decrees of the Church herself in her representative assemblies have in such restorations or reformations as have been accomplished in her structure preceded the civil sanctions accorded to them, then it is a perversion of facts to regard the latter as having originated those re-edifications. Such a method of regarding history is to assume the condition of a spectator who views objects through a lens which inverts his vision, or who looks at a picture turned upside down.

Nor is the study of the biographical records of individuals more likely to exhibit a true view of the Church's history. No doubt minute details of the lives of men who have been prominent in Church or State among their contemporaries are highly interesting, and instructive too; the lives of good men holding up patterns for imitation, of bad ones examples for warning. But however interesting and instructive such a method of treating the historic past may be, even if personal characters are faithfully represented [which, by the way, is not always the case, for all historians have not wholly emancipated themselves from servile hero-worship on the one hand, and unreasoning prejudice on the other], yet neither the virtues nor the vices of individuals can reasonably be adopted as reliable factors in working out the problem of the Church's history. For true results we should rather employ the Acts of the Church herself.

The main object, then, of the following pages will be directed to shew—that the Reformation of the Church of England was inaugurated, promoted, and completed by her own Acts in her proper representative assemblies, i.e. the Provincial Synods of Canterbury and York, or, as we now term them, Convocations—that in spiritual matters Synodical Decrees have preceded civil ratifications—and that the whole structure, as existing at the present hour, has been built up from the foundations mainly by her own hands.

For distinctness sake the subject will be treated under five heads :—

    I. The Origin, Constitution, and proper Functions of the Church's representative assemblies.

    II. The Inauguration, Promotion, and Completion of the Reformation in doctrine, ritual, and discipline by the Convocations of the Church of England.

    III. A Survey of some of their memorable Acts the date of the completion of the Reformation to the suspension of Synodical action in England.

    IV. A Survey of their history after the revival of Synodical action.

    V. A Digest of the present regulations and methods of proceeding in the Convocations of Canterbury and York, the Provincial Synods of the Church of England.

PART I.

THE ORIGIN, CONSTITUTION, AND PROPER FUNCTIONS OF THE CHURCH'S REPRESENTATIVE ASSEMBLIES.

I.

ANCIENT TERRITORIAL DIVISIONS FOR CHURCH GOVERNMENT.

THE ancient territorial divisions of the Church for her government were—(1) Diocese (παροικία). (2) Province (ἐπαρχία), a combination of Dioceses. (3) Exarchate or Patriarchate (διοίκησις), a combination of Provinces. Each division had its proper Synod, the Bishop presiding in that of the Diocese, the Metropolitan in that of the Province, the Patriarch, Exarch, or Archbishop [for these words appear to have been used synonymously] in that of the Exarchate or Patriarchate.

Of Œcumenical Councils, to which of course the Decrees of all other Synods are subordinate, it is not needful here to write, as not being immediately connected with our present subject.

II.

DIOCESAN SYNODS.

EARLY HISTORY.

Constitution of a Diocesan Synod.

In the Diocesan Synod the Bishop sat in conjunction with all the Presbyters of his Diocese. The earliest example we have is that mentioned in Acts xxi. 18—25, when St. James, Bishop of Jerusalem, convened his Presbyters, and when the previous decisions of the Apostolic Council of Jerusalem recorded in Acts xv. were recited and enforced. In the Primitive Church, though the Bishop had a ruling superiority, yet he was wont in all weighty matters to consult his Presbyters, as we know from the example of St. Cyprian. So it is that St. Ignatius describes Presbyters as "the Counsellors "and Assistants of Bishops;" St. Chrysostom as "the Court and Sanhedrim of the Presbyters;" St. Cyprian as the "Venerable Bench of the "Clergy;" St. Jerome as "the Church's Senate;" and Origen as "the Council of the Church." As the Bishop was thus wont to sit in council with his Presbyters, special places of honour were assigned to them in those early assemblies. The Bishop sat in the centre on a high throne, and the Presbyters on either side of him on somewhat lower thrones. And so universal was this custom, that the expressions "they of the "second throne," or the "Corona Presbyterii," were synonymous with Presbyters. Conformably with these facts, there is a vision recorded by Gregory Nazianzen, poetically describing his Diocesan Synod, of which he writes thus: "I thought "I saw myself sitting on the high throne, and "the Presbyters, that is, the guides of the Chris- "tian flock, sitting on both sides by me on lower "thrones, and the Deacons standing by them."

<small>EARLY HISTORY.</small>

The ancient forms of holding Diocesan Synods in England may thus shortly be described. The Priests of the Diocese went in solemn procession to the church appointed by the Bishop, taking their seats there according to the priority of their respective ordinations. Deacons were then admitted, and laity who might have grievances to present, or who might be allowed to witness the proceedings. When the Bishop had entered and taken his seat, a Deacon exclaimed, "Pray ye;" and after prayer again exclaimed, "Rise up." Then the Bishop, turning towards the East, said in subdued tones, "The Lord be with you." The appointed Deacon then read a portion of Scripture taken from the Gospels, after which the hymn "Veni Creator" was sung. The Bishop addressed an allocution to the assembly, after which a sermon was preached. The Clergy then submitted their complaints to the Bishop, and the laity afterwards submitted theirs. In the next place the Bishop laid before the Synod Constitutions for Diocesan Government. A Pastoral exhortation of the Bishop addressed to the Clergy followed, and

<small>Ancient form of holding an English Diocesan Synod.</small>

EARLY HISTORY.

Benedictions.

then a solemn benediction. The benedictions were somewhat different at the close of each day's session; that for the first day will give a sufficient idea of their spirit and language, and was as follows: "May He Who gathereth toge-
" ther the dispersed of Israel defend you, both
" here and everywhere. Amen. And not only
" may He defend you, but make you faithful
" shepherds of His sheep. So that with Christ
" the Chief Shepherd ye may rejoice in heaven,
" being of the pasture of His flock. Amen.
" Which may He deign to grant."

Duration.

Three days were assigned for the duration of these early Diocesan Synods in England, though the assembly separated earlier if all necessary business had been sooner completed.

Borromeo's address.

The eloquent and touching address of Borromeo to his Eleventh Diocesan Synod testifies to the high estimation in which he held such an assembly, and pourtrays the blessing which might be expected to ensue if it were convened and attended under the influences of like sentiments with those which inspired the language of that holy man.

"What do we here, my brethren?" were his words. "We hold a Synod; and what does that
" name import? A congregation and an assembly
" of whom? Even of the most excellent and emi-
" nent in the Holy Church, such as her Bishops
" and the members who are joined to Him by

"bonds of the closest union. But what are those
"who are here assembled? Alas! my speech
"faileth me. Who is able to conceive, much
"less to express, their dignity and their excellent
"greatness! These are they which season all the
"people; the fathers of the multitude; the guides
"and teachers of those souls; spiritual physi-
"cians; in this militant condition generals of
"Christ their Lord; suns to lighten and salt to
"give savour to these people. Christ indeed is
"the Sun of Righteousness. Yet of these it may
"be said, 'Ye are the light of the world.' Clouds
"they are, charged and laden with the showers
"of God's grace, which they shed over all. They
"are the consecrated property of Christ their
"Lord. Great indeed is such a congregation as
"this! But these are not all; for [what is
"greater still] with them is present the very
"Son of God Himself, the Lord Jesus, unless
"we put a bar against Him. For if, where two
"or three are gathered together in His Name
"He hath promised to be in the midst of them,
"how much rather will He be present in the
"midst, not of two, but of nine hundred and
"more, when we are not an indiscriminate mass,
"but His own Priests, united in one to His
"Name; when our affection is one, and we
"shall breathe but as one; when we shall
"direct all our aims and intentions to seek His
"grace and His Holy Spirit! If two of you

Early History.

"[they are our Lord's own words] shall agree
"on earth touching anything which they shall
"ask the Father in My Name, it shall be done
"for them—how much more may not we hope
"to obtain in proportion to our being more
"eminently favoured of God, if we agree in one
"aim, and with one mind promote His honour
"and His glory, Who hath Himself enjoined us
"to invoke His Holy Spirit in these Congrega-
"tions of our Synods!"

Objects of a Diocesan Synod.

One of the main objects of a Diocesan Synod in early times was, that the Bishop might make known to his Clergy the Acts of the Synod of the Province in which his Diocese was situated. The absence of such information officially communicated has been a serious want in our times. When in this generation, for instance, the lectionary was revised, shortened services approved, and Canons on Clergy Subscription enacted by Convocation, it appears—to speak softly—short of seemly that the Clergy should be apprized of such events merely through the columns of the ephemeral press. And as a fact many Clergy long remained ignorant of the remodelling and re-enactment of the Subscription-Canons, and perhaps all are not yet aware of the fact.

English Diocesan Synods.

Records of Diocesan Synods held in England before the Reformation may be found abundantly in the pages of the "Concilia Magnæ Britanniæ," and the forms with which they were celebrated may be seen in Vol. iii. p. 681 of that work. The book "Reformatio Legum Ecclesiasticarum," compiled at the period of the Reformation, directed the annual convention of such assemblies by the respective Diocesan Bishops; but yet few have been held in this country since that time, and thus a valuable part of Church organization has been disregarded. Some instances, however, have occurred. For there is some casual evidence of Diocesan Synods having been convened in Durham and Norwich Dioceses since that epoch. And some special instances are fully recorded, as Diocesan Synods were convened by Bishop Davies at St. Asaph in 1561, by Bishop Freake at Norwich about 1580, by Bishop Lloyd at St. Asaph in 1683, by Bishop Wilberforce at Oxford in 1850, by Bishop Phillpotts at Exeter in 1851, by Bishop Wordsworth at Lincoln in 1871, by Bishop Maclagan at Lichfield in 1884, and by Bishop Ridding at Southwell in 1885. EARLY HISTORY.

Of late years many Diocesan "Conferences" have assembled. Those are mixed assemblies of Clergy and laity. As these institutions, however, do not come within the scope of the subject now in hand, it is not here needful to write of them at any length. It may be well, however, shortly to point out the difference between these assemblies and Diocesan Synods. And this cannot be better done than by transcribing the words of an original letter, now before the writer, from Diocesan Conferences.

EARLY HISTORY.

Bishop C. Wordsworth's Letter.

the late most learned and revered Bishop Wordsworth of Lincoln: "It is my intention," wrote the Bishop, "to have two distinct institutions in " this Diocese—(1) The Diocesan Synod, consti-
" tuted in the manner and on the principles
" received by the Church for seventeen centuries;
" (2) The Diocesan Conference, a mixed body
" [conventus] of Clergy and laity. The Synod is
" to take its part in all matters concerning 'divine
" 'learning,' and the discipline and sacred offices
" of the Church; the Conference to deal with
" mixed matters—the relation of the State and
" the Church, finances Ecclesiastical, maintenance
" of the Clergy, &c."

III.

PROVINCIAL SYNODS.

In an ascending order the next Ecclesiastical assembly to be considered is a Provincial Synod, or Synod of combined Dioceses; and as our Convocations are of this character the subject requires especial attention.

Primitive Provincial organization.

Provincial organization, which is emphatically that of the Church of England, may be traced to the earliest, even to apostolic times. Timothy is

Hom. xv. in 1 Tim.

reported by St. Chrysostom to have been entrusted with the supervision of the whole of

Proconsular Asia, in which were several Bishops. And it is affirmed moreover that Titus was charged with the oversight of the Churches of Crete, and to have superintended the whole island. In the Second Century there are some further evidences of Provincial organization, and of Metropolitical authority exercised over Diocesan Bishops. Irenæus of Lyons, in the year 177, superintended the Gallican Dioceses. Philip of Gortyna was styled "Bishop of the "Dioceses of Crete;" and that there was at that time more than one Diocese in the island is certain, from the fact that then Pinytus was Bishop of Gnossus, the inevitable conclusion being that Philip was Metropolitan. Towards the decline of the Second Century the plainest proofs of this Provincial organization and of Metropolitical authority appear in one passage of Eusebius' history (lib. 5, c. 23). Provincial Synods were at this time convened to consider the proper time for celebrating the Paschal festival. And that historian informs us that in the Synod of Palestine Theophilus of Cæsarea presided; in that of Rome, Victor; in that of France, Irenæus of Lyons; in that of Proconsular Asia, Palmas as senior Bishop. This arrangement of Provincial organization is, moreover, canonically authorized by the 33rd, sometimes numbered the 35th, of the Apostolical Canons, which runs thus: "The Bishops of

marginal notes: EARLY HISTORY. St. Chrys. Hom. i. in Tit.

EARLY HISTORY.

"each Province ought to own him who is "chief among them, and own him as their head, "and to do nothing extraordinary without his "consent, but each one those things only which "concern his own parish [i.e. Diocese], and the "country subject to it." And again, the Fifth Canon of the Council of Nice decreed that "in "each Province Synods should be held twice "every year, so that, all the Bishops of the "Province being gathered together to the same "place, disputed questions might be investigated."

Ancient form of holding a Provincial Synod.

The ancient forms of proceeding in holding Provincial Synods may be found in full detail laid down in the Fourth Canon of the Fourth Council of Toledo, A.D. 633. They are well worthy of study, as they define the proper constituent members of such assemblies, and the part which the Deacons and laity took as spectators of the proceedings or as complainants of injury; and may be read in Neander, ed. Bruns. pp. 222 seq. The Canon being translated decrees as follows:

"At early dawn, before sunrise, let the church "where the Synod is to assemble be cleared of "all manner of persons. And all the doors "having been shut, let doorkeepers stand at "one door through which the Priests may enter, "and also all the attending Bishops may like-"wise come in and take their places according to "the dates of their consecrations. After all the "Bishops have entered and taken their seats let

"the Presbyters who have a right of entrance be
"called in, but let no Deacon intrude among
"them. After these let the approved Deacons
"enter who have received order to attend; and
"the Bishops sitting in a semicircle, let the Pres-
"byters sit behind them, and the Deacons stand
"in front of the Bishops. Then let the laity
"enter, who by election of the Council have
"been deemed worthy to be present. Then let
"the notaries enter, whom the order of business
"requires for reading or taking notes. Let the
"doors then be locked, and while the Clergy
"are sitting in continuous silence, having their
"whole minds fixed on God, let the Archdeacon
"say, 'Pray ye.' All shall immediately prostrate
"themselves on the ground, praying long and
"silently with tears and lamentations. Let one
"of the Bishops then rise and pray aloud to
"God, all the rest still remaining prostrate.
"After this prayer is ended, and all having
"responded 'Amen,' again let the Archdeacon
"say, 'Rise ye up.' Let all then immediately
"rise up, and in the full fear of God, and in
"due order, let both Bishops and Presbyters
"take their seats. Thus while all are sitting
"in their proper places in silence, let a Deacon
"vested in an alb bring forward a volume of
"Canons, and read the Chapters on the hold-
"ing of Councils. When these titles have been
"finished, let the Metropolitan Bishop address

EARLY HISTORY.

"the Council, saying, 'See, most holy Priests, "'from the Canons of the Ancient Fathers the "'regulations for holding a Council have been "'read; if therefore any one of you is moved "'to action let him make his proposition in the "'presence of his brethren.' Then if any one "shall have preferred any complaint in the "audience of the priestly assembly of a breach "of the Canons, let no other matter be entered "on until the proposed matter be first concluded. "Further, if any Presbyter, Deacon, cleric, or "layman, who has not been admitted to the "assembly, should think that he has cause of "appeal on any matter to the Council, let him "intimate his case to the Archdeacon of the "Metropolitan Church, let him declare it to the "Council, and then let leave be granted to the "complainant to enter and state his case. No "Bishop may depart from the common assembly "before the regular hour for separation arrives. "No one may dare to dissolve the assembly un- "less every question shall have been settled. So "that whatever has been decided on by common "deliberation may be subscribed by the hands "of the individual Bishops. Then may God "be believed to have been present with His "Priests, all tumult may carefully be avoided, "and Ecclesiastical business be concluded with "tranquillity."

British Provincial organization.

Provincial organization was established here

in England in very early times. There were originally three Provinces before the Saxon invasion, A.D. 445—(1) London; (2) York; (3) Caerleon-upon-Usk. Indeed it is certain that at the Council of Arles, A.D. 314, these three English Prelates, Restitutus of London, Eborius of York, and Adelsius of Caerleon-upon-Usk, subscribed to the Acts. EARLY HISTORY.

On the arrival of Augustine the Monk, about A.D. 600 [Ranulphus gives as the date 599, Angelocrator 601, Spelman 601, Balæus 602, Vigornensis 603], Christians of the two first named Provinces had been persecuted by their invaders well-nigh to extermination, Theonas, Metropolitan of London, and Thadiocus of York, having fled to Wales and taken refuge there from the Saxon conquerors about the year 586 or 587. But in the Western Province of Caerleon-upon-Usk, or as sometimes called, St. David's, Christianity still flourished. This is plain from the fact that at the interview at the Apostles' Oak, between Augustine and the authorities of the British Church, seven Bishops from the West attended, the Bishops of Bangor, Hereford, Llanbadern, Llandaff, Margam, St. Asaph, and Worcester. It is right here to inform the reader that some antiquarians believe that the Dioceses of Hereford and Worcester at that time had other names. But however this may be, the seven Bishops attending this meeting Mission of Augustine.

EARLY HISTORY. were accompanied by many most learned Clergy; of these one of the chief was Dinoth, Abbot of Bangor Iscoed. The points discussed referred first to the time proper for the celebration of the Paschal festival, which here differed from the Roman calculation, and was originally derived from the Eastern Church [though a miscalculation had been made after the Council of Nice by the Britons]; secondly to the proper form for the administration of Baptism; thirdly to a union with Augustine for preaching the Gospel to the Anglo-Saxons.

The points of difference between the British and the Roman Church as discussed at this interview, are conclusive as to the fact that this Church of England is of Eastern and not of Western origin, and that she rightly claims as her Spiritual Mother the ancient Apostolic Orthodox Church of the East.

Augustine disinclined the Britons from accepting his propositions, first by his haughty demeanour in receiving them as he was sitting, and then by insisting on their obeying him. So finally they declined his proposals, saying that they could not satisfy him "nor receive him "for their Archbishop."

Independence of British Church on Rome. For the conditions he demanded of them were not so much terms of brotherly communion as confessions of submission and inferiority. "If," said he, "in these three things you will obey "me, then will I bear with all other things." And the decision of the assembly was tersely summed up in the words of Dinoth above mentioned, who said, "Be it known and without "doubt unto you, that we all are and every "one of us obedient and subject to the Church "of God, and to the Pope of Rome, and to every "godly Christian, to love every one in his degree "in perfect charity, and to help every one of "them by word and deed to be children of God; "and other obedience than this I do not know "due to him whom you name to be Pope, nor to "be the father of fathers to be claimed and to be "demanded. And this obedience we are ready "to give and to pay to him and to every Chris-"tian continually. Besides, we are under the "government of the Bishop of Caerleon-upon-"Usk, who is to oversee under God over us, and "to cause us to keep the way Spiritual." Indeed, to have transferred their allegiance to Augustine from their own Metropolitan would have been a grave offence, for to the ancient Metropolitan See of Caerleon-upon-Usk they owed obedience. And though that See had been removed to St. David's about eighty years previously, i.e. by the Council held at Llandewy Brevi A.D. 519, yet the ancient title of Caerleon and its jurisdiction was still retained.

The exact spot where this interview between the seven British Bishops and Augustine the Monk

<small>EARLY HISTORY.</small>

<small>Spelm. Conc. i. 708, from Mostyn MSS. See Still. Orig. Brit. pp. 370, seq.</small>

<small>Locality of interview between British Bishops and Augustine.</small>

EARLY HISTORY. took place has afforded matter for some discussion. For it cannot fail to be a question of considerable interest to those who anxiously maintain the right and original independence of the English Church. Spelman thought that the scene of this assembly was near a village named "Ausric," as being a name contracted from "Austin's-ric." Others have written of the place as "Haustake" or "Ossuntree," i.e. the village of "Martin Hussingtree," near Droitwich.

But there is, not far from the present highroad leading from Ludlow in the County of Salop to the city of Worcester, a spot called "The Apostles' Oak," which local tradition marks as the place of this memorable interview. On the road above mentioned there is an old inn named "The Hundred House," and about a mile short of it as one approaches from the Ludlow side is a hill called "The Apostles' Oak Bank." At a little distance to the left of the ascent stands now in a wood an oak tree, which is known to have been planted during the earlier half of the last century to mark the spot where the hollow trunk of an exceedingly aged oak formerly stood, but which had been burnt by a fire carelessly lighted within it. That aged trunk was known as "The Apostles' Oak," and was in the neighbourhood always believed to have been the remains of the tree under whose shadow the seven British Bishops and Augustine met. In

1732 that original trunk was certainly standing in a state of great decay—quite hollow—and in it was placed a seat for the accommodation of the keeper of an adjoining turnpike gate. The gate was denominated the "Apostles' Oak Gate;" and it is said that in a local Act of Parliament passed for the management of the road, "The Apostles' Oak" was nominally specified. The present road is diverted from its former course, so that a traveller does not see the spot unless he purposely seeks it.

In a letter dated May 31, 1797, Dr. Percy, Bishop of Dromore, after mentioning some of the facts above stated, adds: " I remember being told "this by the Rector of 'The Rock,' when I was "on a visit at his Parsonage house. That parish, "which originally extended to this celebrated "oak, was called 'Aca' in Latin [so it is still in "the ' Valor Beneficiorum ' from it], and the Eng-"lish name 'The Rock' is only a corruption "of the old Anglo-Saxon 'Ðæɲ Ӕc'—'ther Oak,' "or 'the Oak.'" Some objections have been raised against this locality; but in a MS. copy of Dr. Percy's letter [which I have had an opportunity of reading] that Bishop says: "I formerly considered the subject, and think "I can answer every objection, and confirm the "tradition." An auxiliary fact giving additional credibility to the local tradition must not be overlooked. That ancient oak marked the

<small>EARLY HISTORY.</small>

boundary between the Dioceses of Hereford and Worcester, and therefore was not unlikely to be chosen as a spot where Bishops from different Dioceses might assemble. This fact also may readily account for the statement in Spelman, "Conc." i. 107, and in the "Conc. Mag. Brit." i. 125, that this meeting took place on the borders of Worcestershire and Herefordshire; though, in fact, the boundaries of the Dioceses and Counties not being here exactly conterminous, the County of Hereford does not really approach within a few miles of the place.

<small>Metropolitan jurisdiction finally confined to Canterbury and York.</small>

Not long after this interview at "The Apostles' Oak," some of the Dioceses of the Welsh Bishops became subject to the Metropolitical See of Canterbury; but it is plain that the Provincial jurisdiction was attached to the See of Caerleon or St. David's through many subsequent centuries at least over some of the Welsh Dioceses. And Giraldus Cambrensis, a Welshman born, and one whose evidence on this point may be accepted without dispute, proves from authentic records that the Bishops of St. David's consecrated Suffragans and exercised all other branches of Metropolitical authority till the reign of King Henry I. At that time Bernard, who had been Chaplain to Adelais, that monarch's second queen, upon being raised to the See of St. David's, submitted to the Metropolitan of Canterbury; and thus about A.D. 1115 the Western Province of Caerleon became merged into the Southern Province. The Convocations of Canterbury and York are consequently now the Provincial Synods representing the Church existing in England and Wales. By them alone she acts in her corporate capacity; by them alone can her authoritative voice be heard.

<small>EARLY HISTORY.</small>

That Provincial Synods consist exclusively of the Bishops of a Province with conjoined Presbyters, and that this was their constitution from the earliest ages of the Church, is plain from manifest proofs too long to be here inserted; but the evidence is as clear as the evidence of any fact can be. Such is the constitution of the Convocations of the Church of England, and has been from time immemorial.

<small>Constitution of Provincial Synods.</small>

There is, indeed, an absurd fallacy which has been current in some quarters that these Provincial Synods originated in the reign of King Edward I., and by that monarch were created. This error has been published chiefly by legal writers, never backward in endeavours to subordinate the Church to the State; and credulous members of another profession have been simple enough to believe them and reproduce their blunders. The confusion has arisen from the fact that King Edward I. called the Clergy to Parliament in order that they might there vote their subsidies, which they had formerly assessed in their Synods. This he did by citing the Clergy to parliamentary assemblies at Northampton and York

<small>Error touching the origin of Convocations. The "Præmunientes clause."</small>

EARLY HISTORY.

in 1282, which proved a failure; and subsequently in 1295, by a clause inserted in the writ which summoned each Bishop to Parliament as a Peer of the Realm. That clause began with the word, "Præmunientes," a barbarism for "Præmonentes," forewarning each Bishop to bring with him some Clergy to Parliament. And those whom he should so bring were specified in the same order as they had before that time attended in their Convocations. Hence the error; for it is hardly necessary to remind anyone that Convocations and Parliaments are very different assemblies. But this call to Parliament is in no way further connected with our Synods. In fact it can be shewn by authentic original records that King Edward I. had no more to do with originating the Convocations of the Church of England than he had to do with convening an Œcumenical Council, or constituting an assembly of independent Tartars in Samarcand.

When the Sovereign in previous times had desired a Provincial Synod to be convened, he directed a writ to each Metropolitan requesting him to cite his proper Convocation. But the writ above mentioned, containing the "Præmunientes" clause, was directed personally to each Bishop, citing him to attend with some of his Clergy in Parliament, being a wholly different instrument and directed to a different end. Indeed, that King Edward I. did not originate our Provincial Synods is manifest from the simple fact, not to mention earlier proofs, which are abundant, that even in his own time three Provincial Synods had been convened under their present condition before such call to Parliament as he was able to enforce was ever issued. That is to say, one in 1273 and one in 1277 by Archbishop Kilwarby, and one in 1283 by Archbishop Peccham. And it is at this point observable that Archbishop Kilwarby's mandate for the Provincial Synod of 1277 inclusively, exclusively, and exhaustively prescribes the members who were to attend, being men exactly the same as those who now at this hour constitute our Convocations, i.e. the Bishops, the greater persons of the Chapters, the Archdeacons, and the Proctors for the Clergy. But the writ containing the call to Parliament by the "Præmunientes" clause was not issued till eighteen years after, i.e. in the year 1295. The original mandates calling together the Convocations in 1273 and 1277, just mentioned, are now preserved in the Diocesan Registry at Worcester Cathedral [Reg. Giffard, folios 41–71], and have been perused personally by myself. The latter, precisely and exactly defining the present constitution of our Convocations, proves conclusively and incontestably how unfounded is the notion that our Convocations were inaugurated by King Edward I.

The conclusion of the whole matter is this.

EARLY HISTORY. King Edward I. in calling the Clergy to tax them in Parliament, imitated exactly and precisely the order in which they had been previously called to their Convocations by their Metropolitans. If anyone takes the trouble to compare Archbishop R. Kilwarby's mandate for Convocation in 1277 and King Edward the Ist's writ for Parliament in 1295, it will be seen that the persons summoned were exactly the same, without the slightest variation whatsoever. But as legal gentlemen who have treated this subject—one, by the way, a Lord Chancellor of our own day—pay greater respect to Parliaments than to Synods, they have read the writs for the former, but disregarded the mandates for the latter; and to this method all their confusions may be traced which ascribe the origin and constitution of the Convocations to King Edward I.

The lower Clergy still called to Parliament by the "Præmunientes" clause. Curiously enough, this call of the Clergy to Parliament by the "Præmunientes" clause in each Bishop's writ of summons to Parliament is continued to this hour. And were any Bishop now to execute the writ in accordance with the Royal commands, and were the Clergy summoned by it to attend, it would be interesting to know what place would be assigned by the officials to the Clergy who presented themselves at the doors of Parliament, where usually Royal commands are not lightly respected. It might, perchance, be pleaded by the bewildered officials, as an excuse for not finding accommodation for the Clergy presenting themselves, that their exclusion had been decided in Horne Tooke's case, and that provisions had been carefully made for shutting out Clergymen below the rank of Bishops from seats in Parliament, whatever privileges may be allowed in this respect to Nonconformist preachers. But this plea would constitutionally be worthless. This prerogative of the Crown to summon certain of the lower Clergy to Parliament is derived from a date anterior to the reign of King Richard II., the time of legal memory, and has been exercised by the Sovereign, as records prove, in comparatively recent times. Under such circumstances it is a maxim of constitutional law that no prerogative of the Crown can be annihilated save by specific statutable words, directed to that particular effect. No such specific annihilation of this Royal prerogative has in this case ever taken place. The prerogative, therefore, to summon the Clergy to Parliament still abides; and if the Royal prerogative still abides, I suppose the duty of obeying it, when exercised, abides still also.

Any curious enquirer on this subject may find information in Coke's IV. Inst. 4, 5, and also in a treatise, " De modo tenendi Parliamentum," signed R. Duddeley, Earl of Leicester [British Museum Add. 15191, MS. Vellum of the 16th century], and also in Bibl. Cotton. Julius. B. 4,

EARLY HISTORY.

p. 4, pl. xviii. c. after Archbishops' and Bishops' summonses, folio 21. It is further here observable that in the Statutes 21 Rich. II. c. 2, and 21 Rich. II. c. 12, the preambles state that these Statutes were made by the assent of the Procurators of the Clergy, as well as of the other constituent members of Parliament [Pearce, "Law Conv." p. 18].

The reader must pardon this somewhat long digression on the subject of the "Præmunientes" clause in the Royal writs of summons calling the Bishops to Parliament, because reliance has been placed on that clause, and on King Edward the Ist's struggles to raise money by taxation, in order to persuade simple people that the Provincial Synods of this Church are of secular origin, and to debase them to the level of the Corporation of a chartered borough town. The very stones in the wall may reasonably cry out against such dishonour done to this Church of England. No; the Provincial Synods of this Church most certainly did not originate with King Edward I. They are of far, far older date, as national records indisputably prove. Their origin must be sought among the deepest foundations of the British Church, in the remotest ages of our country's history,

" . . . . . facta Patrum, Series longissima rerum
" Per tôt ducta viros antiquæ ab origine gentis."
VIRG. Æn. i. 641-2.

As above said, from the time when the **EARLY HISTORY.**
Province of Caerleon-upon-Usk was merged into
Canterbury, the two Provincial Synods of Can- Constitution of the
terbury and York became the representatives of Provincial Synods, or
the whole Church in England and Wales. From Convocations of
a consideration of their ancient origin and extent Canterbury and York.
of jurisdiction the reader may now pass on
to consider their present constitution, remembering at the same time that while severally
representing the Church in their respective
Provinces, they constitute when acting in concert—to use the words of the 139th Canon—
"the sacred Synod of this nation;" "the true
"Church of England by representation."

The Provincial Synod of Canterbury consists Canterbury.
of the Archbishop and the Diocesan Bishops
within his jurisdiction; with these assemble all
Deans of Cathedrals in the Province, the Dean
of Westminster, the Dean of Windsor, the Provost of Eton, all Archdeacons in the Province,
one Proctor elected by each Cathedral Chapter,
a Proctor for the Westminster Chapter [and old
records specify a Proctor for Wolverhampton],
and two Proctors elected by the beneficed Clergy
of each Diocese. On account of the addition
of new Dioceses this Provincial Synod has of
late slightly varied in respect of number. At
the present time [1885] it consists [including the
new Bishopric of Southwell] of the Archbishop
of Canterbury, twenty-three Diocesan Bishops,

EARLY HISTORY.

three Bishops not having territorial Sees, and one hundred and fifty-one Presbyters.

York.

The Provincial Synod of York in like manner consists of the Metropolitan, Bishops, Deans of Cathedrals, Archdeacons, Chapter and Clergy Proctors of the Dioceses within the Province, together with two Proctors for the officialty of the Chapter of Durham. But in one respect York differs from Canterbury, as two Proctors are elected by each Archdeaconry in the former Province, whereas in the latter two are elected by each Diocese. The York Provincial Synod at this time consists of the Metropolitan, eight Diocesan Bishops, one Bishop not having a territorial See, and sixty-eight Presbyters.[1]

The Bishops not having Sees who are found in the Convocations sit not as Bishops but in virtue of Archdeaconries which they hold. Whether all Bishops actively engaged in these two Provinces, even if they do not hold territorial Sees, should be summoned to the Provincial Synods—and whether when appearing there they should sit in the Upper Houses, respectively—are questions which, according to Ecclesiastical principles, could only receive one answer, and that is an affirmative one. So far as Civil requirements go, each Metropolitan is requested by the Royal Writ to summon to his Provincial

---

[1] Not including Proctors for the Archdeaconry of Cleveland, omitted in the official list, 1883.

Synod "totum clerum." Under these circumstances to omit the name of a Bishop, whether an Archdeacon or not, in active work within a Province would seem to be a solœcism on the part of any Metropolitan when issuing the mandates for convening his Provincial Synod.

<small>EARLY HISTORY.</small>

Having now considered the origin and constitution of the Provincial Synods or Convocations of the Church of England, it is time to pass on to a consideration of their proper functions and duties.

The proper functions and duties of our Provincial Synods, and such as have been discharged by them in the Church of England in times past, may generally be ranked under five heads— (1) Prescription of the Canon of Scripture. (2) Promulgation of Symbols of Faith. (3) Condemnation of False Doctrine. (4) Enactment of Canons. (5) Authorization of Liturgical Formularies.

<small>Proper functions and duties of Provincial Synods or Convocations.</small>

(1) So early as in the 84th of the Apostolic Canons, in the 60th Canon of the Synod of Laodicea, and in the 47th Canon of the Third Council of Carthage, we find prescriptions of the Scriptural Canon; and so late as at the Convocation of both our Provinces held in London in 1562–3, we find the Canonical Scriptures defined by the 6th of the Thirty-nine Articles then ratified.

<small>Prescription of the Canon of Scripture.</small>

(2) The promulgation of symbols of doctrinal belief has been one of the prime duties of Synods in all ages. It was a function here exercised in the promulgation of the 8th Article

<small>Promulgation of symbols of faith.</small>

EARLY HISTORY. of the Church of England, which specifies the three Creeds as symbols of faith which "ought "thoroughly to be received and believed."

Condemnation of false doctrine. (3) The condemnation of false doctrine by Provincial Synods is a duty which has been discharged by them continually in past ages, as all early Ecclesiastical records abundantly prove. So late as in Queen Anne's time, on application being made to the Judges of the Civil Courts on this subject, eight out of the twelve, together with the Attorney and Solicitor-General, decided that this was a proper part of the functions of our Convocations. It was then exercised by the Synodical condemnation of Whiston's book, and on late occasions in this generation by the condemnation of Dr. Colenso's volume on "The Pentateuch and Book of Joshua," and of the book entitled "Essays and Reviews."

Enactment of Canons. (4) The next office of Provincial Synods—the enactment of Canons—requires rather fuller consideration, on account of some peculiarities in this country which affect such proceedings. Before the year 1534, our Provincial Synods enacted Canons at their will. In that year the Statute 25 Henry VIII. 19 was passed, which provided that Canons might not be here "enacted, "promulged, executed, or put in ure" without a licence from the Sovereign. The proceedings in such a case are now as follows. First, the Synod debates the subject-matter of the proposed

Canon or Canons. Drafts made of the conclu- **EARLY** sions arrived at are then submitted to the Crown. **HISTORY.** If the Sovereign approves of the proposals, a licence issues to "enact." On the receipt of this instrument the Canons proposed are engrossed on parchment and the Synod meets. In the presence of the whole assembly, both houses being joined in session for the purpose, the Metropolitan, standing, holds the parchment in his right hand; the Prolocutor, standing on his left side, holds it with his left hand. The contents are then read out by the Metropolitan, and the document being placed on the table, is signed, first by himself, then by the Provincial Bishops present, and lastly in order by the assembled Clergy. Such Canons are thus "enacted" and become law. No parliamentary approval is constitutionally required, and they are "promulged" to be "executed and put in ure" by the Ecclesiastical Judges in Ecclesiastical Courts; and their judgments founded on such Canons will be sustained by the Civil Courts so long as the contents do not contravene Royal prerogative, common, or statute law. The above was the course taken in the year 1865, when the 36th Canon and others were remodelled and re-enacted in the Convocation of Canterbury.

(5) The last general duty to be mentioned of Provincial Synods is the authorization of Liturgies and Ritual. In early times, and notably Authorization of liturgical Formularies.

EARLY HISTORY. in this country, liturgies sometimes varied in different Dioceses of the same Province, as is testified by the different "Uses" which here prevailed. But it was, perhaps, more common in the Church that each Province or combination of Dioceses should conform to one use, and measures for this purpose were at times taken, as history testifies. At the Reformation this latter principle was adopted in England, and the first Prayer Book of 1549 was issued for the use of both Provinces. The compilers were certainly all members of Convocation; but the records of the Canterbury Synod having been burnt in the disastrous fire in London in 1666, the authentic records of the authorization of the first Reformed Prayer Book are not forthcoming. There is, however, ample evidence of the fact from other sources; and all trustworthy historians who have written on the subject do not doubt, but on the contrary positively assert, that it had Convocational sanction. The second Reformed Prayer Book was distinctly authorized by the 35th Article of 1552–3. And our present Prayer Book, compiled from the earlier ones, with additions, had the sanction of both our Provincial Synods in 1661, given in the most formal and emphatic manner imaginable; that is, by the personal signatures of all the members of the Canterbury Synod, fortified by the signatures of the Northern Prelates, and six delegates deputed by the York Synod to attend in London, as shall hereafter be shewn in detailing that event.

<small>EARLY HISTORY.</small>

One jurisdiction which has been conferred on our Provincial Synods is a peculiar one, not common to Synods of the Church generally, but here consequent on two Statutes of the realm— the 24 Hen. VIII. 12, as confirmed by 25 Hen. VIII. 19. By the 9th section of the first-mentioned Act, as confirmed by the 3rd section of the second and subsequently ratified by 1 Eliz. 1, it was enacted that in all Ecclesiastical cases "touching the King" an appeal should lie to the Upper House of Convocation of the Province in which the cause arose, and thither only. Such causes certainly came under Convocational jurisdiction in the cases of the divorces of Catharine of Arragon, Anne Boleyn, and Anne of Cleves. Notwithstanding the decisions of the Courts of Q. B. and C. P. in the Gorham Case that this jurisdiction has been superseded, it is impossible to reconcile such a conclusion with the terms of the statutes above quoted; and it is moreover quite contradictory to the positive assertions of our text writers—Dyer, Bacon, Comyn, Woodeson, Blackstone, Ayliffe, and Burn—who with one voice affirm that the jurisdiction was never abolished. Moreover, it is within the certain knowledge of the writer of these lines that in the opinion of some of the highest legal authorities in this generation, the forementioned decisions

<small>Statutable jurisdiction of Convocations over "Kings' Causes."</small>

of two of our law courts should be, to say the least, carefully reconsidered. It is manifest that the above jurisdiction might be a great safeguard to the Church in the case of a man of unsound doctrine being nominated to a Bishopric or a benefice in the gift of the Crown.

IV.

SYNODS OF THE EXARCHATE.

In an ascending order the next Ecclesiastical assembly to be considered is a Synod of the Exarchate. The constitution of Exarchates, or combinations of Provinces, is of later date in the Church than that of Provinces. But at any rate as early as the beginning of the 4th century the territorial division of Exarchate had been generally established. As the Bishop was Chief Ecclesiastical Officer in his Diocese and the Metropolitan in his Province, so the Exarch, Patriarch, or Archbishop was chief in his Exarchate; and under his presidency Synods of the Exarchate or Διοίκησις were convened. That to these Synods of the Exarchate the judgments of Provincial Synods were subject, we have plain proof in the 6th Canon of the Second Œcumenical Council, which defines at length the order of jurisdiction, and indeed enacts that in the case of a Bishop arraigned, he shall have no appeal from the decision of a Synod of the Exarchate, not even to an Œcumenical Council. The authority of Exarchs over the Metropolitan Bishops within their Exarchate is very distinctly shewn by the letter of summons convening the Second Council of Ephesus, A.D. 449. To that Council Dioscorus, Exarch or Archbishop of Alexandria, was bidden to bring with him ten Metropolitans of that Exarchate. From this and other like circumstances, the reader will understand why, throughout these pages, a distinction is maintained between the terms Archbishop and Metropolitan.

<small>EARLY HISTORY.</small>

It is interesting to trace what has been our national practice in this respect. This union of our Provincial Synods into one body, that is, a Synod of the Exarchate, has been effected in England on many occasions. An early and very notable illustration is found in the Council of Whitby A.D. 664, convened for the consideration of the introduction of Romish practices into the Church here; and from that time downwards as many as forty-five occasions at least may be reckoned when this union has occurred [on some of those occasions a Legate presiding], ranging down to the year 1540, when the members of the Canterbury and York Synods assembled together in London for the investigation of the legality of the marriage of Anne of Cleves to King Henry VIII.; and reaching on to the year

<small>English Synods of the Exarchate.</small>

EARLY HISTORY.
1562-3, when members of both Synods united for the ratification of the 39 Articles, as appears from their heading.

Authority to convene a Synod of the English Exarchate.
The authority to unite our two Provincial Synods into a Synod of the Exarchate was specially given to the Archbishop of Canterbury at the Council of Windsor, A.D. 1072, and was confirmed by subsequent Synods, as may be learned by consulting " Conc. Mag. Brit." vol. i. pp. 325, 391, 493 ; and vol. iv. app. 786.

The following is an extract from the Constitution passed at Windsor, A.D. 1072, above referred to—

Conc. M. B. i. 325.
Coll. Rec. V, bis,
Vol. ix. 12.
" So that if the Archbishop of Canterbury should " wish to convene a Council, wherever to him " may seem fit, then at his command let the " Archbishop of York, with all those subject to " him, present themselves, and be obedient to his " Canonical directions." In order that this Constitution might be fortified both by Ecclesiastical and Civil authority it was subscribed not only by the Archbishop of Canterbury, the Metropolitan of York, and thirteen Bishops, but by the King and Queen, with many other persons of high degree. It is a grave question, moreover, whether its provisions might not now be even *statutally* enforced under the 7th Section of 25 Henry VIII. 19, which enacts that such Constitutions and Canons as " were not contrariant or repugnant to the laws, " statutes, and customs of this realm, nor to the " damage or hurt of the King's prerogative royal,"

should still be in force and executed, until a review of those instruments had been effected, and certain acts done which have never been yet concluded to this hour. A copy of an original document of the Conqueror's time, referring to this Constitution [if not the Constitution itself], was exhibited at a meeting of the Royal Archæological Institute at Canterbury in the year 1875.

EARLY HISTORY.

The authority residing in the Archbishop of Canterbury to cite the Metropolitan of York and his Suffragans, with their associated Presbyters, to a Synod of the Exarchate, involves a somewhat intricate historical enquiry. The story is a very long one. It shall be here condensed to the briefest possible space. As regards the earliest period of the British Church, before the Saxon invasion, there are no records to guide enquiry. In 634, Pope Honorius I. granted to his namesake, Honorius, Archbishop of Canterbury, jurisdiction over all England; and this was confirmed by Gregory II. in 730. Theodore, Archbishop of Canterbury, exercised authority over the whole of this country, and convened three Synods of the English Exarchate in 673, 680, and 685 respectively. But Egbert, succeeding to the throne of York in 731, and being a man of somewhat enterprising genius, and impatient of inferiority, obtained the pallium from Rome, and so secured at least his own independence; whether, however, that passed beyond

Subordination of York to Canterbury.

Soames, Anglo-Saxon Ch. p. 78.

Godwin de Præsul. Pt. 2, p. 14.

EARLY HISTORY.

the term of his natural life may, of course, be questioned. For shortly after, without doubt in 796, the Metropolitan of York did profess obedience to Athelard, Archbishop of Canterbury.

After the Norman Conquest, the Constitution of Windsor, A.D. 1072, above quoted, distinctly confirmed the jurisdiction in question on the See of Canterbury. And in 1075 Lanfranc, Archbishop of Canterbury, convened both Provinces to a Synod of the Exarchate at St. Paul's, London, when the decrees of the Council were signed by himself, the Metropolitan of York, twelve Bishops, and sundry Presbyters. Indeed, it is further recorded by competent authority, that Lanfranc convened five of these Synods of the Exarchate.

In the year 1092, when, after the death of Lanfranc, a Synod of Bishops was held for the consecration of Anselm to the See of Canterbury, the instrument of his election was objected to by the Metropolitan of York. This was Thomas I., who is represented as having been a very paragon, in body, of fine stature, comely in youth and handsome in age, with ruddy complexion, and hair white as swan's-down; in philosophy, comparable with the ancients; in music, skilful in composition and execution, both vocal and instrumental, as he played the organ well; and withal affable in manner. But his affability seems to have vanished when he objected to the instrument of Anselm's election,

Godwin de Præsul. Pt. 2, p. 23, quoting Guil. Malmesbur.

inasmuch as it designated the Church of Canterbury "Totius Angliæ Metropolitana." And it must be confessed that Thomas I. had some grounds for checking at this nomenclature, which would logically have excluded his Church of York from being Metropolitan at all. This was more than Thomas Ist's temper, however fine, could bear; for even though his Metropolitan Church might be subject to the See of the Exarchate of Canterbury, yet to deny it the honour of Metropolitan, even by implication, was noway justifiable. So reason prevailed in Thomas Ist's favour, the objectionable word "Metropolitana" was excised from the instrument, and the word "Primas" substituted. From that time the Archbishop of Canterbury has been designated "Primate of All England;" and Thomas I., as a fact, now that his mind was set at rest, did afterwards make submission to Anselm of Canterbury. EARLY HISTORY.

Collier, Rec. Vol. ix. p. 12.

In 1109, Thomas II. was designated as Metropolitan of York—a man youthful in age, and proportionably vigorous in enterprize; and though exceedingly fat, by no means lazy in action. Indeed the preponderance of his bulk does not seem to have repressed the vaulting motions of his ambition; for he challenged independence, and resisted the authority of the aged Anselm of Canterbury, by refusing to signify obedience to that See in prospect of consecration. Anselm addressed the English Episcopate on the subject, Resistance of York to jurisdiction of Canterbury. Godwin de Præsul. Pt. 2, p. 28, quoting Guil. Malmesbur.

G

<small>EARLY HISTORY.</small> and there was a general consensus among those Prelates, that "they would rather part with all "they had" than transgress the rights and decisions of Anselm.

<small>Godwin de Præsul. Pt. 2, p. 29, quoting Guil. Malmesbur.</small> However, about the year 1119, the most vigorous endeavours were made to emancipate the York Province from any subordination to Canterbury. At that time Thurstan, a man at least of a very persevering if not obstinate character, being designated for the See of York, was called on before consecration by Ranulphus of Canterbury to make profession of obedience to that See. This Thurstan refused to do, and proceeded to Rome to plead his cause in the matter. Pope Paul put him off. His successor in the Papal chair, Calixtus, was about to hold a Council at Rheims. Thither Thurstan proposed to betake himself, to secure a victory over Ranulphus. But the King, Henry I., refused him transit, unless he would pledge himself to "contrive nothing against the honour "of the Church of Canterbury." Notwithstanding, however, the assurances of Thurstan himself, and the promise of the Pope's Vicar Apostolic that the "dignity of the Church of Canterbury should "not be humiliated," Thurstan was consecrated to York by the Vicar Apostolic without making submission to Canterbury, John, Archdeacon of <small>Ibid. p. 35, quoting-</small> Canterbury, making formal protest.

<small>Neubrigensis and Stubbesius.</small> In 1176 a somewhat exceptionable method for asserting his independence on the See of Can-

terbury was adopted by a York Metropolitan. This was Roger, of whom an unfriendly writer has recorded that he was more intent on shearing his flock than finding them pasture; while a friendly one maintains that his memory is honourable on account of his having constructed anew the choir of his Cathedral Church, and also the Metropolitan Palace; for having built anew St. Sepulchre's Chapel near that palace; and, further, for having endowed it with large revenues, and founded a College of thirteen persons to minister divine offices therein. It does not, however, appear that these benefactions were supplied from his own resources in largest measure. At any rate, he seems not to have been quite forgetful of his own personal interests, as we are informed that he obtained this privilege from Pope Alexander III., that if any Clerk in the York Province should die without distributing his goods with his own hands, the assets should fall into the Metropolitan Treasury. Indeed, his managements on his own account were clearly somewhat effective, as at his death his coffers were found to contain eleven thousand pounds of silver, three hundred of gold, and a very large amount of coined money. At any rate, this Prelate's method of asserting his equality with the Archbishop of Canterbury was certainly somewhat odd. For being cited to attend at a Council at West-

EARLY HISTORY.

Godwin de Præsul. Pt. 1, pp. 112–13.

EARLY HISTORY.

minster before Hugo, the Pope's Legate, a seat was designed for the York Metropolitan on the left of that personage, one for Richard, the Archbishop of Canterbury, being placed on the right. Roger, indignant at this arrangement, endeavoured to intrude himself between the Legate and Richard; but the latter not giving way, the Metropolitan of York sat in the Archbishop of Canterbury's lap. The Bishops present were amazed, and remonstrated in vain, whereupon Richard's servants dragged Roger from his resting place, stamped on him, beat him with their fists, and tore to rags his Episcopal vestments; whereon the Legate and the Archbishop of Canterbury departed the place, leaving Roger prostrate on the ground. On his personal complaint of this usage to King Henry II., when the truth of the matter transpired, that monarch burst into irrepressible convulsions of laughter; and when Roger further appealed to Rome for satisfaction he found no redress whatever there. And so this proceeding was not favourable to the pretensions of York's equality with Canterbury.

Godwin de Præsul.
Pt. 2, p. 52.

Improving on Thurstan's example, above recorded, William de Greenfield, having through two years been disappointed of consecration to the See of York, after his election prevailed on Pope Clement by a bribe of 9,500 marks to consecrate him at Leyden in 1305. Improving again on this Papal authority, William de Greenfield in the very next year, 1306, promulged at Ripon a Canon, "excommunicating any of his "flock who should make an appeal to Canterbury." EARLY HISTORY.

Of this matter such is the briefest possible account, stress not having been laid on the United Synods of the Exarchate held under foreign Legates, such enquiry not being pertinent to the present purpose.

Now the Canon of Ripon, last mentioned, manifestly [so far as it was of force] annihilated all subjection of York to Canterbury. At the time when the Statute Hen. VIII. 19, now "in viridi observantiâ," was passed, that Act made all existing Constitutions and Canons statutably binding at the time of its enactment, 1534, which were not repugnant to "Sta-"tute law, Custom, or Prerogative Royal." Statutably, therefore, the real question now to be decided is this, a very short one: Did 25 Hen. VIII. 19 confirm the Windsor Constitution first, above quoted, or the Ripon Canon? But, however short the question, the arguments, without any doubt, would be alarmingly long which would be addressed in the High Court of Justice on this matter, were gentlemen of the long robe to be engaged upon it. And the answer, if ever arrived at and pronounced by the learned judges, would decide whether or not the Archbishop of Canterbury could statutably convene a Synod of the Exarchate whenever he thought fit, Present state of the case.

EARLY HISTORY.

and whether or not the Metropolitan of York and his Provincial Synod would be bound to give attendance, under penalty of being guilty of a misdemeanour at Common Law for breach of Statute, in case of disobedience to the Canterbury mandate.

Thus stands the case statutably. Looking at it from an Ecclesiastical point of view, considerable light is thrown on the subject by the two facts. First, that in the Canterbury Synod which enacted the Thirty-nine Articles of Religion in 1562--3 the Metropolitan of York and the Northern Bishops of Durham and Chester, if not other members of the York Convocation, certainly did make their appearance. And, secondly, that at the Canterbury Synod of 1661, which authorized the present Book of Common Prayer, the Metropolitan of York and the Bishops of Durham and Carlisle, together with eight delegates from the York Province, attended; and, further, that the book was subscribed synodically at Westminster by the three Prelates and six of the delegates just mentioned. Nor should it be overlooked that in the title page [1] of the Form of Prayer to be used in Convocation, as printed both in 1689 and in 1703, it is specified that the form is meant either for one Provincial Synod, or for the two Provincial Synods united.

[1] Forma Precum in utraque domo Convocationis sive Synodo Prelatorum et cæteri Cleri seu Provincialis seu Nationalis in ipso statim cujuslibet sessionis initio solemniter recitanda. Londini, typis Car. Bill et Tho. Newcomb, Regiæ Majestati typogr. 1689. 4to.

The forms of proceeding in a Synod of the Exarchate in England are specially described in various parts of the "Concilia Magnæ Britanniæ," and may thus be condensed: On arriving at the church, the place of meeting, where preparations had been previously made by providing seats rising in the form of steps from the ground, the members took their places in defined order. The Archbishop of Canterbury, as President, occupied the chief seat. On his right hand was placed the Metropolitan of York, and on his left the Bishop of London. Next the Metropolitan of York sat the Bishop of Winchester. But if the Metropolitan of York was absent, then the Bishop of London sat on the right of the Archbishop of Canterbury, and the Bishop of Winchester on his left. After these Prelates had taken their places, the other Bishops seated themselves according to the dates of their respective consecrations. These rules of precedence were settled in the Synod of London, A.D. 1075, in accordance with the tenor of some old Canons and after consultation with aged and experienced men who could remember the ancient practice of the Anglo-Saxon Church. When the members had taken their places, and silence obtained, the Gospel "I am the Good Shepherd," &c., was read. Collects were then offered up and the hymn "Veni Creator" sung. Next followed the sermon, at the end of which the Archbishop

EARLY HISTORY.

Forms of proceeding in a Synod of the English Exarchate. Conc. M. B. i. pp. 648, 363, 391, 493; and App. 786.

EARLY HISTORY.

explained the cause of the meeting; formal business was introduced by the officials, and the matters thus introduced discussed. After discussion the opinions of the members were taken, their decisions reduced to writing, signed and sealed by the Archbishop, and signed by the other members of the assembly.

Should our authorities see fit at any time hereafter to unite our two Provincial Synods for any special purpose in a Synod of the Exarchate, there may, as above stated, be found ample precedents for the regulation of proceedings.

In imitation of the example of the early Church, when not merely Provincial but more extended interests have been concerned, the two Provincial Synods of Canterbury and York have, as above described, united in a Synod of the Exarchate. But other methods have been adopted to secure the authority of the Synodical Exarchate.

Various methods for securing the authority of a Synod of the English Exarchate.

A second method has been to hold the two Provincial Synods simultaneously, though separately, each in its usual place, for deliberation on the same business. This plan was pursued when the Canterbury and York Synods were held concurrently and on the same business, the one at Lambeth, the other at Beverley, in 1261; and also in this generation, when the questions relating to the revision of rubrics were discussed in both Convocations simultaneously.

A third method for securing the authority of our two Provincial Synods has been to ratify documents in one assembly and then to transmit them to the other for its authorization. This was the method adopted in passing the Decrees abolishing the Papal Supremacy in 1534, hereafter to be specially detailed; in the enactment of the 141 Canons of 1603–4; in the enactment of the 17 Canons of 1640; and more recently, in our own time, when the Articles of Clergy Subscription in the 36th and following Canons were remodelled and re-enacted; those Canons having been enacted in the Canterbury Synod on June 29, 1865, and in that of York on July 5 next ensuing.

A fourth method has been for the Metropolitan and Bishops of the Northern Province, together with Delegates of the Lower House of their Provincial Synod, to attend the Southern Synod, and there to unite in joint deliberations. This was the case in the review and authorization of the present Prayer Book, when the Northern Metropolitan and Bishops, with Delegates for York, attended the Canterbury Synod in London. To the act of authorization ratifying that book their signatures, appended on December 20, 1661, appear after those of the Archbishop, Bishops, and Clergy of the Canterbury Province, as will be seen hereafter detailed in these pages.

PART II.

THE INAUGURATION, PROMOTION, AND COMPLETION OF THE REFORMATION IN DOCTRINE, RITUAL, AND DISCIPLINE, BY THE CONVOCATIONS OF THE CHURCH OF ENGLAND.

1531—1562-3.

I.

THE REFORMATION INAUGURATED BY CONVOCATIONAL ACTION.

Metropolitans: Warham, Lee.

K. Henry VIII., his courtiers and favourites, unpromising as Reformers.

IT has been a somewhat exceptionable method with historians, certainly an inconsiderate one, to refer the origin and progress of the Reformation of religion in this country solely to the humours of King Henry VIII., the influences of his courtiers, and the proceedings of his favourites. But it is by consulting the records of the Convocations of Canterbury and York that we may discover a more reliable account of the advances which were made towards a true reformation, and a recovery of primitive faith and practice in the Church of England. And these methods of advancement appear to a common capacity to fall in better with Christian maxims, and to square more exactly with the measures of conscience than the managements of King Henry VIII. and the proceedings of his allies in public affairs, whose acts are strangely supposed to have mainly secured the purification of faith and practice.

When that monarch played away at one throw of the royal dice, to Sir Miles Partridge, the peal of "Jesus Bells" hanging in a steeple not far from St. Paul's, London, and renowned for their metal and tone; or when he granted the estates of a religious house to a person who had pleased his palate with a dish of puddings; or when he made havoc for his own purposes of the property of the Church throughout this land, it can hardly be affirmed that he shewed any special or tender regard for the interests of religion. And again, when his courtier the Duke of Somerset erected a scaffolding round Westminster Abbey, with the view of demolishing it for the sake of providing building materials to enlarge his own mansion—for the erection of which, by the way, three Bishops' houses [Coventry, Llandaff, and Worcester] and the Church of St. Mary, Strand, had been already pulled down—it can hardly be supposed that property dedicated to God's ser-

Sovereign:
K. Henry VIII.
1531–1547.

Metropolitans: Warham, Lee.

vice, and temples consecrated to His honour, were very precious in that nobleman's estimation, at least for their proper uses. Most surely, had not the Duke of Somerset's intentions been diverted by timely gifts of land, this country would have experienced, in the demolition of one of her most cherished monuments of antiquity, some sadly sensible evidence of his reforming zeal. No doubt, by these self-appointed reformers the religious were disfurnished in a great measure of their worldly goods, and a vast amount of consecrated property, formerly applied to the promotion of the then received belief, was diverted into profane channels. But it is noway clear that the deprived persons, or indeed any others, would thus be much mended in their faith. Nor can it be reasonably supposed that the people of England generally would be particularly encouraged in the cultivation and improvement of Christian morals by the conspicuous examples of those reformers who, on the comparison between treasures corruptible and incorruptible, certainly made such a choice as was disallowed by our Saviour Himself; and who in practice, too, banished from their code the second great commandment of the Christian Law. And, further, it does not appear from history that by any subsequent rejection of their ungodly gains an example of such repentance as even Judas manifested ever commended their proceedings to public regard. A true reformation in religion is surely not to be set to the account of such apostles as these.

That national blessing, fraught with treasure not of this world, must be ascribed to a very different cause. It must be referred to more scrupulous agents and less suspicious hands. Indeed, the whole career of King Henry VIII.'s own life forbids even the supposition that he could be any true reformer either of faith or morals. Passing over his cruel condemnation to death of those venerable men, Fisher and More; of his once cherished satellite, Thomas Cromwell; and of numerous other victims who failed to bend before his imperious mandates for personal self-assertion—not dwelling now on his barbarous treatment of the inoffensive brethren in the Charterhouse, on his sacrilegious pillages of Church property, or his matrimonial enormities—there was one act of tyranny and avarice perpetrated by him which is specially pertinent to the present subject, and which, moreover, hopelessly disqualifies him from deserving the character of a reformer of religion; at least, if the most flagrant injustice and greedy seizure of other people's goods constitute such incapacity. That act of tyranny and injustice was as follows.

Cardinal Wolsey, when in favour with King Henry, had received a pallium from Rome, and

Sovereign:
K. Henry VIII.
1531–1547.

Royal title, "So far as the law of Christ permits, even Supreme Head."

*Metro-politans:
Warham,
Lee.*

with the King's earnest and active help had, with that Papal flourish of legatine authority, tyrannized over Archbishop Warham and the whole English Clergy to an extent almost unimaginable. But when Wolsey fell out of favour at Court, and his fortunes sank, the King espied a crafty method of enriching his own pocket. So, relying on the Statutes of "Provisors "and Præmunire," he brought an indictment in the King's Bench against the whole body of the Clergy for having submitted to Wolsey's legatine authority—an authority which King Henry himself had previously most strenuously encouraged. However, he offered the Clergy this alternative, that the prosecution against them should be abandoned if the Clergy of the Province of Canterbury would pay to him £100,044 8s. 8d., and the Clergy of the Province of York £18,840 0s. 10d. To this graceful offer the Clergy were obliged to accede, or otherwise they must have been irretrievably all ruined; for the penalties under the Statutes he invoked in the King's Bench were imprisonment and fine at the King's will. But though the Clergy agreed in their Convocations to submit to this imposition, they checked at subscribing the instrument sent to them by the King, which named the amount of money he demanded. It contained these words: "Of the English Church and Clergy, of which "the King alone is Protector and Supreme Head."

This they absolutely declined to subscribe, and were prepared to hazard all results rather than do so. After long and earnest discussions with the King's emissaries on this matter, the above enormous grant, according to the then value of money, being twenty times as large as would now appear from the above recorded sums, was made, the King's title, in the terms of the legal instrument, being changed into these words: "So far "as the law of Christ permits, even the Supreme "Head." This event took place in the year 1531, and inferentially discharged the Clergy from the yoke of obedience to Rome by their own vote. *Sovereign: K. Henry VIII. 1531-1547.*

It is not surprising that a virtual abjuration of Papal Supremacy should have been expressed on this occasion by the Convocations. For from the earliest times downwards continual protests against the encroachments of Rome had been common on the part of this Church and her chief authorities. The memorable refusal of the Seven British Bishops to acknowledge the Pope as their superior, when urged to do so by Augustine on his first arrival in England, has above been recorded. In rather more than half a century afterwards, at the National Council of Whitby, A.D. 664, the most strenuous opposition was exhibited again by the representatives of the British Church against the intrusion of Roman usages. And this resistance was subsequently more successfully carried out at the *Continual resistance of the Church of England to the encroachments of Rome. Sup. pp. 17—19. Spelman, Conc. i. 145. Soames, Anglo-Sax. Ch. p. 72.*

<small>Metropolitans:
Warham,
Lee.

Spelman,
Conc. i. 201.
Labb. &
Coss. vi.
1382–5.</small>

National Synod of Osterfield, A.D. 701, under Archbishop Berthwald, when Wilfrid, the champion of the Pope's cause, reproached the members of the Synod with having openly opposed the Papal authority for "twenty-two years together." But the National Synod of Osterfield, notwithstanding this boastful flourish of reproach, decreed that "the See of Rome could not interfere "with an Anglican Council," nor alter its decisions.

In the year **747**, Boniface, Archbishop of Mentz, but an Englishman by birth, had forwarded to Cuthbert, Archbishop of Canterbury, a copy of a Code of Canons decreed at Augsburg, which enforced with much emphasis the authority of the Roman Pontiff. These were meant to be in some sort a guide for Synodical proceedings in Britain. But, with these Augsburg Canons before it, the National Council of Cliff-at-Hoo, in the year last mentioned, enacted a Constitution as follows: "Every Bishop should be "earnest in defending the flock committed to "him, and the Canonical institutions of the "Church of Christ, with all his might against "all sorts of rude encroachments." Now the Canonical institutions here vouched seem manifestly to point to the Canons of Nice [vi.], 1 Constantinople [ii.], and Ephesus [viii.], on the subject of the independence of Exarchates. And, moreover, the Second Constitution now enacted at

<small>Conc. M. B.
1—95.</small>

Cliff-at-Hoo, notwithstanding Boniface's counsels, looks the same way, and seems directly intended to proclaim the independence of this National Church. *Sovereign:* **K. Henry VIII.** 1531–1547.

A conspicuous instance of the determination of this Church in Britain to maintain her independence on Rome may be found in the proceedings of a National Synod held A.D. 969. Archbishop Dunstan had excommunicated a nobleman for an atrocious offence. This person, by unworthy means, obtained on an appeal to Rome a favourable decision in his case; and the Pope sent a communication commanding Dunstan to restore the offender to the bosom of the Church. But our Archbishop defended his own authority and the independence of this National Church, rejecting all Papal interference, and delivering himself as became the occasion in the following words: "When I shall see tokens of "penitence in that person whose cause is now "under consideration, I will willingly obey the "precepts of the Pope; but so long as the of-"fender continues in his sin, and, claiming im-"munity from Ecclesiastical discipline, insults "my authority, and rejoices in his evil deeds, "God forbid that I should do so. May God "defend me from contravening that law which "my Lord Jesus Christ, the Son of God, has ap-"pointed to be kept in His Church, in deference "to any mortal man, even though it were for Conc. M. B. i. 247–8.

Metropolitans:
Warham, Lee.

"the preservation of my own life." And the Archbishop maintained his determination until the offender submitted to penance.

Not only in regard to discipline do we find these examples of independence on Rome maintained in the British and Anglo-Saxon Church; this independence extended also to doctrinal questions. The seasons of some of the Church's fasts here were quite different from those appointed by Roman authority, as may be seen by reference to Johnson's "Canons," i. 362, and to Heylin's "History of the Sabbath." And, further, as regarded the translation of Holy Scripture into the vulgar tongue, the practice of this Church was entirely opposed to that of Rome. Aldhelm, Bede, and Elfric translated the Scriptures into the vernacular, and Alcuin continually in eloquent terms commended their perusal.

S. Turner, Hist. Anglo-Saxons, iii. p. 431.

On the doctrine of transubstantiation, moreover, the Anglo-Saxon Church differed widely from that of the Roman. The Roman doctrine on this subject is emphatically contravened by the Canons attributed to Elfric, and usually assigned to the year 957. In the 37th of that Code these words occur: "That housel is Christ's Body, not "corporally, but spiritually," &c.; and in like strain this Canon proceeds. And the same doctrine is taught in an Easter Homily of Elfric Putta, Metropolitan of York; and also in one of his letters to his Clergy, in which these words of plain

Inett, Orig. Ang. pp. 350 seq.

significance are found: "This sacrifice of the "Eucharist is not our Saviour's Body in which "He suffered for us, nor His Blood which He "shed upon our account; but it is made His "Body and Blood in a spiritual way, as the "manna was which fell from the sky, and the "water which flowed from the rock." And here the reader may pause to consider how exactly the doctrine on the subject of the Eucharist held by the ancient Church of this land coincides with that taught by the Church of England at the present hour.

Sovereign: K. Henry VIII. 1531– 1547.

Again, in the matter of solitary Communion, or "Low Mass," celebrated by a single priest, as now practised in the Roman Church, the Anglo-Saxon Church was opposed to any such service. This may be learnt from the 7th of those called Theodulf's "Capitula," translated into Anglo-Saxon by Elfric, Archbishop of Canterbury, for the use of the National Church. The words of that Canon are: "Mass Priests "ought by no means to sing Mass alone by "themselves without other men. . . . He ought "to greet the bystanders, and they ought to "make the responses. He ought to remember "the Lord's declaration in the Gospel, 'When "'two or three are gathered together in My "'Name, there am I in the midst of them.'"

Inett, Orig. Ang. p. 355.

From the above facts it may be seen that both in discipline and doctrine the British and

Anglo-Saxon Church did differ from the Roman obedience, and did from time to time assert and maintain her independence. It is observable that such manifestations of independence were continued down to the time of the Norman Conquest, and just before that event were asserted in a very conspicuous instance. For Stigand, the last of the line of Anglo-Saxon Archbishops, vehemently resisted the Pope's authority for eight years consecutively; and though interdicted by the Roman Pontiff, maintained his just independence in his See, and exercised all his Archiepiscopal functions until the arrival of William the Norman.

That conqueror of our land not only expelled this last Anglo-Saxon Archbishop, but also his brother Agelmar, Bishop of the East Angles; and also deprived many other Anglo-Saxon Bishops of their Sees, and native Ecclesiastics of their offices, in order to find places and preferment for his Norman favourites, who were wholly devoted to Rome. In truth, the Norman Conquest introduced and inaugurated that successful and fatal Papal aggression which, by the connivance and even assistance of English Sovereigns, subsequently assumed portentous dimensions. Pope Alexander II. was engaged on the side of King William I., and had conferred on him a standard and a consecrated ring before the attack on England was made; and thus Pope and Conqueror were banded together in common

Metropolitans: Warham, Lee.

Conc. M. B. i. 315.
Thierry, Nor. Conq. i. 144.

Conc. M. B. i. 322.

cause against the Anglo-Saxon nation and Anglo-Saxon Church. Not only were the Anglo-Saxon Prelates, including the Archbishop of Canterbury and other high Ecclesiastics in office, expelled to make room for Normans, but in the very first Council held under the Conqueror, at Winchester, A.D. 1070, in the place of a native Archbishop there is found a Swiss Bishop with the flourish of "Papal Legate" attached to his name. And, as though this were not a sufficient humiliation for the National Church, the names of two "Presbyter Cardinals" are added as conspicuous members of the assembly.

For fresh aggressions of Rome on the independence of this Church and nation some of our subsequent Sovereigns were mainly chargeable. These aggressions they countenanced for political and fiscal reasons. Not only did William the Conqueror call in the Pope's aid to eject the Anglo-Saxon Prelates; the usurper Stephen obtained from Rome the confirmation of his claim to the throne. King Henry II., to promote his ends, accepted at the hands of Pope Adrian the title to the Kingdom of Ireland. King John, at the bidding of Pope Innocent III., humbled himself in a manner as abject as can be imagined before the feet of Pandulf, the Roman Legate. King Henry III. forwarded the designs of the Papacy by encouraging legatine Synods in this country, ten of which were held during his

Sovereign:
K. Henry VIII.
1531–1547.

Metropolitans: Warham, Lee.

reign. And he made himself notorious by taking part with the Legates Otho and Rustand on some of those occasions, against the loud and honest remonstrances of the English Prelates.

Conc. M. B. i. 647.

Nothing could exceed the contumely with which the English Clergy were treated by these Roman emissaries. On one occasion the English Prelates, in company with all the Scholars of the University of Oxford, were compelled to walk from St. Paul's to the house of the Bishop of Carlisle, and thence, having divested themselves of their caps and gowns, to go in procession, not only bareheaded but barefoot too, to the Legate's

Coll. Eccl. Hist. ii. 484.

residence, a mile from the cathedral. Matthew Paris describes in a most tragical strain the state to which this Church was reduced by such a course of policy. He laments "that the daugh-"ter of Zion was become, as it were, an harlot;" that "persons of no merit or learning came "menacing with the Pope's Bull into England, "hectored themselves into preferment, trampled "upon the privileges of the country, and seized "the revenues designed by our pious ances-"tors for the support of religion, and for the "benefit of the poor, and for the entertainment "of strangers." And then this chronicler continues his reasonable complaints by adding that whereas formerly the offices in the Church were held by natives of birth and character, the land is now pestered with obscure rapacious persons, no better than farmers and servants to the Court of Rome, who glean up the wealth of the country for the pride and luxury of their masters; and that thus England, aforetime so illustrious, was made a prey to foreigners, and sunk in ignominious degeneracy.

<small>Sovereign: K. Henry VIII. 1531–1547.</small>

But, notwithstanding the royal patronage conceded to these excesses, the English Clergy from time to time resented this Roman tyranny. Edmund, Archbishop of Canterbury, protested vehemently against the aggressions made against his Metropolitan See. Sewall, Archbishop of York, directed a sharp remonstrance on the like subject to Pope Alexander IV., taking occasion to remind that Pontiff that "when our Saviour commissioned "St. Peter to feed His sheep, He did not give him "authority to flay or eat them." When the Legate Rustand, appearing in a Synod at London, A.D. 1255, attempted to exercise unwarrantable jurisdiction over this Church, Fulco, Bishop of London, most unmistakably delivered his mind, after several days' debate, as follows: "I will certainly "bear to have my head cut off before I will "consent to such slavery on the part of our "Church, and to such injustice effected by in- "tolerable oppression." Nor was his brother Bishop of Worcester, Walter, less emphatic in his language when he added: "I would sooner "be condemned to be hanged than that the "liberty of our holy Church should be subject

<small>Coll. Eccl. Hist. ii. 548.</small>

<small>Conc. M. B. i. 709-10.</small>

_{Metro-
politans:
Warham,
Lee.}

"to such an overthrow." And, further, against this union of Royal and Papal power for the degradation of the Church, the Bishop of London, declining pacific remonstrance, adopted quite a martial tone. For when King Henry III. made bold to say that neither the Bishop nor any of those who acted with him loved their King, and that "he would take good care that "the Pope should both rebuke and punish such "conduct," the Bishop, nothing daunted, replied:

_{Conc. M. B.
i. 710.}

"The Pope and the King, stronger than I, may "deprive me of my Bishopric; yet let them take "my mitre, I shall change it for a helmet."

In the reigns of King Henry V. and King Henry VI. we again see this resistance by the Clergy to Roman aggression conspicuously shewn. When it was proposed that the uncle of King Henry V. should be made a Cardinal and "Legate à latere" from the Pope, the Archbishop of Canterbury, Chicheley, forbade and prevented this encroachment on his See; for, in the words of his letter to the King, "he was bound to "oppose it by his ligeance, and also to quit "himself to God and the Church of this land." And, further, this Archbishop again maintained his independence on Rome, when the Pope required him to endeavour to obtain a repeal of the Statutes of Præmunire which forbid appeals to Rome. With this request Chicheley absolutely declined to comply, which so exasperated Pope

Martin V. that he issued a Bull to suspend the Archbishop from his office. But this document the Archbishop wholly ignored, and continued in the discharge of his duty. And his courageous conduct in this respect was so far gratifying to the country at large, that the Lords Spiritual and Temporal, the University of Oxford, and the Commons, addressed the King in favour of one who had incurred the displeasure of the Pope by opposing these aggressive inroads on the independence of the National Church. Not only did Archbishop Chicheley thus oppose Martin V., but he equally defended the rights of this Church against Pope Eugenius IV., by refusing to consecrate to the Bishopric of Ely a person nominated for the See by that Pontiff.

This resistance to Roman aggression was not merely manifested by the words and acts of individual Archbishops, Bishops, and Ecclesiastics, but sometimes also by more formal Synodical action. In the Synod of London, held under Archbishop Boniface, A.D. 1246, the subject of Papal interference was brought before the assembly, when, "as regards the state " of the English Church"—it was decided that— " contradiction should be signified to the Pope, "and that an appeal should be made to the " presence of our Lord Jesus Christ, and to " a General Council, by God's grace" at some time to be convened. And again, in the eighteenth year

Sovereign: K. Henry VIII. 1531–1547.

Metropolitans:
Warham,
Lee.

of King Henry VI., A.D. 1439, when the Canterbury Provincial Synod met in London under Archbishop Chicheley, a Bull from Rome was laid before the assembly with a view to its adoption by the English Church. But this Papal instrument the Synod absolutely refused to confirm or even to allow.

A return must now be made to our immediate subject. Considering the constant remonstrances which had been here made and persisted in, both in Anglo-Saxon and later times, against the aggressions of Rome, and the pretensions of the Roman Pontiff to be the head of this Church, it is not surprising that both Convocations in 1531 should have granted the style and title to the Sovereign of this country, as before detailed, which proclaimed the Church of England free from usurped Roman jurisdiction. The abolition of that jurisdiction by the Convocations, so far as Ecclesiastical authority reached, now put an end to all appeals from the native Ecclesiastical Courts of England to Rome.

The present was a notable era in our national history. For, however strange it may appear, it is nevertheless a fact, that notwithstanding the Statutes of Provisors and Præmunire, which absolutely forbid such proceedings, English subjects, when worsted here in their legal contentions before their country's proper Ecclesiastical Courts, did from time to time carry appeals thence to Rome. And it has been thought that this was done on occasion by the connivance of our Sovereigns; otherwise, in face of the stringent provisions of the Statutes just mentioned, it is hard to understand how such appeals to a foreign jurisdiction could have been promoted. But, however this may be, it is clear that from this time, 1531, by the grant of this title to the Sovereign—" so far as the law of "Christ permits, even Supreme Head"— the Clergy, as far as they were concerned, declared that all Curial jurisdiction was to be restrained within the borders of the land. While at the same time, by adding the proviso—" so far as "the law of Christ permits"—they retained to themselves all authority over doctrine and ritual, which the law of Christ would allow them to concede to no mortal man.

_{Sovereign:
K. Henry
VIII.
1531–
1547.}

Indeed, that King Henry VIII., a monarch not specially prone to construe anything whatsoever to his own disadvantage, did himself so understand this grant of title with its proviso is quite clear from his reply to the York Clergy who interrogated him on the subject. His Majesty's words were these: " As to spiritual " things .... forasmuch as they be no worldly " or temporal things, they have no worldly nor " temporal head, but only Christ that did institute " them, by Whose ordinances they be ministered " here by mortal men, elect, chosen, and ordained,

_{Conc. M. B.
iii. 764.}

<small>Metropolitans: Warham, Lee.</small>

"as God hath willed for that purpose, who be "the Clergy." And again, when the Royal style and title was afterwards confirmed by Statute, we learn the same from a MS. discovered by Mr. Froude in the Rolls' Records. That MS. runs as follows: The King does not "pretend there-"by to take any power from the successors of the "Apostles that was given to them by God . . . ;" nor did "the King's Grace, his nobles, or subjects, "intend to decline or vary from the Congre-"gation of Christ's Church in anything concern-"ing the Articles of the National Faith."

<small>Froude's Hist. Eng. Vol. ii. p. 326.</small>

<small>Convocation invokes aid of the Civil power for repressing Roman exactions.</small>

It was about this time, moreover, that a direct proposal was made, in a petition directed to the Crown by Convocation, that statutable measures might be taken for emancipating this nation from Roman exactions. So that in that assembly such measures were promoted as we shall hereafter see were both synodically and statutably taken for securing national independence. The objection at this time of the English Clergy to the imposition of Roman authority over them was no less incisively expressed now than it had been in earlier times, as before recorded. On the present occasion the Clergy in their Convocation protested most vehemently against the unjust and tyrannical exactions of the Roman Curia. They complain to His Majesty, in a somewhat satirical strain, that the fees exacted for legal instruments sealed at the Court of Rome and thence issued were excessive; assuring the King that "parchment and lead be very dear "merchandize at Rome, and in some cases an "hundred times more worth than the weight "or counterpoise of fine gold." Further, they inform His Majesty that the Court of Rome "getteth by this means and many other much "goods and profits out of this Realm, and never "departeth with any portion thereof hither again;" and so the Convocation prays His Majesty to cause such unjust exactions "to cease and to "be foredone for ever by Act of this His Grace's "High Court of Parliament." And, finally, the Convocation prays His Majesty, in case the Pope should take measures for continuing these exactions, then, that "as al good Christen men be "more bound to obey God than any man; and "forasmuch as St. Paul willeth us to withdraw "ourselves from al such as walk inordinately, "it may please the King's Most Noble Grace to "ordain in this present Parliament, that then "the obedience of him and the people be withdrawn from the See of Rome." Thus the Clergy were manifestly willing to abjure any obedience, and desired that such abjuration on the part of the Crown and country should be fortified by Act of Parliament. On this occasion they sought subsequent Civil sanctions for the aid of the Spiritualty—a course common in the Church in all ages, as will hereafter appear.

Sovereign:
K. Henry VIII.
1531–1547.

Strype's Mem. Vol. i. Pt. 2, p. 158.
Cleopatra, E. 6, p. 263.

Metropolitans: Warham, Lee.

"Submission of the Clergy."

In the year 1532 an event occurred familiarly known as "The Submission of the Clergy," which now requires attention. On April 12, in the year last mentioned, Archbishop Warham introduced into the Canterbury Convocation as a subject for discussion a supplication from the Lower House of Parliament which had been presented to the King. This supplication is by some supposed to have been forged on the Royal anvil by a workman who designed in the collision of forces some advantage to himself. And as to its presentation at a time when Parliament so far demeaned itself as to agree that Royal Proclamations should override Statutes, no one can be surprised that that assembly would present anything which the Sovereign might provide. But, however this may be, the contents of this supplication were somewhat doleful; the chief complaints of alleged grievance being, first, that the old Ecclesiastical Canons in force were injurious to the King's prerogative and burdensome to the subject; secondly, that the Clergy claimed to enact Canons of their own sole authority.

Into the almost interminable discussions which ensued between the representatives of the Convocation and the emissaries of the King on this subject it would be wearisome to enter. They must be read in the pages of the "Conc. "Mag. Brit.," if anyone is so much interested in the subject as to engage in the task of wading through such controversial details. It must suffice here to say, that from April 12 to May 16, 1532, the conferences between the two parties and the debates in the Synod continued; and that on the last-named day the Convocation finally agreed to what is known in history as "The Sub-"mission of the Clergy." This, to sum the matter up shortly, consisted in the following promise, viz.: That they would not enact any new Canons without Royal licence to do so; and that, as regarded the old Canons, they should be revised by the King and thirty-two persons to be chosen by him, sixteen to be Members of Parliament and sixteen to be Clergymen. Grounded on this "Submission of the Clergy," the Statute 25 Hen. VIII. 19, commonly called the "Clergy Submission Act," was enacted rather more than a year and a half afterwards in Parliament, as we shall hereafter see. Sovereign: K. Henry VIII. 1531–1547.

The events last recorded were preparations for the coming Reformation in Religion, as regarded doctrine and ritual. The ground was thus cleared for the building, and active work for the erection of the edifice soon after began in Convocation. But some secular enactments in Parliament must be first considered in their chronological order.

The two Acts named in the margin, and denominated "The Great Statute of Appeals," and "The Clergy Submission Act," were passed Parliamentary legislation. 24 Hen. VIII. 12. 25 Hen. VIII. 19.

Metropolitans: Cranmer, Lee.

in 1533 and 1534 respectively. The 9th section of the first, confirmed by the 3rd section of the second, must be shortly here considered, as having a material bearing on the constitutional powers of the Convocations, and also as having given rise to three of the most important State trials ever recorded in our country's annals.

Convocational jurisdiction in causes "touching the King."

By Section 9 of the first-mentioned Statute, all Ecclesiastical causes "touching the King" were referred, not to any Ecclesiastical or Civil Court in the realm, but in every case to Convocational jurisdiction. This provision took speedy and notable effect, and was carried out in the cases of the trials for divorce between King Henry VIII. and three of his wives—Catharine of Arragon, Anne Boleyn, and Anne of Cleves. Indeed, it is clear, beyond any reasonable doubt, that the provision in question was introduced and enacted specially with a view to the case of Catharine of Arragon. This may be surely learned from a comparison of dates and events. The Parliament in which this provision became law met on Feb. 4 [1533]. The Convocation to which Queen Catharine's case was submitted for judgment, met at St. Paul's on March 26

Conc. M. B. iii. 756.

next following, and on that day Archbishop Cranmer brought into the Synod the documents necessary for the enquiry. Thus it is plain that the clause above mentioned was introduced into the Act in order to give statutable as well

INAUGURATION OF THE REFORMATION. 73

as Ecclesiastical authority to the conclusions which should be arrived at in Convocation.

The enquiry in the case of Catharine of Arragon in truth succeeded immediately upon the enactment of the clause in the "Great Statute of Appeals," which referred all Ecclesiastical causes "touching the King" to Convocational jurisdiction. The chief question submitted to the two Convocations was whether Queen Catharine was the King's lawful wife, inasmuch as before her marriage to him she was the widow of his elder brother, Prince Arthur. Pope Julius II. had given King Henry VIII. a dispensation to contract this marriage, notwithstanding the affinity of Catharine; and the main question which the Convocations had to try was whether this dispensation was beyond the Pope's power. If it was "ultra vires," then the marriage between King Henry and Queen Catharine was illegal, and he was free to marry another. If, on the other hand, the Pope's dispensation was valid, then the King was Catharine's lawful husband, and he could not enter into another marriage contract. The decision of both Convocations on the point above mentioned was worthy of English Provincial Synods. It was decreed in the Canterbury Convocation, by 263 votes to 19, that "it "was unlawful to marry a deceased brother's "wife;" and that such a "prohibition of the

Sovereign:
K. Henry VIII.
1531–1547.

Queen Catharine of Arragon's divorce.

Conc. M. B. iii. 756-8.

L

> "Divine law could not be dispensed with by "the Pope." The same conclusion was arrived at in the York Convocation by 51 votes to 2. Subsequently, Archbishop Cranmer held a Court at Dunstable to pronounce the nullity of marriage between King Henry and Catharine, which was the direct result of these Convocational decisions; and they were specially recited in the body of the judgment. It was of this Court that Shakspeare thus wrote: The Archbishop

> > "Held a late Court at Dunstable, ten miles off
> > "From Ampthill, where the Princess lay; to which
> > "She oft was cited by them, but appear'd not."
> > HEN. VIII. Act iv. Sc. 1.

Metropolitans: Cranmer, Lee.
Conc. M. B. iii. 767.
Coll. Records, Vol. ix. in loco.

A State trial of more significant importance than this can hardly be imagined; for if it had not been adjudged by competent authority that King Henry VIII. was free to marry Anne Boleyn, it is clear that Queen Elizabeth, their daughter, would have been illegitimate, that the English Crown in her person would have been bastardized, and that the persistence of a writer of this generation in designating that renowned Sovereign of this realm as Miss Elizabeth Boleyn, would be fully justified.

Q. Anne Boleyn's divorce.

A second instance of the exercise of this Convocational jurisdiction in "Kings' Causes" was exemplified in the case of Anne Boleyn's subsequent divorce three years afterwards, in

1536. In June of that year the sentence of divorce was agreed to in the Canterbury Convocation, and the necessary seals and signatures of the members were attached to the instrument.

A third instance of the exercise of this Convocational jurisdiction in "Kings' Causes" occurred in 1540. So far as the arrangements for the prosecution of this matter [which involved the question whether a pre-contract of Anne of Cleves with a son of the Duke of Lorraine annulled her marriage to King Henry VIII.], and the high figure of the persons examined as witnesses, a more imposing State trial was perhaps never witnessed in this country. Both Convocations were united in London for the purpose. A Committee was appointed of Bishops and other Ecclesiastics from both Provinces, who met at the Royal Palace, Westminster, for the examination of witnesses. Those witnesses were the most notable persons in the realm, comprising, among others, the Lord Chancellor Audley, the Dukes of Norfolk and Suffolk, the Lord High Admiral Russell, Sir Anthony Browne Master of the Horse, Lord Southampton, Lord Cobham, with others of high degree. These noblemen and gentlemen put in written depositions, swearing to the truth of their contents; and those documents were filed as schedules for the guidance of the Convocations in coming to a final judg-

Sovereign: K. Henry VIII. 1531–1547.

Conc. M. B. iii. 803.

Nullification of the marriage of Anne of Cleves.

Conc. M. B. iii. 851.

Ibid. iii. 852.

ment. To add solemnity of circumstance, among the papers was a deposition of the King himself, with a declaration upon the matter under Thomas Cromwell's hand. Finally, after long investigations, it was decided by the united Convocations, and by an overwhelming vote, that the King's marriage to Anne of Cleves was not binding; and the instrument to that effect, sealed with the seals of the Archbishops of Canterbury and York, and subscribed by the hands of the other members of the Synod, bears date July 9, 1540.

Bearing the foregoing facts in mind, it is somewhat surprising that the learned Justices of the Court of Common Pleas should have in our times affirmed that, "after due enquiry and "investigation, no instance has been found of "an appeal in such cases [i.e. Kings' Causes] to "the Convocation." The enquiry, one imagines, must have been of a very superficial character which did not discover some of the most imposing State trials ever witnessed in the country, both as regards their circumstances and their consequences. Nor was the announcement of the learned Barons of the Exchequer less astonishing, especially considering that they had affirmed that they should themselves carefully examine the subject before giving judgment on it. However, after this promised examination, they announced to the world that it was a "fact "that no appeal to Convocation ever has taken "place during the three centuries which have "elapsed since the passing of these Statutes." As this due enquiry and careful examination produced such remarkably slender results, in presence of some of the most important national events that ever occurred, it must be presumed that this enquiry and examination was confined to the records of the Law Courts. But some people will be apt to remember that those records do not wholly exhaust the historic annals of England.

It would not condone the above judicial misapprehensions to plead that these cases "touching the King" were not tried by the Convocations on appeal from a lower Court, but in first instance; because, as is well known in Ecclesiastical jurisprudence, applications are often made to the higher Court "primâ vice."

If the world was not pretty well accustomed to strange deliverances from the secular tribunals on Ecclesiastical subjects, the reader would hardly give credit to the fact that the foregoing announcements have been judicially pronounced. However, many late experiences in this respect may easily reconcile him to the belief. As we proceed he will have such belief confirmed by some very assuring and instructive examples.

The chief corner-stone of a true reformation in the doctrine, ritual, and discipline of

Sovereign: K. Henry VIII. 1531–1547.

Formal rejection of Papal Supremacy by the Convocations of Canterbury and York, the chief corner-stone of the Reformation.

Metropolitans:
Cranmer,
Lee.

the Church of England was really laid by the Convocations of Canterbury and York in the year 1534. On March 31 in that year the Canterbury Convocation, with only four dissentients in the Lower House; and on May 5 the Convocation of York unanimously, decreed that—

"THE POPE OF ROME HAS NO GREATER JURIS-"DICTION CONFERRED ON HIM BY GOD IN HOLY "SCRIPTURE IN THIS KINGDOM OF ENGLAND THAN "ANY OTHER FOREIGN BISHOP" ["Conc. Mag. "Brit." iii. 769, and Wake's MSS., Ch. Ch. Library, ad ann. 1534].

Thus by the Synodical Decrees of our two Convocations the Papal Supremacy in England was formally discharged, and thus the primitive independence of the British Church was canonically restored.

It is impossible to overestimate the importance of this fact, as it was the real foundation of the Reformation. The renunciation of the Papal Supremacy, after these Synodical Decrees on the subject had been promulged, became general throughout the English Church and nation. Original Decrees and transcripts of those Decrees declaring such renunciation remained for many generations preserved in the Exchequer. The learned Mr. Wharton had no less than one hundred and seventy-five authentic copies thence obtained. Those transcripts contained the subscriptions

Coll. Eccl. Hist. iv. 267.

INAUGURATION OF THE REFORMATION. 79

of all the Bishops and Members of Chapters, Monasteries, Colleges, and Hospitals of thirteen Dioceses. That learned person also declared that he had certain knowledge that the original subscriptions from the remaining Dioceses were lodged elsewhere. So universally did the mass of the national Clergy and people join in formally protesting against the Papal Supremacy as soon as it had been synodically renounced by the authority of the two Convocations.

Sovereign: K. Henry VIII. 1531–1547.

This renunciation of the Papal Supremacy, and this vindication of the primitive independence of the British Church by her Provincial Synods, were a rightful assertion of the principle known in Ecclesiastical history as the JUS CYPRIUM, and were strictly warranted by those Canons and rules governing Ecclesiastical territorial jurisdictions which were decreed by Œcumenical Councils.

Rejection of Papal Supremacy warranted by the JUS CYPRIUM.

Thus the Sixth Canon of the first Œcumenical Council [Nice] specially confirms the independent rights of the Egyptian, Lybian, Pentapolitan, and Antiochian Exarchates, as being in conformity with the "ancient customs, which " should prevail."

Again, the Second Canon of the Second Œcumenical Council [Constantinople, I.] is very clear on this head, forbidding usurpations such as the English Church had been subjected to by the Roman Pontiffs. "Let no Bishops," runs that Canon, "go beyond their Diocese [Exarchate]

Metropolitans: Cranmer, Lee.

"to Churches beyond their bounds, nor disturb "the Churches. According to the Canons, let "the Bishop of Alexandria administer the affairs "of Egypt; and the Bishops of the East govern "the East alone; the rights and privileges of the "Church of Antioch sanctioned by the Nicene "Canons being preserved inviolate. Let the "Bishops of the Asian Diocese administer the "Asian affairs only; and the Bishops of the "Pontic Diocese the affairs of Pontus only; and "they of Thrace the affairs of the Thracian "Diocese only. But let not Bishops go out of "their Diocese for ordination or any other "Ecclesiastical administration uninvited. The "superscribed Canon touching the Dioceses being "observed, it is manifest that in each Province "the Synod of the Province will rule, according "to the Decrees which were defined at Nice."

And still again, the Eighth Canon of the Third Œcumenical Council [Ephesus], as quoted by high authorities, is very clear on this head. It runs thus: "The same rule shall be observed "in all other Dioceses and Provinces whatsoever, "so that no Bishop shall occupy another Pro- "vince which has not been subject to him from "the beginning; and if he shall have made any "such occupation or seizure, let him make "restitution, lest the Canons of the Holy Fathers "be transgressed," &c.

It is here admitted that this last-mentioned

Canon does not appear in all editions of the Ephesine Canons. But when it is remembered that to defend an unwarrantable usurpation in Africa a local Sardican Canon was impudently vouched by the Roman Curia for an Œcumenical Canon of Nice, it is easier to believe that this Eighth Canon of Ephesus has under the like influences been surreptitiously excised, than to imagine that it could by any influences whatsoever at any time have been surreptitiously inserted into the Ephesine Code.

Sovereign: K. Henry VIII. 1531– 1547.

Neander, Ed. Bruns. pp. 157 D, 160 I, 202.

A true reformation having been thus inaugurated by the Convocations, the next step is to trace the course of events by which that reformation was promoted.

II.

THE REFORMATION PROMOTED BY CONVOCATIONAL ACTION.

It will at this point be needful to enter into a somewhat long enquiry, shewing by comparison of dates that Synodical Acts preceded Civil sanctions during the reign of King Henry VIII. in matters connected with doctrine, ritual, and discipline. But, before doing so, it is desirable to point out that this principle of confirming preceding Acts of the Church by subsequent Civil sanctions was familiar to the early ages of Christianity, was the practice adopted in this country, and had been continued without intermission down to the times now under consideration. And it is the more needful to do this because the most fanciful misapprehensions are in our own times current on this head, some people oddly supposing, in their undistinguishing conclusions, because they find Ecclesiastical matters the subjects of Civil ordinances, and of Acts of Parliament, that therefore the matters involved were originated by secular authority. We will, then, take a retrospect of this matter.

Metropolitans: Cranmer, Lee.

The heads of the Church have frequently, from earliest times, themselves sought the help of the Civil power to corroborate their Spiritual authority. It was to add the force of Civil to Ecclesiastical authority that Ambrose appealed to Theodosius I. The words of that Father, among others, were these: "My words will not "have such force as your Edict." The Count Candidian was despatched by Theodosius the Younger and Valentinian III. to the Ephesine Council, for the very purpose that Imperial authority might fortify the proceedings there. That emissary was yet strictly charged by the Emperors not " to enter into any disputations, for " that it was unlawful for him who was not in " the holy order of the Episcopate to intermix " in Ecclesiastical discussions." "Princes," we learn from Justinian, the Nestor of Jurispru-

Ecclesiastical corroborated by Civil authority in early times.

Labb. et Coss. Tom. iii. pp. 443–4.

dence, "have rightly promulged laws conform- "able to the Synodical Canons, indicating that "the sanctions of the Spiritualty are deservedly "corroborated by the approbation of Royal Ma- "jesty." Our own Sovereigns have followed in the same course as that laid down by Justinian. William I. by his charter distinctly superadded Royal authority to antecedent Ecclesiastical jurisdictions; and, further, commanded by Edict "that every Sheriff should execute justice for "the Bishop and for God, according to the "Canons and Episcopal laws, so that if after "excommunication satisfaction was not made "to the Church, the power and justice of the "Crown should be exercised."

Sovereign: K. Henry VIII. 1531–1547.

It is equally clear that in spiritual matters it was not the practice to permit Civil intervention to precede Ecclesiastical action. In King Edward III.'s reign, when the Commons desired an Act of Parliament to remedy an alleged grievance in an Ecclesiastical matter, that monarch's reply was: "The King will charge the Bishops to see "it remedied." And again, when a similar petition was presented to King Richard II., his reply was that "he will charge the Clergy to "amend the same." In the eleventh year of King Henry IV., on a similar occasion, the Royal answer was: "This matter belongs to "Holy Church, and has been remedied in the "last Convocation." Again, in the third year

Metropolitans: Cranmer, Lee.

of King Henry VI., to a Parliamentary petition on an Ecclesiastical matter, that Sovereign replied that "he had delivered the Bill to the "Archbishops of Canterbury and York, charg- "ing them to provide means of remedy."

This practice of committing matters Ecclesiastical to the jurisdiction of the Spiritualty, and corroborating their Acts by Civil sanction, having been adopted in this country from early ages, and continued down to the time we are considering, was not now abandoned. For the Ecclesiastical laws enacted in the reign of King Henry VIII. had not their first rise in Parliament, but—to use the words of our most learned Ecclesiastical historian—"It is mani- "fest, by the dates of the Acts in Convocation, "that they had first in that place their originals." Of the absolute truth of this statement any unprejudiced reader must be convinced who has patience to peruse the statement of facts now following.

The chief corner-stone of the Reformation having been, as before said, laid by our Convocations in the matter of jurisdiction, it is interesting to trace how in matters of doctrine, ritual, and discipline the Reformation was carried on by degrees, and promoted under the sanctions of the same authority. The summary of that progress shall be here first set down in brief, and then some details respecting the most important matters specified shall follow.

In the reign of King Henry VIII., Convocations compiled or sanctioned in 1536 the Ten Articles of that year. In 1537, the "Institution "of a Christian Man." In 1542, "The New and "Expurgated Edition of the Sarum Use." In 1543, "The Necessary Doctrine and Erudition "of any Christian Man." In 1544, "The English "Reformed Litany." In the reign of Edward VI., in 1547, the authority "to administer the "Communion in both kinds." In the same year "The Abrogation of the Cœlibacy of the Clergy." In 1548, "The Order of the Communion." In 1549, "The First Reformed Prayer Book." In 1552–3 the 42 Articles of Religion of that date. In the same year, as ratified by the 35th of those Articles, the Second Reformed Prayer Book. And, finally, in the reign of Queen Elizabeth, in 1562–3, the present 39 Articles of Religion, at which date the English Reformation may be said to have culminated.

Such is a brief summary of the acts and events which really constituted the Reformation in doctrine, ritual, and discipline in the Church of England. But, as in such a national movement Civil authority of necessity was frequently involved, it shall be shewn by a comparison of dates that in spiritual matters at this epoch of our history Acts of Parliament, Royal Proclamations, and Civil Ratifications did not precede, but followed in point of time,

Sovereign: **K. Henry VIII.** 1531–1547.

Summary of Synodical Acts promoting and completing the Reformation.

the decisions of the Spiritualty, and were merely ancillary to the Acts of the Convocations. This will be plain to any reader who has patience enough to peruse the following very dry details.

<small>Metropolitans: Cranmer, Lee.</small>

<small>Comparison of the dates of Synodical Acts and Civil ratifications.</small>

This enquiry shall begin with the first Acts of Parliament touching doctrine, ritual, or discipline, passed in the reign of King Henry VIII., and be carried on chronologically through the series of Civil instruments connected with religion to the last hour of that monarch's life. Of course, notice need not be taken of those Statutes which merely affected the temporal interest, and legalized the sacrilegious pillage of Church property, as these do not come directly within the scope of an enquiry into the circumstances attending a reformation in doctrine, ritual, and discipline.

The first two Statutes of this reign connected with the present subject affected discipline only. These were "The Great Statute of Appeals," 24 Hen. VIII. 12, and "The Clergy Submission Act," 25 Hen. VIII. 19. The first of these Statutes recognized in its preamble, in the most emphatic language imaginable, the authority of the Spiritualty over all matters spiritual. The effect of the two Acts in combination was, first, to withdraw all Ecclesiastical appeals from Rome and refer them to the Sovereign of this country; secondly, to subject the Clergy to these three disabilities: (1) That they should not be convened in their Convocations without the previous issue of a "Royal Writ." (2) That they should enact no new Canons without a "Licence" from the Crown. (3) That the old Canons should be subjected to a revision by a Commission of sixteen Clergy and sixteen laymen—but that meanwhile those Canons should abide in force until such revision should be completed.

Sovereign: K. Henry VIII. 1531–1547.

Before giving detailed proofs that in questions of doctrine, ritual, and discipline, the Synodical Acts of Convocations preceded at this period of our history the Civil Acts of the State, it is well to quote the preamble of the first Act just mentioned, 24 Hen. VIII. 12; and for this reason. It is "The Great Statute of Appeals," acknowledged on all hands to be one of the fundamental Constitutional Statutes of the realm. Now nothing can be plainer than the language of its preamble, as testifying what was the sense of the nation at that time on the subject before us, and what, it may be added, its sense would be now, if reason instead of silly prejudices prevailed among us. Here, then, are the words of the preamble of that Great Statute, 24 Hen. VIII. 12, when treating of this "Realm of England:" "The body spiritual whereof, having power "when any cause of the law Divine happened "to come in question, or of spiritual learning,

Metropolitans: Cranmer, Lee.

"then it was declared, interpreted, and shewed, "by that part of the said body politic called "the Spiritualty, now being usually called the "English Church, which always hath been re-"puted and also found of that sort that both "for knowledge, integrity, and sufficiency of "members it hath been always thought, and is "also at this hour sufficient and meet of itself, "without the intermeddling of any exterior per-"son or persons, to declare and determine all "such doubts, and to administer all such offices "and duties as to their rooms spiritual doth "appertain."

Let us see, then, by comparison of dates, how the principle here emphatically laid down was adhered to in public managements at this epoch.

The two Statutes above mentioned were passed respectively in the spring of the years 1533 and 1534. Now first, as regards the withdrawal of appeals from Rome therein specified, and the relegation of them to the Crown of England: that was subsequent to and consequent upon the Acts of the Canterbury Convocation on Feb. 11, 1531, and the Acts of the York Convocation on May 4, 1531; for on those occasions each Convocation respectively subscribed an instrument recognizing the Sovereign of this realm to be "of the "English Church and Clergy ... Supreme Head, "so far as the law of Christ permits." Secondly, as regards the disabilities to which the

Coll. Eccl. Hist. iv. 180. Conc. M. B. iii. 744-5.

Clergy, as above specified, were subjected: those were disabilities to which they had themselves consented; and, moreover, were defined in the Statute—"ipsissimis verbis"—in the very words which the Clergy had themselves used and authorized in Convocation on May 15, 1532. *Sovereign: K. Henry VIII. 1531–1547.*

[1] "The King's Proclamation for the Abolishing of the Usurped Power of the Pope" was signed by His Majesty on the 9th day of June, 1534. But the Papal authority had been already synodically discharged in the most emphatic form imaginable on the 31st day of March preceding by the Convocation of Canterbury, and on the 5th day of May preceding by the Convocation of York, as above recorded. *Conc. M. B. iii. 749–754.* *Sup. p. 78.*

The Statute authorizing the King's Grace to be "Supreme Head," was enacted in that Parliament which met at Westminster, Nov. 3, 1534. But the title, "Supreme Head, so far as "the law of Christ permits," was accorded to His Majesty in the Convocation of Canterbury, on the 11th of February, 1531, and in that of York on the 4th of May in the same year, as above stated. *Sup. p. 88.*

At the end of the year 1534, the King's Proclamation "to bring in seditious books" was issued. But the Convocation of Canterbury had previously, on the 19th of December, addressed the King that such a course might be pursued. *Conc. M. B. iii. 770–6.*

---

[1] A fuller detail of the following matter has already appeared in "England's Sacred Synods," by the same author. (Rivingtons, 1855.)

<small>Metropolitans: Cranmer, Lee.</small>

To the next Royal Proclamation, concerning "Heresies," the same argument wholly applies.

The Statute 27 Hen. VIII. 15, giving the King authority to nominate thirty-two persons of the Clergy and Laity for making of Ecclesiastical Laws, was enacted in the Parliament held between Feb. 4, 1536, N.S., and the following April. But the provisions of this Act were merely ancillary to 25 Hen. VIII. 19, passed in 1534, N.S. And the authority specified in both <small>Conc. M. B. iii. 749-54.</small> was accorded in Convocation finally on May 15, 1532.

The Royal Letters to the Archbishop of Canterbury "Against Preachers" were signed by the King on July 12, 1536. But these letters were directed to enforce such doctrines as were contained in the Ten Articles [familiarly known as <small>Ibid. iii. 803-17.</small> the Articles of 1536], which had been subscribed on the previous day, that is, on July 11, 1536, by both Houses of the Canterbury Convocation. Nor did His Majesty forget to recite their Synodical authority, for in the body of the document issued by him these words occur: "We have caused "all you, the Bishops with the Clergy of our "realm, in solemn Convocation, deliberately "disputing and advising the same, to agree to "certain Articles, most Catholic," &c.

The King's Proclamation "For Uniformity in "Religion" next followed in 1536. But this document states upon the face of it that the

King intendeth, "by advice of his Prelates and "Clergy" [a term notoriously signifying Synodical authority], "to enforce uniformity."

<small>Sovereign: K. Henry VIII. 1531-1547.</small>

The Statute [28 Hen. VIII. 7] concerning the "Succession of the Crown," passed in consequence of Queen Anne Boleyn's divorce, was enacted in that Session of Parliament which ended July 18, 1536, and Acts of Parliament then took effect from the last day of session, when they received Royal assent. But this divorce, being a matter of Ecclesiastical cognizance, had been previously adjudged in Convocation, that is to say, on June 21 preceding.

<small>Conc. M. B. iii. 803.</small>

In the same session of Parliament, 1536, the Statute [28 Hen. VIII. 10] for "Extinguishing the "Authority of the Bishop of Rome" was enacted. But that authority had been Synodically extinguished two years previously, in the months of March and May, 1534, respectively, by the Convocations of Canterbury and York, as before stated.

<small>Sup. p. 78.</small>

In the same session the Statute [28 Hen. VIII. 16] "For the Release of such as have ob-"tained pretended Licences, &c., from the Bishop "of Rome" was passed. But in this case the argument under the last head wholly applies.

In this same year, 1536, "The King's Injunc-"tions" were put forth, proclaiming that certain Articles should be declared, that certain holidays should be abrogated, and that certain restraints should be placed on devotions paid to images. But the Articles referred to had been previously ratified by Convocation, a fact to which these Injunctions themselves bear witness, on the preceding 11th of July; the question of holidays had been previously settled in the same assembly, July 19; and devotion to images had been previously restrained, under the same authority, by the Sixth of the Articles above mentioned.

<small>Metropolitans: Cranmer, Lee.</small>

<small>Conc. M. B. iii. 803–823.</small>

The Injunctions published later in this year, 1536, were chiefly supplementary to the last-mentioned Injunctions. The principal points contained were, that the translation of the Bible should be set up in every church, and that superstitious regard to images should be suppressed. But the translation of the Scriptures had been previously requested by Convocation on Dec. 19, 1534, and had now lately been completed in accordance with that request. And the question of images had been previously settled by Synodical authority on the preceding 11th of July in this year, as just above stated.

<small>Ibid. iii. 776.</small>

<small>Ibid. iii. 803, 823.</small>

"Articles about Religion ... published by the "King's authority," were issued in 1536. But their very heading states that they were "set "out by the Convocation." Moreover, in the preamble, the King bears this personal testimony to their Synodical authority: We " have caused " our Bishops, and other the most discreet and " best learned men of our Clergy, of this our

<small>Ibid. iii. 817.</small>

"whole realm, to be assembled in our Convoca- "tion, for the full debatement and determination "of the same."

Sovereign: K. Henry VIII. 1531–1547.

The King's "Strait Commandment ... for the "Abrogation of certain Holy Days, sent to all "Bishops," was also issued in 1536. But these documents were only transcripts of the Decree made in Convocation on the subject, on the 19th of July preceding.

Conc. M. B. iii. 803.

"The King's Letter against too many Holi- "days" was signed by His Majesty, Aug. 11, 1536. But this document merely desired that the late Decree agreed to on the subject by Convocation should be enforced. And, moreover, this instrument declares on the face of it, that "The "superfluity of holidays we have, by the assents "and consents of all you the Bishops and other "notable personages of the Clergy of this our "realm, and in full congregation and assembly "had for that purpose, abrogated."

"A Letter written by the King to his Bishops, "directing how to instruct the people," was published on Nov. 19, 1536. But this document is simply a declaration of Episcopal duties, in accordance with the then existing Ecclesiastical law; some reference being also made to the Ten Articles previously agreed upon by the Canterbury Provincial Synod, on July 11, 1536.

"A Proclamation concerning Rites and Cere- "monies to be used in due form in the Church

<small>Metro-
politans:
Cranmer,
Lee.</small>

"of England" was next issued. But this instrument declares upon its face that all such rites and ceremonies are enjoined "as have "been laudably accustomed in the Church of "England."

The Act [31 Hen. VIII. 14] of the Six Articles, "for abolishing diversity of opinions," &c., was the last Statute enacted in that session of Parliament which ended on June 28, 1539. But the whole of the doctrinal matter which that Statute respected had been previously submitted formally to the Canterbury Synod for their de- <small>Conc. M. B. iii. 845-6.</small> cision on the second day of that month; and answers to the several points proposed having been thence returned in detail, the Act was framed in Parliament in accordance with those answers. This has been usually denominated as the "Whip with six strings." And as there was here no progress towards a true reformation in religion, this matter was not included in the condensed summary above given, which was confined to those Acts of the Convocations which tended to such a result.

In 1539, Injunctions were published, by "the "authority of the King, against English Books, "Sects, and Sacramentaries; also the putting "down the day of Thomas Becket." A perusal of these Injunctions shews that they were intended to stop the publication of heretical writings, to promote the observation of certain doctrines and ceremonies, to settle a point of discipline, and to obliterate from the Calendar Thomas à Becket's day. But Convocation had applied previously to the Crown, on Dec. 19, 1534, on the subject of restraining suspected books. As to the doctrines, ceremonies, and points of discipline alluded to, they had severally been synodically settled previously, that is to say, on July 11, 1536, and on June 2, 1539, respectively; and as to the "putting down the day of Thomas "Becket" his canonization, "made only by the "Bishop of Rome," was necessarily extinguished by the discharge of the Papal Supremacy, under the Synodical authority of the two Provincial Synods of the Church of England in 1534, as above specified.

Sovereign: K. Henry VIII. 1531–1547.

Conc. M. B. iii. 770–6.

Ibid. iii. 803, 820, 821–2.

Sup. p. 78.

The Statute [32 Hen. VIII. 15] "Concerning "Archbishops, Bishops, &c., to be in the Com-"mission ... concerning the Abolition of Erro-"neous Opinions in the Christian Religion," was enacted between April 28 and July 24, 1540. But this Act was merely ancillary to the "Act "of the Six Articles" above mentioned, in respect of which, as has been said before, the whole doctrinal matter contained had been previously submitted to Convocation, and the Act was framed in accordance with the answers thence returned.

The Statute [32 Hen. VIII. 25] for "Dissolu-"tion of the King's pretended Marriage with the "Lady Anne of Cleves" was passed July 12,

Metropolitans: Cranmer, Lee.

1540. But the question of this nullification, being a matter of Ecclesiastical cognizance, had been previously decided in a National Synod, or Synod of the Exarchate, that is to say, on July 9, 1540, when the judgment was signed by the Archbishop of Canterbury, the Metropolitan of York, and the other members of the assembly, as above described. This conclusion was arrived at after a most imposing trial, the two Convocations of Canterbury and York having been united for the purpose. The number of voters in favour of the nullification of this marriage appears altogether to have been 294; those against it, 25; in all 319 [Pocock's "Records of the Reformation," ii. 449–59].

Sup. p. 75.

The Statute [32 Hen. VIII. 38] "Concerning "Pre-contracts of Marriages" was passed in this same session of Parliament. But it was wholly framed upon the principle enforced by the two Convocations assembled in united Synod on the 9th of July previously, viz. that pre-contracts only rendered marriages void in cases where they had not been consummated. For on this point the greatest stress was laid in the associated Synods.

A Proclamation for the "Bible of the largest "and greatest volume to be had in every Church" was issued on the 6th of May, 1541. But, as has before been said, a translation of the Bible had been previously requested by Convocation on the

19th of December, 1534. That translation had subsequently appeared, and had been set up in churches. An improved translation had more recently come out, under the auspices of Archbishop Cranmer, in 1539, and this last edition was to be substituted for the former one.

Sovereign: K. Henry VIII. 1531–1547.

The King's Letter "For taking away Shrines "and Images," dated from Hull, is attributed to October 4, 1541. But the reform of such abuses as were here ordered to be removed had been previously initiated by the Sixth of the Articles agreed to in Convocation on the 11th of July, 1536. Furthermore, it is not clear that this letter does not really belong to the year 1542. At any rate, it is dated the "thirty- "fourth yere of our reign." In this case the present contention is fortified, as this Royal letter must then have been subsequent to the debate which took place on this subject in Convocation, on Feb. 24, 1542, N.S.

Conc. M. B. iii. 821, 803.

Ibid. iii. 861.

The Statute [34 & 35 Hen. VIII. 1] "For the "Advancement of True Religion, and for the "Abolishing of all False Doctrines," was enacted in the spring of 1543, N.S. But the very first section of the Act gives us this very salutary information: "Recourse must be had to the "Catholic and Apostolic Church for the decision "of controversies." This Statute, therefore, very justly directs that "Tyndale's translation" should be forbidden in accordance with the decision arrived at in the Canterbury Convocation previously, on Feb. 3, 1542, N.S.

<small>Metropolitans: Cranmer, Lee.</small>
<small>Conc. M. B. iii. 860–1.</small>

The Statute [35 Hen. VIII. 3] "For the Ratification of the King's Majesty's Stile" was enacted in the spring of 1544, N.S. By this Act, to mention the only point which concerns our present enquiry, the title of "Supreme Head" was ratified by Parliament. But this title, as before has been mentioned, had been accorded, with a qualification, thirteen years before by the Convocation of Canterbury, on the 11th of February, 1531, N.S., and by the Convocation of York, on the 4th of May in that year.

<small>Ibid. iii. 725.</small>
<small>Ibid. iii. 744–5.</small>

The Statute [35 Hen. VIII. 5] "Concerning the Qualification of the Statute of the Six Articles" was passed in the spring of 1544, N.S. But this Act was merely declaratory of certain modes of proceeding to be taken under the provisions of 31 Hen. VIII. 14; and upon the doctrinal matter contained in the last-mentioned Act—though, happily, certainly not upon its cruel provisions—the decisions of Convocation had been given, as above stated, on the 2nd of June, 1539, and that moreover at the express request of the King and his Vicar-General.

<small>Ibid. iii. 845–6.</small>

The Statute [35 Hen. VIII. 16] "Concerning the Examination of the Canon Laws by two and thirty persons" was also enacted in the spring of 1544, N.S. But this Act was only ancillary to a provision in 25 Hen. VIII. 19, respecting a review of the Canon Law, which had previously been agreed to by the Clergy in Convocation, on May 15, 1532. Moreover, the subsidy lately voted on Feb. 23, 1543, N.S., by the Canterbury Convocation, had been accompanied by a request, which, taken with its substantial concomitant, was not unlikely to meet with the King's and the Parliament's very favourable joint consideration. This request was, "for the Ecclesiastical laws of this realm "to be made according to the Statute made in "the 25th year" of this reign. And, still further, the question of a review of the Canon Law had been discussed in Convocation in this very year, on Feb. 1, 1544, N.S., and deliberation had been then held upon an address to the King in furtherance of the specific purpose which the Statute before us contemplates.

Sovereign: K. Henry VIII. 1531–1547.

Conc. M. B. iii. 749–754.

Ibid. iii. 863.

Ibid. iii. 868.

"The King's Letters to the Archbishop of "Canterbury, for publishing Royal Injunctions" for using "certayne godly prayers and suffrages "in our natyve Englyshe tongue," were put forth June 11, 1544. But these Injunctions without doubt refer to that Reformed Litany in English, very similar to the one now in use, in regard to which there is internal evidence to prove that it was sanctioned by the Convocation which rose on March 31, 1544.

Atterb. Rights, &c. p. 193.

"An Injunction given by the King ... for the

<small>Metropolitans: Cranmer, Holgate.</small>

"Autorisyng and Establishyng the Use of his "Primer," was issued on the 6th of May, 1545. The chief complaint here insisted on was—"that "the youthe by divers persones are taught the "Pater Noster, the Ave Maria, Crede, and Ten "Commaundementes, all in Latin and not in En-"glyshe;" and this Primer was chiefly intended to rectify such disadvantage. But on the 17th and 24th of February, 1542, this subject had been debated in the Convocation of Canterbury, and on the latter day Archbishop Cranmer had treated with the Upper House on the advisability of the "people's learning and reciting in "the vulgar tongue the Lord's Prayer, the Creed, "and the Ten Commandments." And all this leaves little doubt that the Primer was the result of those debates.

<small>Conc. M. B. iii. 861.</small>

On the 8th of July, 1546, King Henry VIII.'s last Proclamation connected with religion was published. It was directed against Wiclif's, Tyndale's, and Coverdale's translations of the Scriptures; and also against some other books containing matter contrary to the Statute 34 & 35 Hen. VIII. 1. But on the 3rd of February, 1542, N.S., the Bishops in the Canterbury Convocation had decided against those earlier translations of Scripture, and joint Committees of both Houses of Convocation had subsequently been appointed for amending them. The intention, therefore, of this Proclamation

<small>Ibid. iii. 776.</small>

was to enforce the use of such a translation only as had proper authority. And, as regards the books referred to in this Proclamation, the language of the Act invoked plainly specifies that they were such as impugned the established religion, or were contrary to the previous Proclamation on the subject. And that Proclamation, before mentioned, was issued at the express request of the Convocation, made on the 19th of December, 1534.

Sovereign: K. Henry VIII. 1531–1547.

Conc. M. B. iii. 770-6.

Strype's Cranmer, p. 24.

Now, from the date of the Synodical discharge of the Papal Supremacy by our Provincial Synods in 1534 down to the death of King Henry VIII., the foregoing list contains the principal Civil Acts which touched religious faith and practice. And if any patient reader has been so persevering as to peruse the matter contained in it he will see good reason to be convinced that on such occasions the Acts of our Convocations preceded those of the Civil power; that Royal Proclamations were only the embodiment of preceding Convocational determinations; and that Acts of Parliament were merely the Civil authority conceded to antecedent Convocational Decrees.

As matter of fact, we have King Henry VIII.'s own testimony on this head. In his commissional letter of business to the united Convocations of Canterbury and York, in London, July 6, 1540, these words occur:—" We, who are wont

Metropolitans: Cranmer, Holgate.

Burnet's Hist. Reform. Rec. in loco.

"to adopt your judgment in the other more "weighty matters of this English Church which "affect discipline and religion, have thought fit "to take care that explanation and communi- "cation should be made to you, so that what "you may have decreed to be lawful by the "laws of God We may, by the authority of our "whole Church, venture lawfully to do and carry "out." The testimony of Jewell in his "Apology" is to the same effect [See "Apol." pp. 115, 138; also "Recapitulated," p. 153. London, 1852]. This matter, finally, may be summed up in the words of the Church historian Fuller, an author not pecu- liarly favourable to Ecclesiastical authority, but who yet writes as follows:—"Upon serious con-

Church Hist. Bk. v. p. 188.

"sideration," are his words, "it will appear that "there was nothing done in the Reformation "of religion save what was acted by the Clergy "in their Convocations, or grounded upon some "act of theirs precedent to it, with the advice, "counsel, and consent of the Bishops and most "eminent Churchmen, confirmed on the postfact, "and not otherwise, by the Civil sanction, ac- "cording to the usage of the best and happiest "times of Christianity."

III.

THE REFORMATION COMPLETED BY CONVOCATIONAL ACTION.

HAVING traced the history of the inauguration and promotion of the Reformation from 1534 to the end of the reign of King Henry VIII., it is time now to turn attention to the completion of that movement. This completion was effected by seven several events, which shall be here presented in their chronological order. *(Sovereign: K. Edward VI. 1547.)*

(1) The Synodical Restoration of the Cup to the Laity in Holy Communion. (2) The Compilation of a Liturgical Office for the Administration of the "Holy Communion in the English Tongue, " under both Kinds, of Bread and Wine." (3) The Synodical Abrogation of the Cœlibacy of the Clergy. (4) The Compilation and Synodical Authorization of the First English "Book of "Common Prayer." (5) The Review of that Book, and the Synodical Authorization of the Second English "Book of Common Prayer." (6) The Synodical Authorization of the 42 "Articles of Religion" of 1552-3. (7) The Synodical Authorization of the 39 "Articles of "Religion" of 1562-3. Each of these seven events shall be treated of in order, and in each *(Seven events which completed the Reformation.)*

*Metro-
politans:
Cranmer,
Holgate.*

*Restoration
of the Cup
to the
Laity.*

*Conc. M. B.
iv. 16.*

*Atterb.
Rights, &c.
p. 197.*

will be found Convocational authority primarily and fully exercised.

(1) The first event under this head to be considered is the return to primitive practice in ordering the administration of the Holy Communion in both kinds. On Nov. 30, 1547, an ordinance received from Archbishop Cranmer, which had been promoted among the Bishops of the Upper House, was read in the Lower House of the Canterbury Convocation, for the receiving of the Body of our Lord under both kinds. It there received some signatures; and in the following session, Dec. 2, a Synodical Act on this point was carried without a dissentient voice. "This session, all this whole "session, in number sixty-four, by their mouths "did approve the proposition made in the last "session of taking the Lord's Body in both "kinds, 'nullo reclamante.'"

Thus this ordinance received first and full Synodical sanction; and on the very next day, Dec. 3, a Bill brought into the House of Lords by Archbishop Cranmer was read a second time, which subsequently passed into the Act 1 Ed. VI. c. 1, in which it was enacted that the Communion should be administered in both kinds. Never was a more distinct proof that Synodical decisions at this period of our national history preceded Civil ratifications in matters of religion than this event supplies.

We have indeed been assured by a modern writer of some celebrity, that "Act of Parliament in 1547 alone ordered the giving of the "Cup to the laity." How false such an assertion is our national records [to say nothing of trustworthy historians, as Strype and Collier] abundantly prove. King Edward VI. himself had a much truer conception of the exigencies of the case. In his Proclamation, issued about this time, that King forbids all contentions on the subject, "until such tyme as the King's Majesty, by th' "advice of his higher Council and *the Clergy of* "*this Realme*, shall define, declare, and set forthe "an open doctrin thereof." It may also be observed that in the Public Record Office there is a letter from the Privy Council to the Bishops, dated March 15, 1548, requesting them to direct the Clergy to administer the Communion in both kinds. This letter of the Council succeeded the Synodical Decree in Convocation by rather more than three months, another proof of the point before us.

<small>Sovereign: K. Edw. VI. 1547-8.</small>

<small>Conc. M. B. iv. 19.</small>

(2) Consequently upon the above Synodical decision, as ratified by the Civil Legislature, that the Communion should be administered in both kinds, measures were taken, with the Royal sanction, for the preparation of an Office for the purpose. The work was entrusted to a Committee of twenty-four persons, and that Committee was composed entirely and exclu-

<small>Compilation of the first English Communion Office.</small>

P

Metropolitans:
Cranmer,
Holgate.

sively of members of the Convocations of Canterbury and York, an important fact which has generally been overlooked. This is manifest from the styles and titles of the names as given in common histories, with the exception of two, i.e. Robertson and Redmayn. But Robertson was a member of the Canterbury Convocation, as being Archdeacon of Leicester, a fact which may be learned from Sparrow's "Rationale," p. 136. And that Redmayn was also a member is plain, from the fact that he is represented as

Conc. M. B. iv. 16, 17.

having delivered his opinion in writing about this time on the subject of the cœlibacy of the Clergy, because he was not in his place in Convocation at the time when that question was debated. Thus it is plain that this Committee for compiling the first English Communion Service was a joint Committee selected from the two Convocations of Canterbury and York. So unfounded is a fallacious and prevalent notion that it was merely an ordinary Royal Commission selected at large. That the reader may satisfy himself on this point without doubt, a list of the names of this Committee is here given:—

Coll. Eccl. Hist. v. 246-8.

1. The Archbishop of Canterbury (Cranmer).
2. Bishop of London (Bonner).
3. Bishop of Bristol (Bush).
4. Bishop of Chichester (Day).

5. Bishop of Coventry and Lichfield (Sampson).

Sovereign: K. Edw. VI. 1548.

6. Bishop of Ely (Goodrich).
7. Bishop of Hereford (Skyp).
8. Bishop of Lincoln (Holbeach).
9. Bishop of Norwich (Rugg. al. Repps).
10. Bishop of Rochester (Ridley).
11. Bishop of Salisbury (Salcot al. Capon).
12. Bishop of St. Asaph (Purfew al. Warton).
13. Bishop of St. David's (Barlow).
14. Bishop of Westminster (Thirlby).
15. Bishop of Worcester (Heath).

With the foregoing Prelates of the Canterbury Convocation were joined from the York Convocation these, viz.:—

16. The Metropolitan (Holgate).
17. Bishop of Durham (Tunstall).
18. Bishop of Carlisle (Aldrich).

With the above Prelates there were associated in this Committee the following members of the Lower House of the Canterbury Convocation:—

19. Taylour (Dean of Lincoln, and Prolocutor of the Canterbury Convocation).
20. Cox (Dean of Ch. Ch.).
21. Heynes (Dean of Exeter).
22. May (Dean of St. Paul's).
23. Redmayn (Master of Trinity College, Cambridge).
24. Robertson (Archdeacon of Leicester).

Metropolitans:
Cranmer,
Holgate.

Heylin,
Hist. Ref.
p. 57.

Coll. Eccl.
Hist. v.
247 seq.

As before said, nothing can be clearer than that this was a joint Committee, selected from the two Convocations of Canterbury and York. The Committee met in due course, to "consult "about one uniform Order for administering the "Holy Communion in the English tongue, under "both kinds, of bread and wine." They proceeded tenderly in their work, being unwilling needlessly to offend those of the Roman persuasion. It was therefore arranged that the older Office should be used in the Latin tongue up to the point where the celebrant received the Communion himself. A new portion was there added in English, beginning with an Exhortation [in effect the same as the second of those now existing in our present Prayer Book], and containing the Invitation, the General Confession, the Absolution, the Comfortable Sentences, the Prayer of Humble Access, the form of the distribution of the elements to the people, together with a dismissal in the peace of God. A rubric was also added respecting the bread, and another for consecrating more wine, if needful. This Order of the Communion was published on March 8, 1548, N.S., together with the King's Proclamation, giving Civil sanction for its use.

Thus, by a formal Synodical Act in the first place, there was restored to the Church of England the primitive practice of Communion in both kinds; and, in the second place, an Office for the purpose was prepared by a joint Committee, selected exclusively from the two Convocations of Canterbury and York. Sovereign:
K. Edw. VI.
1548.

This Synodical emancipation of this Church from the comparatively modern corruption of denying the Cup to the laity, is an era in her history which calls for thankfulness. The innovation of half Communion was of comparatively recent date, and its rejection by the authority of the English Church bears her testimony against one of the strangest abuses of the Church of Rome. The Christian laity were not generally denied their right to a participation in "the Communion of the Blood of Christ" until after the Chapter defining the Roman doctrine of transubstantiation was presented by Pope Innocent III., at the Lateran Council, A.D. 1215. William the Conqueror caused his army to communicate in both kinds, according to the usage of his time, immediately before the battle of Hastings, A.D. 1066. Thomas Aquinas, about A.D. 1260, says that in his time the Cup was not given to the people in *some* Churches, and by thus limiting the practice his evidence proves that the general practice of the Western Church was then otherwise. It was not till the Thirteenth Session of the Council of Constance, begun A.D. 1414, that this abuse finally passed into a Synodical Decree of the Roman Church.

Margin notes: Bing. Ant. B. XVI. c. vi. § 27. Landon's Man. p. 295. Heylin, Hist. Ref. p. 30. Ibid. p. 50.

<small>Metropolitans: Cranmer, Holgate.</small>

Meanwhile, all history proves how modern this innovation comparatively is, and how little of primitive practice, or ancient authority, can be pleaded for its adoption.

<small>Abrogation of the Cœlibacy of the Clergy.</small>

<small>Conc. M. B. iv. 16. Strype's Cranmer, p. 156.</small>

(3) The third important event, under the present head to be considered, is the Abrogation of the Cœlibacy of the Clergy. On Dec. 17, 1547, the following resolution was submitted to the Lower House of the Convocation of Canterbury: "That "all such Canons, Laws, Statutes, Decrees, Usages, "and Customs, heretofore made, had, or used, "that forbid any person to contract matrimony, "or condemn matrimony already contracted by "any person, for any vow or promise, of priest-"hood, chastity, or widowhood, shall henceforth "cease, be utterly void, and of none effect." To this resolution fifty-three members subscribed in the affirmative, and twenty-two in the negative. Thus the compulsory cœlibacy of the Clergy was synodically abrogated by a majority of more than two-thirds of the whole number voting. This matter, however, slept for a while, so far as Civil ratification was concerned, for though a Bill on the subject was brought into Parliament and carried in the Commons, it lay unfinished in the Lords for want of time, their session ending a few days after the subject was submitted to their deliberations.

However, in the following year, 1548, the former Synodical decision was again "debated and "earnestly sifted in the Convocation." On this second occasion, a greater number of the Lower House than before voted for the relaxation of the cœlibacy of the Clergy. The former number of fifty-three supporters of the measure was now increased to seventy; and most of the Bishops in the Upper House also subscribed a document in favour of annulling the restraint. In accordance with this second Synodical decision on the matter, the Statute [2 & 3 Ed. VI. 21] was enacted, giving Civil force to the Convocational Act. Thus again we see Civil ratification accorded to antecedent Synodical determinations, and indeed in this Statute the Convocational decision on the subject-matter is specially recited.

<small>Sovereign: K. Edw. VI. 1548.</small>

<small>Strype's Mem. Vol. ii. p. 134.</small>

As regards this Act of Parliament last mentioned, and its successor on the same subject [5 & 6 Ed. VI. 12], that learned historian Jeremy Collier, an accomplished master of subtle humour, thinks fit to be somewhat merry. While generally commending the object of the Statutes, his view seems to be that it was, to say the least, odd management on the part of Parliament to dispossess the religious, as it had done, of a great part of their incomes, and then to legalize an increase of their expenditure. "When," he writes, "the tithes were taken away in many "places, and the parish duties lessened, they "had the freedom of engaging in a more expen-

<small>Eccl. Hist. v. 473.</small>

<small>Metropolitans: Cranmer, Holgate.</small>

"sive way of living. When the revenues were "cut short, it was at their choice to increase "their charge; they had the opportunity of "wanting more things, when the means of pro-"curing them were more slender than ever. "Thus they had liberty without much property. "They might, if they pleased, be legally undone "and starve by Act of Parliament."

And this author's complaint of the extent to which the religious had been despoiled seems noway unfounded, considering that, by the management of the last Sovereign and his <small>Bib. Cott. Cleop. E. 4, 381.</small> sycophant Parliaments and courtiers, the abbeys in England and Wales which had been suppressed and their estates mostly confiscated to <small>Hume, Hist. Eng. ch. xxxi.</small> private uses, amounted to 645, to which must be added 110 hospitals, 2,374 chantries, and 90 colleges. The whole yearly revenue of these establishments is computed to have been £161,000; and, besides this, the sums realised upon the stock <small>Coll. Eccl. Hist. v. 28.</small> on the farms, the timber, and other materials, furniture, plate, church ornaments, jewels, and bells, must have mounted to an almost incalculable sum. Nor should it be forgotten, considering all the circumstances connected with these valuations, that these revenues from land, upon modern computations and according to present management, would probably rise nearly twentyfold. While courtiers were thus enriched by the spoil of the religious, it may also be remembered that these were not the only sufferers. Before this pillage, the poor were relieved or maintained by the religious houses. After their revenues had been transferred to private pockets, it soon became necessary to establish a rate on all real property for the relief of the poor. That has in our time amounted to fourteen millions per annum. So that, however sensibly private families may have been enriched by these managements, it is pretty clear that the nation cannot feel any high regard for the memory of those who were engaged in them, or persuade itself that public interests were greatly promoted by such sacrilege. These proceedings were certainly no sign of zeal for promoting religion, nor any recommendation of such reformers to a nation's gratitude or respect— *Sovereign: K. Edw. VI. 1548.*

> "And yet this act, to varnish o'er the shame
> "Of sacrilege, must bear Devotion's name."
> DENHAM: Cooper's Hill.

(4) The fourth event, and one of an important character, to be considered under this head, took place in the year 1548, and is the compilation and authorization of the First Reformed Prayer Book of Edward VIth's reign. The origination, prosecution, and completion of this work must be certainly attributed to Convocational action. *First English "Book of Common Prayer."*

It should be remembered that, more than six years before the time now under consideration,

Metropolitans:
Cranmer,
Holgate.

Conc. M. B.
iii. 861.
Ibid.
iii. 863.

i.e. on Feb. 24, 1542, N.S., Archbishop Cranmer had moved in the Upper House of the Canterbury Convocation that "Portuises, Missals, and "other Service Books should be reformed." In the following year this matter was again pressed upon the attention of the Synod. For on Feb. 21, 1543, N.S., the Archbishop again suggested an examination and correction of all "Mass "books, Antiphoners, and Portuises," and the desirableness of framing public services "out of "the Scripture and other authentic doctors." Upon this suggestion an order was made that the revision of the Service Books should be committed to Goodrich, Bishop of Ely, and the Bishop of Sarum, with six members to be chosen by the Lower House. That House, however, waived the privilege of appointment, and left the matter in the hands of the Bishops. In the meanwhile the business of a reform in the services was carried on actively and without delay, the Convocation having in the same session ordered that a chapter of the Old or New Testament should be read in English during Divine Service, and having also devoted two succeeding sessions to the prosecution of the same subject. That those to whom the matter was entrusted had now made considerable progress in reforming the Service Books is plain from the contents of a petition sent up last year [Nov. 22, 1547] to the Archbishop from the Lower House of Canterbury. It ran as follows: "That the work of the Bishops and "others, who, *by the command of Convocation,* have "laboured in examining, reforming, and publish- "ing the Divine Service, may be produced and laid "before the examination of this House." As the reform of Divine Offices had been entrusted to a Committee of the Convocation of Canterbury, as above stated, on Feb. 21, 1543, N. S., and as the Lower House had now given an impulse to the enterprize by their late petition [Nov. 22, 1547], measures were taken that the desired event, the completion and publication of a Reformed Service Book, might be brought to a speedy issue—" the "business being continued in the same method," to use Atterbury's words on the subject, "into "which the Convocation had formerly put it."

Sovereign: K. Edw. VI. 1548.

Conc. M. B. iv. 15.

Rights, &c. p. 198.

A body of Divines was therefore now selected and fortified by Royal authority for the purpose. This was a smaller Committee than that which had just settled the "Order of the Communion." That Committee consisted of twenty-four per- sons, as above stated, and was composed of members of both Convocations. The Committee now under consideration consisted of thirteen persons only, and was selected solely from the Convocation of Canterbury. But on comparison of the two lists given, it will be seen that all those engaged in the second Committee had served on the first. The names of members of

Metropolitans: Cranmer, Holgate.

the second Committee for compiling a Reformed Prayer Book are as follows:—

1. Archbishop of Canterbury (Cranmer).
2. Bishop of Chichester (Day).
3. Bishop of Ely (Goodrich).
4. Bishop of Hereford (Skyp).
5. Bishop of Lincoln (Holbeach).
6. Bishop of Rochester (Ridley).
7. Bishop of Westminster (Thirlby).
8. Dr. Cox (Dean of Ch. Ch.).
9. Dr. Heynes (Dean of Exeter).
10. Dr. May (Dean of St. Paul's).
11. Redmayn (Master of Trinity College, Cambridge).
12. Robertson (Archdeacon of Leicester).
13. Taylour (Dean of Lincoln, and Prolocutor of the Canterbury Convocation).

Coll. Eccl. Hist. v. 272-6.

The Committee met on Sept. 1, 1548. Their object was to compile an Order for Morning and Evening Public Prayer, together with forms for celebrating other religious offices in conformity with the faith of the early Church. The "Uses" of Sarum, York, Bangor, and Lincoln, as well as diversities in some parts of Divine Service, were to be discontinued, and uniform offices to be provided for the whole kingdom. The Committee laid down these rules for their own guidance: that nothing should be changed for the sake of novelty; that their work should be grounded on the Word of God, and fashioned according to the best precedents of the Primitive Church. Calvin, it is said, who thought himself charged with the superintendence of the faith of Christendom, offered his services on this occasion to Cranmer; but the Archbishop at this time was too wise to accept them, and happily declined the offer. Had he availed himself of it, we should doubtless have had some baser metal introduced into the composition; but, as Cranmer refused such aid, the work was on this occasion saved from foreign alloy. Martyr and Bucer were indeed about this time invited to come hither to season our Universities, but these foreigners did not arrive till this First Book of Common Prayer was completed. *Sovereign: K. Edw. VI. 1548. Heylin, Eccl. Vind. p. 69.*

The Convocation records of the formal Synodical sanction of this First Reformed Prayer Book are not forthcoming, as the fire of London in 1666 unhappily consumed the Acts of the Canterbury Synod. But the fact that the book was formally and synodically sanctioned can be positively proved by other evidence, and that indisputable.

The first evidence to be produced is that of King Edward the VIth himself. In his letter to Bishop Bonner, dated July 23, 1549, His Majesty thus writes: "One uniform Order for "Common Prayer and Administration of the "Sacraments hath been and is most godly set "forth, not only by the common agreement and *Conc. M. B. iv. 35.*

Metropolitans:
Cranmer,
Holgate.

"full assent of the Nobility and Commons of the "late session of our late Parliament, but also "by the like assent of the Bishops in the said "Parliament, *and of all other the learned men of* "*this our Realm, in their Convocations and Synods* "*Provincial.*"

His Majesty also gave a second assurance to the same effect in his answer to a petition of the Devonshire men, who were displeased at the new Service Book, and indeed had gone so far as to rise in insurrection, being moved to great indignation on the subject. In his reply to these malcontents his words were as follows:

Atterbury,
Rights, &c.
p. 199.

"Whatever is contained in our book, either "for Baptism, Sacrament, Mass, Confirmation, "and Service of the Church, is by our Parlia- "ment established, *by the whole Clergy agreed,* "*yea, by the Bishops of the Realm devised,* by God's "Word confirmed."

To prove that this First Prayer Book of Edward VIth's reign was synodically authorized, the next evidence to be produced is an order of His Majesty's Council by which Dr. Hopkins, the Lady Mary's [afterwards Queen Mary] Chaplain, was instructed to acquaint that Princess with the insufficiency of her reasons for demurring to the Reformed Liturgy. The

Ibid.

Council bid him to use these words: "The fault "is great in any subject to disallow a law of "the King, a law of the Realm by long study, "free disputation, and *uniform determination of* *the whole Clergy*, consulted, debated, concluded."

<small>Sovereign: K. Edw. VI. 1549.</small>

A second item of evidence contributed by His Majesty's Council on this head is to be found in a letter indited by them to the Lady Mary herself, on the subject of her Chaplain's saying Mass in a manner not consistent with the Reformed Communion Office. That letter declares that such a proceeding is "*a contempt of the Ecclesiastical orders of the Church of England.*" Now if the First Prayer Book of this reign, which included a Reformed Communion Service, had not been established regularly by proper Synodical authority, we must here pay His Majesty's Council the ill compliment of believing from their expressed language that they lay under an incapacity of distinguishing between Ecclesiastical and Civil sanctions—a vulgar failing far less common in those times than in these—or we must bear more hardly on their memory by supposing that though cognizant of so patent a distinction, they yet wilfully misstated the facts of the case in hand.

<small>Atterbury, Rights, &c. p. 202.</small>

But we have not only the foregoing evidence of King Edward VI. on two occasions, and of his Council on two occasions also, but we have further the evidence of two Archbishops that the Prayer Book before us was synodically authorized. Archbishop Bancroft, who was born before this book was compiled and promulged, thus

Metropolitans: Cranmer, Holgate.

writes: "The first Liturgy set forth in the beginning of King Edward's reign was carefully compiled *and confirmed by a Synod.*"

Coll. Eccl. Hist. vi. 277.
Strype's Mem. ii. 87.

Dr. George Abbot, Archbishop of Canterbury next in succession, also contributes the clearest evidence on this subject. Thus he wrote: "The "religion which was then and is now established "in England is drawn out of the fountains of "the Word of God, and from the purest orders "of the Primitive Church, which for the or- "dinary exercise thereof, when it had been col- "lected into the Book of Common Prayer by "the pains and labour of many learned men "and of mature judgment, *it was afterwards* "*confirmed by the Upper and Lower House.* Yet "not so but that the more material points *were* "*disputed and debated in the Convocation House by* "*men of both parties.* ... And then, it being in- "tended to add to Ecclesiastical decision the cor- "roboration of Civil Government, according to the "ancient custom of this kingdom (as appeareth "by records from the time of King Edward III.), "the Parliament, which is the most honourable "Court of Christendom, did ratify the same."

Ibid. and i. 133.

One more witness must be produced, the learned and accurate historian Strype, whose language is plain on the point before us. Thus he wrote: "The consideration and preparation "of this Book of Common Prayer, together with "other matters in religion, was committed first "of all to divers learned Divines, as was shewn "before, and *what these had concluded upon was* "*offered the Convocation;* and after all this the "Parliament approved it, and gave it its ratifi-"cation."

Sovereign:
K. Edw. VI.
1549.

Now, notwithstanding the disabling circumstance of the loss of the Convocation Registers, we thus have the evidence of King Edward VI. on two occasions, of his Council on two occasions, of two Archbishops, and of a most accurate historian, that this First Prayer Book of King Edward the VIth's reign was synodically authorized in the most formal manner imaginable. The Act which gave Civil authority to this book [2 & 3 Ed. VI. 1] takes notice that it was set forth by "the aid of the Holy Ghost," enjoining upon the authorities of cathedral and parish churches the duty of providing copies for use before Whitsuntide, 1549, and of using the book within three weeks after such copies were obtained. The book was published in March, 1549, N.S., and was used in some of the London churches on Easter Day, which in that year fell on April 21. And here we have another conspicuous instance that at this period of our country's history Civil ratifications on Spiritual matters were subsequent to Synodical determinations, and consequent upon them.

At this point it is pardonable to ask the reader to make a pause, in order to make a reflection

Metropolitans: Cranmer, Holgate.

and to take a brief retrospect. The reflection is, that the very heart's core of the Reformation of the Church of England is found in these four particulars: (1) The Rejection of the Papal Supremacy. (2) The Restoration of the Communion in both kinds. (3) The Abrogation of the Cœlibacy of the Clergy. (4) The Compilation and Promulgation of a Reformed English Prayer Book. The retrospect is this: that these four particulars were originated, carried forward, and concluded, as above shewn, by the action of our Convocations, synodically, and in accordance with the principles inherited from the Primitive Church.

Second English "Book of Common Prayer."

(5) The fifth event to be considered here is the compilation of the Second Book of Common Prayer. The Prayer Book of 1549 had not long been in use when some of the more uneasy spirits of the day pressed for a revision of that work. These designs were pressed on

Hist. Ref. p. 107.

"by agents in Court," as Heylin tells us, "the "country, and the Universities." Fuel was added to this flaming desire for revision by those foreigners, Peter Martyr and Bucer, who had lately arrived in this country, though it is noway clear why the authorities of the English Church should have indebted themselves for advice to those who did not belong to her.

Collier, Eccl. Hist. v. 397.

However, Archbishop Cranmer applied to Bucer for his thoughts on the subject. Now

Bucer did not understand the English language sufficiently for the purpose in hand; and this at first view appears a considerable disqualification for his interference. The volume was, however, translated for his information into Latin, by one Aless, a Scotchman. Bucer being thus qualified, as he supposed himself, for the undertaking, wrote to the Archbishop at length. At the outset of his communication he gave this remarkable commendation to the book, declaring that "upon perusal of the Service Book "he thanked God Almighty for giving the English grace to reform their ceremonies to that "degree of purity; and that he found nothing "but what was either taken out of the Word of "God, or at least not contrary to it, provided "it was fairly interpreted." Now, if the First Prayer Book was in this commendable state, according to Bucer's own shewing, it seems, to say the least, very odd that he should have begrudged no pains to recommend alterations, for which purpose he lengthened out his strictures to no less than twenty-eight chapters. And it has been thought that his animadversions were somewhat overstrained, and that his mind was overcharged with scruples. Nor do his remarks in the body of his discourse agree tolerably with the concessions made at its beginning. Notwithstanding this, however, Peter Martyr, as appears from a correspon-

Sovereign: K. Edw. VI. 1549.

Collier, Eccl. Hist. v. 397.

Ibid. v. 406.

dence which passed between them, agreed with him.

<small>Metropolitans: Cranmer, Holgate.</small>

There was still another foreigner, of a far more fiery disposition than either of those last mentioned, who did his best to stir up a conflagration. One who deemed himself wiser than the ancients, more authoritative than the Fathers of the Primitive Church, and who, from never having the slightest misgiving as to the correctness of his own singular views, deemed himself qualified "to dictate religion to all Christendom," notwithstanding the horribly immoral doctrines which he taught, shortly condensed in that historical traditional exhortation to his disciples, "Pecca fortiter." That he should contribute very combustible materials on this occasion is no wonder, considering that he did not hesitate to employ the material appliances of fire and faggot for the correction of such as declined to accept his frantic singularities. This foreigner was Calvin, who in his writings at this time took unwarrantable freedoms in making use of very coarse and offensive language with reference to the First Reformed Prayer Book.

<small>Heylin, Hist. Ref. p. 107.</small>

In consequence of this agitation, the question of a revision of the book was brought forward in Convocation in the year 1550. The first debate on the subject among the Prelates of the Upper House, so far as records inform us, referred specially to two points: (1) What holi-

<small>Collier, Eccl. Hist. v. 435.</small>

days in the Calendar should be retained, and which should be abrogated. (2) The form of words to be used, and the manner to be adopted in administering the Holy Eucharist. To a communication from the Upper House the Lower House returned answer "that they had not yet "sufficiently considered of the points proposed, "but that they would give their Lordships "some account thereof in the following session." Their exact final answer is, unfortunately, not on record; but that some agreement was come to seems proved by the evidence of Peter Martyr, who, writing in the early part of 1550, N.S., states that "Archbishop Cranmer told him they "had met about this business, and had con- "cluded on a great many alterations."

This second review of the Reformed Prayer Book was chiefly managed by Archbishop Cranmer, Ridley [at this time Bishop of London], and some associated Divines, but who those were is not certain. It is, however, believed by Fuller, Heylin, and Sparrow, that they were in the main, if not wholly, the same Committee as that which compiled the First Prayer Book. If such is the case, the remarks above made as to the Synodical character and composition of that Committee will here also apply. This Committee, in September, 1551, brought their labours to an end, with the exception of some emendations which were subsequently to be

Sovereign: **K. Edw. VI.** 1550.

Heylin, Hist. Ref. p. 107.

Collier, Eccl. Hist. v. 434.

considered; and, in the opinion of many people quite well qualified to judge, those labours noway mended the original First English Prayer Book, but rather the reverse.

The Canterbury Synod met on Oct. 14 and Nov. 5 next ensuing [1551], and it looks very much as if these meetings were called for the special purpose of considering the foresaid emendations with a view of having the whole work ready for final confirmation by the Synod which met acourse with Parliament in January next following. The Convocation then meeting seems to have held continuous sessions, but the records having been miserably kept, there is no evidence as to the final measures adopted at this moment respecting the Second Reformed Prayer Book, though it may fairly be presumed that those sessions were devoted to the conclusion of so important a matter. And this presumption is fortified by the fact that in the preamble to the Act of Uniformity [13 & 14 Car. II. 4] it is recited that this book was "compiled by the reverend "Bishops and Clergy."

But if the official record of the Synodical authorization at this moment of the Second Prayer Book is not forthcoming, yet it was distinctly and unmistakeably so authorized very shortly afterwards by the 35th Article of 1552–3, N.S., which, treating of this book and the ordinal attached to it, declares that they

"are godlie, and in no poincte repugnaunt to *Sovereign:*
"the holsome doctrine of the Gospel, but agre- *K. Edw. VI.*
"able thereunto, ferthering and beautifying the *1551.*
"same not a little, and therfore of al faithfull *Card. Syn.*
"membres of the Churche of Englande, and cheiflie *i. 31.*
"of the ministers of the Worde, thei ought to be
"received and allowed with all readiness of minde
"and thankes geving, and to bee commended to
"the people of God."

(6) The sixth event here to be considered is the *Forty-two "Articles of* adoption of the "Forty-two Articles of 1552–3." At *Religion."* this period it seemed good to the highest authorities here in Church and State that definitions on certain points of faith and discipline should be promulged. Whether modern definitions on such subjects, specially as touching belief, are desirable or the reverse; whether the cause of religion in Christendom would not have been better served if such instruments had never seen the light, as, for instance, the Augsburg Confession, the Helvetic Confession, the Nuremburg Confession, the Westminster Confession, the Wurtemburg Confession, or the dogmas of the Roman Curia in 1870; and whether the Three Creeds of the Universal Church are not sufficient symbols of unity for Christians, and, when accepted, ample warrant for their claims to the Sacraments and privileges of the Church Catholic—these are very grave questions; but it is beyond the present purpose to discuss

<small>Metropolitans: Cranmer, Holgate.</small>

them. Suffice here to say, that it seemed desirable to our authorities to put forth "Articles "of Religion." The business here is to shew that, such a course having been decided on, the enterprize was carried out under proper Ecclesiastical and Synodical authority. The history of these Articles is briefly as follows:

<small>Strype's Cranmer, p. 272.</small>

In the year 1551, Archbishop Cranmer undertook to frame a Book of Articles for the preservation of peace and unity in the Church. The Archbishop, in due course, delivered his draft for approbation to his Suffragans, as is clear from a letter addressed to him on May 2 of the following year, 1552, by the Lords of the Council. In this letter reference is made to the

<small>Ibid.</small>

"Articles which were delivered last year to the "Bishops." The Archbishop sent his answer to the Lords of the Council, and in September, 1552, was engaged in putting the whole work into shape, affixing titles to the Articles, and making some additions. On the 19th of September, the Archbishop consulted by letter Sir William Cecyl and Sir John Cheke, the former being His Majesty's principal secretary, the latter His Majesty's tutor, as to whether they should lay the matter before the King, or whether the Archbishop himself should open that business.

<small>Ibid. p. 273.</small> The latter course was preferred. Cranmer himself delivered the Articles to the King, and His Majesty returned them to the Archbishop on

Nov. 20, 1552, in order that they might receive the last touches of his pen, and, as Collier tells us, that "they might pass the Convo-"cation" and so be published. The Archbishop made his last remarks upon them, and on the 2nd of March following, according to Wake, "this Book of Articles was laid before Convo-"cation," and the result was "that the whole "body agreed upon them and subscribed to "them." And these statements of Collier and Wake agree perfectly with the title of the Articles themselves, which thus runs: "*Arti-*"*cles agreed on by the Bishoppes and other learned* "*menne in the Synode at London, in the yere* "*of our Lorde Godde MDLII.*" [O. S.], "*for the* "*avoiding of controversie in opinions, and the esta-* "*blishment of a godlie concorde in certaine matiers* "*of religion.*"

Sovereign: K. Edw. VI. 1552-3.

Eccl. Hist. v. 437.

Present State, p. 599.

Card. Syn. i. 18.

With all this evidence before the world, it is nothing short of very strange that doubts should have been raised in some quarters as to the Synodical authorization of these Forty-two Articles of 1552-3. One would have thought that their very title had been conclusive on the point, because the expression "the Synode at London" would notoriously mean, in that age, Convocation, as may be shewn from like expressions elsewhere used. But further than this, there is ample confirmatory evidence on the point. The Articles were promulged with Royal authority ap-

s

pended, and so pledged the King to the veracity of the title of the code as above given; and were that untrue, then, in Heylin's words on this subject, "a most pious and "religious prince must needs be looked on as "a wicked and most lewd impostor, in putting "such a horrible cheat on all his subjects by "fathering these Articles on the Convocation, "which begat them not, nor ever gave consent "unto them."

But not only is there thus the King's evidence on the subject; when the Articles were sent for subscription to the University of Cambridge it was particularly specified that they had been "concluded on in the Synod of London." Again, in the beginning of Queen Elizabeth's reign, in a dispute connected with the London Ministers, the Synodical authority of these Articles was admitted on all hands and by both parties; and this matter, having occurred so soon after the promulgation of the documents in question, must have found those engaged in discussion fully possessed of all the facts needful for coming to a true conclusion. And, lastly, we have the evidence of the Synod which, in 1563, N.S., reduced these Forty-two Articles to the present tale of the Thirty-nine Articles of the Church of England. For in the session held Jan. 19 of that year, these Articles of 1553, N.S., are specially designated as "Articles published in

Marginal notes: Metropolitans: Cranmer, Holgate. Hist. Ref. p. 122. Card. Syn. i. 5, note. Wake, State, p. 599. Atterb. Rights, &c. p. 408.

"the Synod of London in the late reign of "King Edward VI."

During the following reign of Queen Mary it is plain that no true Provincial Synods or Convocations of the Church of England could be convened, inasmuch as shortly after her accession to the throne the two Metropolitans were committed to prison, eleven Diocesan Bishops deprived or forced to resignation, and at least nine thousand, some authorities say twelve thousand, Clergy suffered the like fate. The proper Provincial Synods of this Church being thus silenced, the Crown and the Parliament seized the opportunity to reform backwards to a surprising degree, and took some gigantic strides into the region of exploded error. And it is worth observation, that under like circumstances just a century afterwards, when the voice of the Church in her Provincial Synods was silenced, Oliver Cromwell and his Parliament made an equally sensible retrogression, but in a worse direction still — the members of the House of Commons then swearing, in St. Margaret's Church, Westminster, to the "Solemn League and Covenant" with hands uplifted to heaven; and the Westminster Assembly, that ricketty, ill-favoured offspring of Parliament, promulging dogmas of faith to supersede by a novel "Confession" the Christian Creeds of the Church Universal. These were the blessings

Sovereign:
Q. Mary.
1553–1558.

Interruption of true Provincial Synods.

Warner's Eccl. Hist. ii. 347.
Coll. Eccl. Hist. vi. 63–4.
Hist. Ch. of Great Britain, p. 185.
Gladstone, Church and State, p. 121.

with which this nation was then favoured; these were events which in their results have left indelible stains on the character of this nation, which ages cannot obliterate nor time bury in oblivion. But more of this hereafter. And so we pass on to the times of Queen Elizabeth.

<small>Metropolitans: Parker, Young.</small>

(7) The seventh event for consideration under the present head is the Synodical authorization of the Thirty-nine Articles of 1562-3. Authentic records so indisputably prove that these Articles of the Church of England were synodically authorized in due Canonical form that for the present purpose it is unnecessary to dwell long on the subject. The history of that event, which on many accounts is one of interest to English Church people, is shortly as follows. The Synod which authorized those Articles assembled on Wednesday, Jan. 13, 1563, N.S., at St. Paul's Cathedral. Archbishop Parker presided. Mr. William Daye, B.D., Provost of Eton, preached the Latin Sermon, on the text, "Feed the flock of God which is among you," &c. [1 Pet. v. 2]. The Holy Communion was administered by Grindal, Bishop of London; and Dr. Alexander Nowell, Dean of St. Paul's, was elected Prolocutor. And it is observable that on this occasion the Metropolitan of York, together with the Bishops of Durham and Chester, attended, so that the assembly assumed the character of a Synod of the Exarchate.

<small>Thirty-nine "Articles of Religion."</small>

<small>Syn. Ang. p. 193. Strype's Parker, p. 121; and Annals, i. 280.</small>

In the fourth session, held Jan. 19, the business of a review of the Forty-two Articles of 1552–3 was begun in the Upper House, and on the same day a report was brought up by the Prolocutor of the Lower House, stating that a Committee had been there appointed, and that copies of the last-named Articles had been supplied to it, with a view to reconstruction and consideration by the whole House. On the following day the Upper House was engaged on the copy submitted to it, and after three more sessions devoted to the discussion, the body of Articles, i.e. the Thirty-nine now received by the Church of England, was agreed to unanimously, and there subscribed by Parker, Archbishop of Canterbury, together with eighteen Diocesan Bishops of the Southern Province, and by Young, the Metropolitan of York, together with the Bishops of Durham and Chester, from the Northern. The document was transmitted to the Lower House, and on the 5th of February following was returned to the Upper, bearing upwards of one hundred signatures of the Lower Clergy, a number which was increased by a large list of subscribers presented to their Lordships on Feb. 10. The Thirty-nine Articles were thus synodically authorized duly in the proper Canonical manner, and were published with this title: "*Articles whereupon it* "*was agreed by the Archbishoppes and Bishops of*

Sovereign: Q. Elizabeth. 1562-3.

Syn. Ang. p. 201.

Conc. M. B. iv. 237-8.

Card. Syn. i. 53.

Metro-
politans:
Parker,
Young.

"*both the Provinces and the whole Cleargie, in the
" Convocation holden at London in the yere of our
" Lorde God MDLXII."* [O. S.], "*according to the
" computation of the Churche of Englande, for the
" auoydyng of the diversities of opinions, and for
" the stablishying of consent touchyng true religion.
" Put foorth by the Queenes aucthoritie.*"

York assent to the "Thirty-nine Articles."

A few words must be added as regards the assent of the Lower House of York to these Articles. It appears from the " Concilia Mag. " Brit." iv. 243, that that assembly had at this time " weighty business " on hand " concerning the " public good, the order of the Church, and the " glory of God;" and that it was there determined " that their Metropolitan should be con- " sulted upon certain Articles" touching the matter. It is therefore pretty certain that the Thirty-nine Articles were then and there debated, and we must suppose that the members of the York Synod must either have sent up their signatures [which have not been recorded], or, if not so, that they must have signified their assent to their Metropolitan, who signed on their behalf. This much is quite certain, that the York Clergy approved of these Articles, or we should have heard more of the matter. And if the York Clergy had not agreed to them, the titles of these Articles, both in the English and Latin copies, would not have declared, as they do, that they were " agreed upon by the Archbishops "and Bishops of both the Provinces, and the whole Clergy."

Sovereign: Q. Elizabeth.
1562-3.

At this point the Reformation of the Church of England may be said to have culminated; and, on consideration of the facts above recorded, it will appear to an unprejudiced mind that its Inauguration, Promotion, and Completion must be set to the account of her representative assemblies, the Convocations or Provincial Synods of Canterbury and York.

If, however, the main structure was now completed, some subsequent additions have been made, and some further improvements effected, which shall hereafter be considered.

PART III.

SURVEY OF SOME MEMORABLE ACTS OF THE CONVOCATIONS, FROM THE DATE OF THE COMPLETION OF THE REFORMATION TO THE SUSPENSION OF SYNODICAL ACTION.

I.

GENERAL REVIEW OF SYNODICAL ACTS AFTER THE COMPLETION OF THE REFORMATION.

Metropolitans: Parker, Grindal, Whitgift. Grindal, Sandys, Piers, Hutton.

THE Reformation of the Church of England, as above detailed, was now completed. But, as castles and houses ever and anon require some repairs, so it is with the structure of the visible Church. Thus in Queen Elizabeth's long reign from time to time regulations were made for Ecclesiastical government by Convocational authority. A brief summary shall here be given of some Synodical events which took place between the date of the ratification of the Thirty-nine Articles of Religion and the close of that Sovereign's life, omitting the ever-recurring business of subsidies which does not touch our special subject.

Review of some Synodical events in Q. Elizabeth's reign.

In 1571, ten Canons on Church Discipline were promulged, which were also signed by the Prelates of the Northern Province. In 1576, fifteen more Articles were synodically ratified, on the "admission of apt and fit persons to the "Ministry, and the establishing good order in "the Church."

In 1584, one Hilton was convened for a most scandalous offence before the Canterbury Synod. This renegade Clerk had preached a sermon in the Church of St. Martin-in-the-Fields, in which he depraved the Bible, blasphemed our blessed Lord's Name, and, in fact, proclaimed himself a heathen. For this hideous misbehaviour he was cited before the Canterbury Synod. There he confessed his impiety, and in writing abjured his errors. Besides an admonition, the penalties imposed on him were, that he should attend during the delivery of a sermon at St. Paul's Cross on the following Sunday, there standing with a faggot on his shoulders before the preacher; and also that he should make in the church, where he had proclaimed his heathenism, a recantation of his blasphemous teaching in presence of the Lower House of the Convocation. Further, he was forbidden again to preach without a licence from the Archbishop.

In the same year, 1584, six Articles on Church Discipline were promulged; and in 1597 twelve more Constitutions on the same subject.

Sovereign:
Q. Elizabeth.
1558–1603.

Conc. M. B. iv. 263.
Sparrow's Collections, p. 223.
Strype's Grindal, p. 194; and App. p. 59, n. 4.
Strype's Whitgift, pp. 210-11.

Card. Syn. p. 139.
Ib. pp. 147, 161.
Conc. M. B. iv. 352-6.

Metro-politans:
Parker, Grindal, Whitgift.
Grindal, Sandys, Piers, Hutton.
Ecclesiastical Essays in Parliament.
Prophetic mutterings of a future tempest.

Throughout the whole of Queen Elizabeth's reign there were constantly heard the distant mutterings of that desolating storm which burst over this Church and nation in the second succession of the Crown after that monarch's death. Well-nigh without intermission these warning sounds ominously echoed within the walls of the House of Commons. They were the voices of those members who constituted themselves the champions of the disloyal and disaffected section of malcontents out of doors. Their assaults were not so directly delivered against the Crown as against the Church. The Church was the constant object of their attack; and it may be a warning to Sovereigns to remember at what point the assault was first made which resulted in the murder of an Archbishop, the martyrdom of a King, the temporary wreck and ruin of the happiness of a great nation, and the miseries inflicted on a long-suffering people by hypocritical and fierce fanatics.

However, our heroic virgin Queen during her lifetime repressed these agitators with becoming fortitude and perfect success. Indeed, that monarch constantly and unmistakeably delivered her mind to the Commons on the subject of their Ecclesiastical enterprizes. She treated with undisguised contempt and deserved scorn those restless and meddling members of that House who were continually seeking a vulgar popularity by proposing measures for reforming religion, and, indeed, so far transgressing the bounds of their proper functions as to endeavour to introduce new liturgical forms of public worship.

Sovereign:
Q. Elizabeth.
1558–1603.

It is not uninteresting to contemplate some of the extinctions which these firebrands in Parliament had to endure at the Queen's hands. In 1572, on May 22, the Speaker brought down a message to the Lower House from Her Majesty, declaring that it was Her Highness's pleasure that "no Bills concerning religion shall be pre-"ferred or received into this House unless the "same should be first considered and liked by "the Clergy." Notwithstanding this, in 1587, on Feb. 27, one Mr. Cope had the modesty to commend a liturgy of his own composition, so far as appears, or at least of his own selection, for adoption; and he was seconded in his endeavours for such Ecclesiastical reform by Mr. Lewknor, Mr. Harleston, Mr. Bainbrigg, and Mr. Wentworth. And this notwithstanding that a message had been sent by the Queen to the Lower House that they "should not meddle "in such matters."

Commons' Journals, i. 97. Ibid. p. 213. Dewes, p. 410.

In 1593, one Mr. Morrice, entering on the same forbidden ground, had again to be reminded by Sir R. Cecil of Her Majesty's injunctions on the matter. And in the same year the Queen somewhat rose in her language when deprecating such essays. For when the cus-

Metropolitans: Whitgift, Piers.
Dewes, Journal Lords, p. 460.

tomary liberty of speech was requested for the Commons by Sir E. Coke, then Speaker, this answer was returned in Her Majesty's name by the Lord Keeper Puckering: "Privilege of "speech is granted; but you must know what "privilege you have, not to speak every one "what he listeth, but *your* privilege is 'yea' or "'no.' Wherefore, Mr. Speaker, your privilege "is, that if you perceive any idle heads . . . . "which will meddle with reforming the Church "and transforming the Commonwealth, and do "exhibit any Bills for such purpose, that you "receive them not until they be viewed and "considered by those who it is fitter should "consider of such things, and can better judge "of them."

And subsequently, when the Queen had been advertised of some approaches in the House of Commons towards these forbidden subjects, she sent for the Speaker himself, Sir E. Coke, into her presence, and commanded him to deliver a message to the Commons, which he did on Feb. 28, 1593, in the following words: "Her Majesty's "present charge and express commandment is, "that no Bill touching the said matters of State "or reformation in causes Ecclesiastical be ex-"hibited." "And upon my allegiance," added the Speaker, "I am commanded, if any such Bill "be exhibited, not to read it."

It is by no means clear that the justice at

Dewes, p. 479.

least of such reproofs might not on occasion have found proper place in times much nearer our own than those of Queen Elizabeth.

<small>Sovereign: K. James I. 1603-1625.</small>

During the years which elapsed between the accession of King James I. and the suspension of Synodical action in the Church of England [1603–1718], events occurred of much importance connected with the Convocations. A few of the most memorable of those events shall be now briefly summarized; and the most important of them hereafter considered in detail.

In King James I.'s reign, the enactment of the 141 Canons of 1603–4, and the trial of Crashaw for false doctrine in 1610, took place. In King Charles I.'s reign, the enactment of the Seventeen Canons of 1640. In King Charles II.'s reign, the compilation and Synodical authorization of our present Prayer Book in 1661. In King William III.'s reign, the rejection of the "Comprehension Liturgy," which would have reduced the Prayer Book to a Puritan standard, and was proposed by that monarch and some of his sycophant Bishops in 1689. On this occasion it is observable that, even at this somewhat unpropitious season for Church authority, a joint address of both Houses of Parliament was presented to the Crown requesting that Convocation should be consulted, " according to the ancient practice and

<small>Summary of Synodical Acts from the accession of King James I. to the suspension of Synodical Action.</small>

Metropolitans: Various.

"usage of this kingdom." In Queen Anne's reign, a letter of business from Her Majesty having been directed to Archbishop Tenison, expressing a desire that Convocation would repress loose principles, Whiston's book, "An "Historical Preface," &c., was brought before the Canterbury Convocation and synodically condemned in 1711. In King George I.'s reign, in 1717, Bishop Hoadley's books, "The King-"dom of Christ" and "The Preservative," and his "Sermon" before the Court, were delated. The above brief summary of some events, which it would require volumes to describe in full, will suggest what are the proper functions of our Convocations, what duties they have discharged in past times, what engagements are proper for them now, and what will continue to be so while the Church of England abides in her pristine character.

Among the events mentioned in the above summary there are four which demand here special attention. (1) The Enactment of the 141 Canons of 1603–4. (2) The Enactment of the 17 Canons of 1640. (3) The Compilation and Synodical Authorization of the present Book of Common Prayer of the Church of England. (4) The Rejection of the "Comprehension "Liturgy" by the Canterbury Convocation. These shall be considered in their order.

II.

ENACTMENT OF THE 141 CANONS OF 1603-4.

The continual recurrence of the voting of subsidies, and of the ordinary Synodical business transacted at this time, does not call for any special attention. But the enactment of the 141 Canons, being the groundwork of the present proceedings in the Ecclesiastical Courts, must be considered at some length. *Sovereign: K. James I. 1603–1625.*

Before, however, entering on that enquiry, it may be worth while to take a brief survey of some other events which occurred during King James I.'s reign.

In 1610, Mr. Crashaw, Preacher at the Temple, was convened before the Canterbury Synod for having published a book containing erroneous doctrine. This performance was entitled, "News from Italy of a Second Moses." The volume was a translation of the life of the Marchese Carraccioli, an Italian, who, having abjured the Roman persuasion, adopted the cruel and fanciful singularities of Calvin. In a dedication prefixed to his work, Mr. Crashaw took occasion to draw a parallel between this Italian *Review of some Synodical events in King James I.'s reign. Strype's Annals, iv. 398. Card. Syn. p. 591, n.*

Marquis and the Jewish Lawgiver. But on the most cursory inspection of Mr. Crashaw's pages the comparison between Moses and the Italian does not hold good; and this indeed the author must have himself discovered, at least if his retractation was honest which he made when he expressed contrition for his publication and abjured the tenets contained in the work. Upon his confession of error this preacher at the Temple was dismissed by the Archbishop. In like manner, in the following year, one Griffin, who had been guilty of some horrid blasphemies, recanted, confessed his impieties, and submitted himself to the Synod.

In 1624, by Dr. Young, Dean of Winchester, and again in the ensuing year by Dr. James, the learned writer on the texts of the Fathers, a proposition was made in the Canterbury Synod which unfortunately was never carried into practical effect. It was this—that the most remarkable scholars of Oxford and Cambridge should be selected by Convocation for the purpose of collating with the best MSS. the Greek and Latin editions of the Fathers, the records of Councils, and the works of ancient Ecclesiastical writers. It was the purpose of this examination to compile an index which might assist in determining the true reading of passages where doubt had existed, or where fraud had been practised. The Prolocutor informed the Lower House of Canterbury that the plan had been submitted to the King, who approved it. And the Deans, Capitular Proctors, as well as other members of the Synod, were requested to search the libraries of their respective churches, and to prepare catalogues of their MSS. and best editions for presentation to the assembly, with a view to the prosecution of the enterprize. An examination of the "Indices Expurgatorii" also formed part of the plan. Had this scheme been carried out, it would have contributed much to strengthen the cause of the Church of England. For though this country, by the sacrilegious enormities of King Henry VIII. and his followers, and by the plunder of the abbeys, had more MSS. destroyed than any kingdom of like size ever possessed; yet still, enough were left here to have furnished, if rightly made use of, the evidence of truth to the world and to posterity. The enterprize, however, from some unknown cause, was unhappily abandoned. *[margin: Sovereign: K. James I. 1603–1625.]*

The most important Synodical act, however, of this reign, at least in its results, was the enactment of the 141 Canons of 1603–4. *[margin: Canons of 1603–4.]*

The Convocation of Canterbury which enacted the present Code of Canons of the Church of England met on March 20, 1604, N. S., and is reported by the quaint historian Fuller to have "been shot between the joints of the harness;" *[margin: Conc. M. B. iv. 378. Church Hist. Bk. x. p. 28.]*

Metropolitans: Cant. vacant. Hutton.

by which somewhat dark metaphor that worthy meant that this Provincial Synod was held between Archbishop Whitgift's death and the promotion of Bancroft, Bishop of London, to the See of Canterbury. In consequence of the vacancy in this Metropolitan See, Bishop Bancroft presided in this Convocation, under a Commission issued by the Dean and Chapter of Canterbury as being guardians of the Spiritualities. There was no Latin sermon preached at the opening session, an event contrary to usual custom, the appointment of the preacher on such occasions resting with the Archbishop. Dr. Ravis was elected Prolocutor of the Lower House.

Constructions of Law to the disadvantage of the Church by the learned profession.

The Canons of Discipline enacted in the later part of Queen Elizabeth's reign were confirmed only for the term of her natural life by that monarch. And here it should be remarked, that it is noway clear that such confirmation is constitutionally necessary subsequent to enactment by a Convocation. At least it does not appear to be so, if the provisions of the Statute [25 Hen. VIII. 19] are rightly interpreted, which alone governs this whole matter. The Act in question provides that the Convocations, for the purpose of enacting Canons, shall have Royal "Assent and "Licence." This means one instrument; it specifies one proceeding, i.e. permission to enact. And so the matter was understood at the time this Statute was passed and for many years after, and this method was adopted on the occasion of the first licence ever issued in compliance with the terms of the Act. Subsequently, however, legal ingenuity, favourable to Royal jurisdiction but not equally zealous for the protection of Ecclesiastical authority, in construing this Statute transposed its terms, and converted "Assent and "Licence" into "Licence and Assent," and so made two proceedings needful, first, "Licence," and secondly, "Assent" afterwards. Thus the Crown Office secured, without warrant of law, a double action: (1) The issue of the Royal "Licence" before enactment; (2) The issue of an instrument of "Assent" after enactment. What larger amount of legal fees accrued by this management it would be impossible for one not versed in official and Crown Office secrets to divine. At any rate, the contrivance was more subtle than honest. However, let this pass, though it is only a fair example of the disabling encumbrances to which the Church has been on occasion subjected by the ingenious performances of the learned profession.

_{Sovereign: K. James I. 1603–4.}
_{Atterb. Rights, &c. Add. pp. 642–5.}

As another instance of the same character, it may here be remarked that the Statute [25 Hen. VIII. 19] governing the whole of the relations between the Crown and the Convocations, specifies that those assemblies shall not "enact, promulge, execute, or put in ure" any new Canons without licence from the

Metropolitans:
Cant. vacant.
Hutton.

Coke, Rep. xii. 70; Wake, Auth. C.P. p. 108; and Wake, State, p. 534.
Atterb. Rights, &c. p. 637.

Crown. This, again, has by legal ingenuity been improved backwards to the Church's detriment. And we have had a decision of the judges that a Convocation cannot "confer to constitute "any Canons without 'license del Roy,'" an assertion widely different from the terms contained in the Statute. Of course, the absurdity of this decision is patent on its face. For how can a Convocation propose Canons in precise terms to the Crown, requesting a licence to enact them without having previously "conferred" on the contents of the documents to be presented? What King in his senses would grant his licence before the precise words of the proposed Canons were submitted to him? And who ever heard of two licences being needful for the same set of Canons? If the above decision of the judges was correct, I am afraid the Lower House of Canterbury, and large and important committees of that body, have been over and over again subject to all the pains and penalties of præmunire in very late years indeed.

As above said, the Canons passed in the later part of Queen Elizabeth's reign were only confirmed for that monarch's natural life. It was therefore thought fit by the legal authorities that a Code should now be re-enacted in Convocation. Consequently, on April 13, 1604, Bishop Bancroft, acting as President, the see of Canterbury being still vacant, took measures for the

Strype's Annals, iv. 396.

enactment of Canons, and on May 2 he delivered to the Prolocutor a Book of Constitutions, collected, it is said, by the Bishop himself, out of Articles, Injunctions, and Synodical Acts previously passed and published, especial regard being had to the Canons of 1571 and 1597. After a Committee of the Lower House had been appointed for considering this draft, and after some clashing on the subject had taken place in the Upper House, a joint Committee of both Houses was eventually appointed to prosecute the matter. Sundry conferences having taken place, and many sessions having been devoted to the subject, the whole Code of Canons, numbering 141, was finally approved, confirmed, and "de-"livered from the hands of the Synod to the "care of the printers." These Canons were published with the following title : "*Constitu-*"*tions and Canons Ecclesiastical, treated upon by*"*the Bishop of London, President of the Convocation*"*for the Province of Canterbury, and the rest of the*"*Bishops and Clergy of the said Province, and agreed*"*upon with the King's Majesty's Licence, in their*"*Synod, begun at London, Anno Dom.* 1603" [O.S.], "*and in the year of the reign of our Sovereign Lord*"*James, by the grace of God, King of England,*"*France, and Ireland, the first, and of Scotland*"*the thirty-seventh.*"

In the Royal ratification [i.e. the unstatutable "assent" above referred to] appended to these 141

Sovereign: K. James I. 1604.

Conc. M. B. iv. 379.

Ibid. iv. 380–406. Gibson's Codex, p. 993.

York Synod enacts the 141 Canons. Supra, pp. 146–7.

Metropolitans:
Bancroft,
Hutton.

Gibson's Codex, pp. 993-5.

Canons enacted by the Convocation of Canterbury, King James I. inserted this clause, that they "should be diligently observed, executed, "and equally kept by all our loving subjects of "this our kingdom, both within the Provinces of "Canterbury and York." Now, considering that at this time the York Convocation had not only never enacted, but had not even viewed these Canons, His Majesty appears for the moment to have been guilty of very great inadvertence, to have disabled the authority of the York Provincial Synod to a very unreasonable extent, and to have overstepped the bounds of the regale, in a manner most undistinguishing. The York Bishops and Clergy, as might be expected, checked at this aggression on their ancient rights. They thought if they submitted that they would always be held obliged to approve and be governed by whatsoever the Southern Synod should think fit to determine. And, indeed, the King himself on due recollection discovered his error, and made just reparation for his incautious and hasty confusion between Ecclesiastical and Regal authority. This he did by sending down a licence to the Northern Convocation to enact such Canons as should seem "fit and convenient for the "honour and service of Almighty God, the good "and quiet of the Church, and the better government thereof," within the Province of York.

Wake's State, p. 507.

Conc. M. B. iv. 426-8.

The York Convocation, to which this licence

was sent, met on Nov. 9, 1605, but was prorogued on account of the illness of the Metropolitan Hutton, whose end was approaching. In consequence of his death, which occurred about the end of the year, Dr. Thornborough, Bishop of Bristol and Dean of York, was chosen to act as President of the Northern Synod; and shortly afterwards Dr. William Goodwin was appointed Prolocutor, on March 5, 1606, N. S., on which day the licence for the enactment of Canons was produced. And in subsequent sessions, the 141 Canons of the Canterbury Synod were examined and considered, and finally, with unanimous assent and consent, ratified, and commanded to be " observed in and throughout the Province "of York." The nominal subscription of the President and other members may be seen in "Conc. Mag. Brit.," iv. 428. *Sovereign: K. James I. 1605-6.*

Notwithstanding these patent facts of history, it was stated in the House of Lords, July 11, 1851, at a time when in both Houses of the Legislature the most unreasonable jealousy of the revival of the Convocations was, one may say, ridiculously manifested, that these Canons never received the sanction of the Northern Province. And this announcement was received with approving and joyous cheers by the assembled peers. The reader will, I fear, look in vain into "Hansard," vol. cxviii., under the date above given, for a record of this odd an- *An odd announcement in the House of Lords.*

Metropolitans: Bancroft. York vacant.

nouncement, as for very shame it has been expunged; but it was most assuredly made, as every contemporary report of the debate testified, even to the consenting cheers which rang through the House.

While on the subject of these Canons, it may be excusable to make a short digression from the main argument and to insert here a few remarks on a matter of interest connected with them— that is, the extent of authority and amount of obligation which belong to them. Now there are several decisions and announcements of learned judges on this subject, which appear to sum up sufficiently the views on either side which have been held.

Legal obligation of Canons. Contradictory decisions of the learned Judges. Cory v. Pepper, Levinz, ii. 222.

(1) In the 30th year of King Charles II., the Court of Queen's Bench decided that these Canons " are good, by the Statute 25 Hen. VIII., " so long as they do not impugn the Common Law " or the Prerogative Royal." And these judges appear to have more exactly stated the truth of the case than any others who have approached the subject. Their position would have been absolutely impregnable if only their sentence had been supplemented by a few words, and had concluded thus—"impugn the King's Preroga-"tive Royal, or the Customs, Laws, or Statutes " of this Realm." For their judgment would have then been in strict and absolute accordance with the very letter of the 2nd section of the Statute

which governs the whole case, and which they themselves quoted; and it is hard to see how anyone with reason could then have gainsaid their conclusion.

Sovereign:
K. James I.
1605-6.

(2) The second judgment noticeable is that of Chief Justice Vaughan, whose words were : " A " lawful Canon is the law of the kingdom as " well as an Act of Parliament; and whatever is " the law of the kingdom is as much the law " as anything else that is so, for what is " law doth not ' suscipere magis aut minus.'" But this Chief Justice certainly assigned too extensive a power to a Canon, when he declared it to be " as much the law as anything " else that is so;" because on all hands it is admitted that it cannot prevail if contrariant among other things to a Statute of the Realm. And, consequently, a Canon is not as much the law as a contrariant Statute.

Gibson's
Cod. p. 995.

(3) Thirdly, Chief Justice Holt thus delivered his mind : " 'Tis very plain that all the Clergy " are bound by the Canons confirmed by the King; " but they must be confirmed by Parliament to " bind the laity." How this learned person could have been misled to trouble his brain with the odd idea of a Canon of Church Discipline being confirmed by Parliament, it is really hard to imagine. Canons of Discipline have existed and have been enforced from a date far beyond the time of legal memory, and very incisively

Bishop of
St. David's
v. Lucy.
Carthew,
p. 485.

x

Metropolitans:
Bancroft.
York vacant.

too, in our own times. But no man ever yet heard or read of a Canon on Ecclesiastical Discipline being confirmed by Parliament, or even submitted to that assembly for such an operation. There is something so whimsical in this fanciful excursion of Chief Justice Holt that it may be discharged from future consideration in the prosecution of the subject before us.

(4) The fourth decision to be considered is that united judgment of the Queen's Bench thus delivered by Lord Chief Justice Hardwicke:

Burn. ii. 26. "We are all of opinion that, 'proprio vigore,' "the Canons of 1603 do not bind the laity." Now, with all respect to the united judgment of the Queen's Bench, it must be said that this judgment, like that of Chief Justice Vaughan above quoted, which looked quite the other way, cannot be accepted without very considerable latitude of reserve. To say that a Canon in no case, "proprio vigore," binds a layman, is altogether too expansive a proposition. Not now to enter upon the question as to how far lay members of the learned profession practising in Ecclesiastical Courts, and other laymen connected with them, are bound by Canonical regulations, let us take a simple case of one noway connected with those Courts as an illustration. Suppose, for instance, an aggrieved lay parishioner to libel his Clergyman in the Ecclesiastical Court for a breach of the 68th Canon [the only law which could be invoked for some specified clerical shortcomings in official duty]; and suppose that, in adjudicating on the complaint, the Court should find that the Clergyman had not committed under the terms of the Canon any breach of duty, and should consequently pronounce him guiltless of the "offence against "the laws Ecclesiastical" charged against him. It is then abundantly clear that in such case the lay complainant would experience a very perceptible assurance of the "proprius vigor" of the Canon under which he had proceeded, combined with the "proprii vigores" of the Canons governing the practice and proceedings of Ecclesiastical Courts, by an appeal to his pocket for the payment of costs incurred. And, further than this, if he did not defray them in due course, the well-known process under the Canon law of a sentence of "Contumacy," followed by a second half Ecclesiastical and half Civil process denominated "Significavit," and by a third wholly Civil one designated "De "contumace capiendo," would impress on his mind, by the stern arguments provided by the walls of a city or county gaol, as the case might be, that the "proprius vigor" of the Canon under which he at first proceeded, and others, had exerted a binding force in which he was himself somewhat sensibly concerned.

(5) The fifth announcement by a learned

*Metro-
politans:
Bancroft.
York
vacant.*

Comm. i. 83.

judge to be considered on this subject, is that of Sir William Blackstone, who thus writes of these Canons: "Where they are not merely declaratory " of the ancient Canon law, but are introductory " of new regulations, they do not bind the laity, " whatever regard the Clergy may think proper " to pay them." Now it must be said that this is altogether an inadequate and a very clumsy representation of the obligatory force of these Canons as regards the Clergy. Their measures of obedience are most certainly not limited by the confines of that regard which they may "think proper to pay." The matter does not lie within their own discretion. That is quite certain, as any one of them would have very incisively commended to his attention by suspension from his benefice [if he had one], under circumstances easily conceivable, though needless here to dilate on.

On a general review of the announcements above recited of the learned in the law, it will be observed that some are contrariant to others. Now contraries cannot both be true together, as Lord Macaulay's familiar schoolboy could very confidently and rightly assert. But contraries may be false together, as the very alphabet of the seductive art of logic assures us. And I venture to think, with all submission, that such is the fate in considerable measure of these legal announcements before us. If judges differ diametrically from each other, it can, I hope, be no offence to differ at least from some of them.

It must further be remembered in considering this question, that the force of a Canon may die out by desuetude. It is a principle of Ecclesiastical Jurisprudence never to repeal a Canon, and that for reasons quite comprehensible, on which it is not needful here to dwell. But the execution of a Canon is sometimes, from various causes and reasons, allowed to lapse, and then it would not subsequently be enforced.

On a review of the whole matter, the following would seem, at least to a common capacity, to state the truth of the case as it stands at the present time. A Canon under licence from the Crown enacted by Convocation, and not being contrariant to the King's Prerogative Royal, or to the Customs, Laws, or Statutes of this Realm, and further, not having fallen into desuetude, is binding directly on the Clergy, and, in certain cases, incidentally on the laity also.

III.

ENACTMENT OF THE SEVENTEEN CANONS OF 1640.

<small>Metropolitans: Abbott, Matthews.</small>

<small>An evil augury.</small>

<small>Fuller, Ch. Hist. Bk. x. p. 109.</small>

King James I. died on the 27th of March, 1625; and on the accession of his son, King Charles I., a slight event, but one of evil augury, occurred, which seemed to portend coming ill. When that monarch sent the officials of the Court to survey the regalia, it was discovered that the left wing of the golden dove upon the sceptre had been broken off: this ornament being one of the emblems among others required for the coming coronation—

> "As holy oil, Edward Confessor's crown,
> "The rod, and bird of peace, and all such emblems."
> SHAKSPEARE: K. Hen. VIII. Act iv. Sc. 1.

Upon this discovery the King sent for Mr. Acton, a goldsmith, whose son reported the circumstance to the contemporary historian Fuller, and desired that the casualty might be repaired, and that the very same broken wing of the dove might be restored and again set on in its place. This the goldsmith affirmed that it would be impossible to effect so fairly as to leave no mark of the accident. Upon which His Majesty replied, "If "you will not do it, another shall." Mr. Acton, being unwilling thus to be superseded in his art, carried home the sceptre and had another new dove of gold set upon it. So the ancient emblem of peace was removed from the royal sceptre of England, and some novel work substituted. Upon its return the King was well pleased with the artificer's supposed success, as not discovering the change. This removal of the emblem of peace was no good omen for the future. That evil genius of discord seems to have been already on the wing which soon afterwards launched itself with malignant fury on this land, and goaded on a misguided people to deeds of unbridled barbarism and fratricidal atrocities which have rarely been equalled in the world's history. For those national horrors the self-constituted parliamentary leaders of the populace were mainly responsible; and for their crimes, aggravated as they were by fantastical cant and revolting hypocrisy, all succeeding generations of honest and good men do ever detest their names and execrate their memories. *Sovereign: K. Chas. I. 1625–1649.*

The foregoing incident was no propitious omen for the State. An event about four years before had occurred, in 1621, which was equally inauspicious for the Church. Being engaged in deer-shooting at Bramshill Park, Archbishop Abbott, using a crossbow, and aiming at a *Three more evil omens.— Collier, Eccl. Hist. vii. 416. Conc. M. B. iv. 462.*

<small>Metro-
politans:
Abbott,
Matthews.</small>

buck, unfortunately struck Peter Hawkins, Lord Zouch's keeper, with an arrow under the left arm, which caused the death of the unhappy sufferer about an hour afterwards. This was sad enough, but another result followed which presaged badly too. As homicide on the part of one in holy orders might be charged by ill friends to amount to "irregularity," which in Ecclesiastical regards lays the sacerdotal powers to sleep, forfeits preferments, and renders the person incapable of any for the future, it was thought right, on advice being taken by the Archbishop, that dispensation should be sought, "ad majorem cautelam," for his deplorable act, however involuntary.

<small>Collier,
Eccl. Hist.
vii. 418.</small>

After advice obtained, the source from which this dispensation was sought is in a high degree surprising. It was none other than from the Crown! and that, too, on the advice of those who ought to have known better. For by the instrument issued from the Crown Office, "the "Canons, in case there was need, are overruled "and dispensed with," the Archbishop's sacerdotal character is revived, and he is fully restored to his sacred functions. This is a marvellous relief beyond question from the Crown, as it "supposes a Patriarchal at least, if not a "Papal authority, vested in the Sovereign." The dove of peace broken and removed, a man killed by an Archbishop, Spiritual authority ignored, and Royal Supremacy burlesqued—these signified four sad warnings of coming calamities to Church and State. So these were noway good omens for the future. Sovereign: K. Chas. I. 1625–1649.

During the earlier part of King Charles the 1st's reign there is not much to record relating to the Acts of the Convocations. On account of the plague then raging in London, both the Canterbury Convocation and the Parliament removed to Oxford in 1625. The Convocation first met at Christ Church, and afterwards held sessions in the Chapel of Merton College, the Parliament then assembling in the magnificent Hall of Christ Church. The Canterbury and York Synods subsequently met from time to time, though with very considerable intermissions; the business for subsidies being on occasion transacted, but no events occurring worthy here of special mention until the enactment of the Seventeen Canons of 1640. Sessions at Oxford.
Fuller, Ch. Hist. Bk. ix. p. 108. Comp. Hist. iii. 6.

It will not be improper under the present head to take some special notice of the Convocations which enacted the Seventeen Canons of 1640, not on account of any influence which those instruments have exercised over subsequent Ecclesiastical Jurisprudence, but on account of the circumstances which attended their enactment. These circumstances are highly instructive, as recording the temper of the times, and as illustrating the germs of those mutinous and rebellious principles which at this time inspired the House of Commons, and betrayed the symptoms of that national disease which soon after entailed the most malignant and fatal consequences on this land. The poet's exhortation, " Discite justitiam moniti," here finds place for acceptance.

Metropolitans: Laud, Neile.

At this period of our country's history the House of Commons seems to have been seized with an irrepressible desire to usurp the functions of a National Synod. Such aspirations, as history testifies, were emphatically repressed in Queen Elizabeth's time by some remarkably incisive messages sent down to the Commons by that determined Sovereign, and there not only delivered, but very sternly carried into effect by their own Speaker. But in the present reign, notwithstanding King Charles the Ist's prohibition of disputes in that assembly about religion, the members took leave to debate on the subject with remarkable freedom. Indeed, that the House of Commons might be incited to ramble beyond the bounds of its proper functions in this direction, a book entitled " Zion's Plea" was dedicated to that body by one Leighton, a Scotchman, by profession a Doctor of Physic, in practice a fiery Puritan. In this frantic performance dedicated to the Commons this professor of the healing art must have sadly forgotten the true ends of his proper

Ecclesiastical aspirations in the House of Commons.
Vid. sup. pp. 138–40.

Cyp. Ang. Pt. i. p. 126.

calling, for he advised the Commons, as regarded the Bishops, " to smite them under the fifth rib," and indeed went so far as to recommend the murder of those Prelates. The Sovereign's Consort, Queen Henrietta, he designated as "an idolatress," "a Canaanite," and "a daugh-"ter of Heth." However acceptable such sanguinary exhortations and coarse railleries may have proved to those to whom they were dedicated, it cannot be said that they reflect much credit on their author, or on the character of that assembly to which any man would dare to address such barbarous and profane expressions.

Sovereign: K. Chas. I. 1640.

Notwithstanding the constant affectation by this House of Commons of functions which one would have thought only pertained to Synods of the Church, it seems that its members were very slenderly qualified for engaging in theological discussion. At least so this appears from the example of one of them, who certainly supposed himself to have been one of the most competent for the purpose in the whole assembly. This was Mr. Pym, who, in wandering out into topics of this character [instead of confining himself to the subjects of tonnage and poundage then rife enough, and with which he was probably quite familiar], missed his way to a remarkable degree, and so lost himself in a labyrinth of some very perplexing mistakes. That gentle-

Coll. Eccl. Hist. viii. 42.

Metro-politans: Laud, Neile.

man vouched the "Lambeth Articles" for the doctrine of the Church of England, and seems to have thought that a contradiction of them was sufficient to subject a man to the charge of heresy. Thus Mr. Pym's essay in divinity discovered overwhelming disqualifications for his enterprize. For it is beyond question that the "Lambeth Articles" were never adopted by the Church of England as exponents of her doctrine; and, further, it is most devoutly to be hoped that such Calvinistic symbols never will be by her accepted, whatever Hibernian stamp of authority may have been conceded to them elsewhere. In fact, this orator floated in discussion, aimed without precision, and struck without force. His arguments resembled those delusive weapons which revert on their projector, and certainly left on Mr. Pym's memory indelible scars of ignorance and incompetence.

Comp. Hist. iii. 102.

While such humours were dominant as above recorded, Parliament met on April 13, 1640; but it only sat for about three weeks. The King sent a message to the Commons reminding them of supplies, at the same time taking notice of the intolerable conduct of which the Scotch had been guilty. It is said that Sir

Ibid. pp. 103–4.

H. Vane, one of the principal Secretaries of State, being desired to propose six subsidies, asked for twelve; and this is a matter not unconnected with our particular subject. The request of the Secretary being considered excessive, surprised the Commons and disturbed their temper. Consequently, as they proceeded to engage in some very unserviceable debates, heaping up complaint on complaint, this Parliament was dissolved by the King, on the advice of his Council, on May 5.

Sovereign: K. Chas. I. 1640.

Concurrently with the meeting of the Parliament just mentioned, the Convocations of Canterbury and York met which enacted the Seventeen Canons of 1640.

On the 14th of April the Canterbury Synod assembled at St. Paul's Cathedral, under the presidency of Archbishop Laud. After the hymn "Te Deum Laudamus" had been sung by the Choir, Dr. Thomas Turner, one of the Canons residentiary, preached an eloquent sermon in polished Latin on the text, "Behold, I "send you forth as sheep in the midst of wolves," &c. [Matt. x. 16]. That Divine certainly chose a very apt theme for his discourse, considering the menacing attitude towards the Church which Parliament was then adopting, and the savage character of the popular temper, which was then beginning to exhibit itself unmistakeably, as will soon be seen. At the close of his discourse the preacher took notice that while some Bishops affected popular applause for qualities of meekness and mildness, it happened that the imputation of rigour and even of tyranny attached

Assembly of the Canterbury Synod. Conc. M. B. iv. 538.

Fuller, Ch. Hist. Bk. xi. p. 167.

<small>Metropolitans: Laud, Neile.</small>

by comparison to others who were more justly severe in their managements; and so he put his hearers in mind that it was desirable that all, with equal care, should secure a like conformity. After the end of the sermon and the singing of an anthem the assembly met in the Chapter House, whence, by the direction of the Archbishop, the Clergy retired to the Chapel of St. Mary-the-Virgin, at the east end of the Cathedral, for the election of a Prolocutor. Their choice fell on Dr. Richard Steward, Dean of Chichester.

<small>Syn. Ang. ii. 16.</small>

<small>Ibid. p. 17.</small>

The next session of the Synod took place three days afterwards, April 17, in King Henry VIIth's Chapel at Westminster, and after some formal preliminaries, and the confirmation of Dr. Richard Steward as Prolocutor, Archbishop Laud proceeded to address the assembly in a Latin speech. His speech lasted for nearly three-quarters of an hour; it was gravely uttered, and, as though the speaker foresaw the impending desolations of this Church and nation so soon to be realised, his eyes were scarcely restrained from weeping. Towards the end of his address the Archbishop called attention to the "Licence" which had been sent down from the Crown for the enactment of Canons for the regulation of the Ecclesiastical state. And he put the members of the Synod in mind of the confidence which His Majesty had placed in

<small>Fuller, Ch. Hist. Bk. xi. pp. 167–8.</small>

their ability and integrity by encouraging them to alter old Canons and frame new ones, the like of which had not for many years been done.

Sovereign: K. Chas. I. 1640.

The Clergy shewed their affection to the throne so substantially, that they voted six subsidies of four shillings in the pound, "for "the support of His Majesty's Royal estate, and "the furtherance of his most royal and extra- "ordinary designs abroad." And, indeed, they promised a more ample supply to the Exchequer if they had power to make a larger levy. This was the act on the part of the Clergy which soon afterwards brought down upon their heads a storm of parliamentary indignation—one may rather say, a storm of parliamentary fury. The House of Commons viewed with no equanimity the supply of the King's needs; the members of that assembly had then schemes under hand, or at least in their heads, which this supply to the Royal Exchequer might countermine.

Subsidies voted to the Crown. Syn. Ang. ii. 21.

After the vote of the subsidies the Synod turned its attention to the enactment of Canons needful, as was thought, for those uneasy times. But while this business was in progress, a constitutional question was raised which caused considerable controversy. As was above said, the Parliament which was convened acourse with this Convocation was dissolved on May 5. So when the Convocation met on May 6, the

Controversy as to whether Convocations are necessarily dissolved by a dissolution of Parliament.

*Metro-
politans:
Laud,
Neile.*

Fuller,
Ch. Hist.
Bk. xi.
p. 168.
Coll. Eccl.
Hist. viii.
183.

day following the dissolution of Parliament, this question was immediately raised—whether a dissolution of Parliament necessarily involved a dissolution of the concurrent Convocations. This question was argued with more heat than learning, on the side at least of those who thought that the Convocations were necessarily dissolved when Parliament was placed under such a disability by the Crown. In answer to these objections it was shewn that there was a wide distinction between the "Royal Writ" for summoning Convocations and a "Licence" to enact Canons; and, even admitting that the "Licence" expired with the Parliament [for this "Licence" was for some unexplained reason so limited], yet that the "Writ of Summons" remained in force until the assembly was dissolved by another document for that purpose. This distinction between a "Writ of Summons" and a "Licence" to enact Canons, which, by the way, seems above the comprehension of some people even in our own day, was so patent, that most of those engaged in the discussion were, at least on that point, convinced and satisfied that the Convocations were still in a condition to deliberate, notwithstanding the dissolution of Parliament.

However, as some uneasy spirits were not yet amenable to reason, His Majesty determined to refer the question to some of the chief lawyers about him. These learned persons returned answer and subscribed an opinion which knocked down the dispute. Their subscribed opinion ran as follows:—

<blockquote>
"The Convocation called by the King's Writ under the Great Seal doth continue until it be dissolved by Writ or Commission under the Great Seal, notwithstanding the Parliament be dissolved.

"Jo. Finch, C. S.   Edward Littleton.
"H. Manchester.   Ralph Whitfield.
"John Bramston.   Jo. Bankes.
"Ro. Heath."
</blockquote>

Sovereign: K. Chas. I. 1640.

Conc. M. B. iv. 540.

The first of these subscribers was Lord Keeper; the second, Lord Privy Seal; the fourth, Chief Justice of the Common Pleas; and the sixth, Attorney-General. Supported by such grave authority, the continuance of the Convocation appeared warranted by the Constitution; so that it proceeded with the business before it. But a fresh "Licence" to enact Canons was prepared, which was to continue during the Royal "will and pleasure."

Just at this time, when the business of preparing the proposed Canons was in progress, the Church and all those connected with her were assailed with violence. Some fanatics broke into St. Paul's Cathedral, tore down the furniture, and raised tumultuous shouts of "No Bishops." Arch-

Riots in London.

bishop Laud became the special object of the fury of a London mob. A rabble rout of Anabaptists, Brownists, and other sectaries, numbering more than five hundred, attacked his palace at Lambeth on the 11th of May for two hours. As these malcontents were, however, unable to carry that position, they determined to divert the assault and play off their batteries on the Convocation. But sensible means of defence were provided for that assembly, and a guard, consisting of some companies of the trained bands of Middlesex, commanded by Endymion Porter, a man well affected to the Church, his country, and his King, were marched down to Westminster for the purpose. Thus fortified, the Synod proceeded with its business and prepared their Canons, despatching that matter with speed and courage.

Metropolitans: Laud, Neile.
Cyp. Ang. ii. 115–16.

The six subsidies of four shillings in the pound were finally concluded on and ratified, with provisions for levying them under Ecclesiastical censures; and here great offence was given, because these subsidies were ratified without any confirmation by Parliament. On many occasions since the 37th year of King Henry VIII. Parliament had confirmed the Convocational subsidies, but not always. According to the ancient constitution of this country the Clergy had most certainly a right to vote their own money for the public needs, and to enforce

Comp. Hist. iii. 110.
Coll. Eccl. Hist. viii. 192.
Cyp. Ang. ii. 123.

payment of it, too, without any parliamentary sanction. And, as a matter of fact, they had exercised this right, without any parliamentary interference, so lately as in the twenty-ninth year of Queen Elizabeth's reign. However, if they were capable of any such honest recollections, perhaps some members of the late Parliament felt reasonable shame that the Clergy had shewn a substantial respect for their Sovereign which they themselves had refused to pay. And hence the ill will.

<small>Sovereign: K. Chas. I. 1640.</small>

It may be observed by the way, that this Synod intended to provide a Pontifical for the English Church, consisting of a Form for Royal Coronations, an Office for Consecrating Churches and Churchyards, and a Form for Reconciling Penitents, which, together with the Confirmation and Ordination Services, were to be bound up in one volume. But this design unhappily came to nothing; if augmented and perfected it would have supplied a want seriously felt to this day in the Church of England.

<small>A Pontifical for the Church of England contemplated. Comp. Hist. iii. 111, note. Cyp. Ang. ii. 122.</small>

The most important work, however, of this Convocation was the compilation and ratification of the Seventeen Canons, popularly known as the "Canons of 1640." These Canons had reference to the Royal power, the suppression of Popery, Socinianism, and Sectarianism, the prevention of innovations in doctrine and Church government, the regulation of some rites and ceremonies by enforcing the restitution of the Com-

<small>Enactment of the Seventeen Canons of 1640. Conc. M. B. iv. 543.</small>

Metropolitans: Laud, Neile.

munion Tables to the east end of the Churches, from which they had been removed in some places, and finally to some particulars touching parochial management and the proceedings of Ecclesiastical Courts. These Canons having been reduced to form, and engrossed, were enacted on *Syn. Ang. ii. 54.* the 29th of May, Archbishop Laud holding a copy in his hand conjointly with the Prolocutor, Dr. Richard Steward, and reading aloud to the assembled Synod the contents, which were signed by the members, according to the constitutional method of enacting such instruments. On the same day this Synod was dissolved by the Archbishop.

It was against the Sixth of these Canons that popular and parliamentary fury was soon afterwards directed. That part of the Canon which is needful for the purpose shall be precisely here set down in full, that the reader may judge of the reasonableness of such commotions. It contained an oath to be taken by the Clergy, and the oath was as follows:—

The "&c." Oath. Conc. M. B. iv. 549.

"I, A. B., do swear that I do approve
" the doctrine and discipline or government
" established in the Church of England, as
" containing all things necessary to salva-
" tion; and that I will not endeavour, by
" myself or any other, directly or indirectly,
" to bring in any Popish doctrine contrary
" to that which is so established; nor will
" I give my consent to alter the government

"of this Church by Archbishops, Bishops, "Deans, and Archdeacons, &c., as it stands "now established, and as by right it ought "to stand, nor yet ever to subject it to the "usurpations and superstitions of the See of "Rome. And all these things I do plainly "and sincerely acknowledge and swear, ac-"cording to the plain and common sense "and understanding of the same words, "without any equivocation or mental eva-"sion or secret reservation whatsoever. "And this I do heartily, willingly, and "truly, upon the faith of a Christian. So "help me God in Jesus Christ."

Sovereign: K. Chas. I. 1640.

In opposition to the " &c." contained in this oath clamorous outcry was raised. It was said to be the "greatest mystery of iniquity "which had ever been invented, at least among "modern generations of men." It was accused of involving such "unfathomable depths of "Satan" as that no man could discover the bottom of it. In fact, it was proclaimed that swearing a man to an "&c." was imposing a mysterious latitude of restraint, tying up the conscience to hidden meanings, and obliging the juror by undiscovered particulars.

Cyp. Ang. ii. 123. Coll. Eccl. Hist. viii. 186.

All these ebullitions of rhetoric, however, were merely the flashes of party heats. The " &c." had no more to do with interpreting the sense of the oath than one of Bentley's eccentric criticisms

Metropolitans:
Laud,
Neile.

on Horace is connected with a translation of the Vedas. In the Third Canon preceding the one now under view these words had been used in describing the gradation of Church government, viz.: "Archbishops and Bishops, Deans, "Archdeacons; all having exempt or peculiar "jurisdiction, with their several Chancellors, "Commissaries, and Officials; all persons en-"trusted with the cure of souls." When, therefore, the Sixth Canon was drafted, containing the oath above mentioned, this "&c." was inserted after the word "Archdeacons" to signify those officials who had previously been nominally described at length, and to avoid needless tautology. Thus we learn how minute a spark may kindle a devastating conflagration.

It may not be out of place to mention that a contemporaneous copy, if not the very copy enacted, of these Canons which caused such national commotions both in and out of Parliament was a few years ago preserved in the old State Paper Office, now pulled down. That copy, one would think, was an instrument of considerable historical interest and value. It is a small quarto volume, dated May, 1640, and stitched with three leather straps and thread. A parchment is attached with the names of the members of Convocation who subscribed. At any rate, whatever its value, it was tied up in a not very cleanly piece of common brown paper, together with some other not uninteresting records. In truth, the whole packet externally looked more fitting for the housemaid's box, and suitable as materials for fire-lighting, than an envelope containing papers of high historical interest. Now that the papers are transferred to the Rolls, it is to be hoped that the packet above mentioned is clad in more suitable garb than when I saw it.

This Convocation, having finished the business connected with the subsidies and the Seventeen Canons, was dissolved by Archbishop Laud on the 29th of May, 1640.

On the 14th of April, 1640, the York Convocation assembled concurrently with the Canterbury Synod last recorded. The Metropolitan of York, Dr. Richard Neile, presided; and Dr. Henry Wickam, Archdeacon of York, was elected Prolocutor. A "Licence" to enact Canons was received on the very day on which Parliament was dissolved, May 5; and, as was the case in the Southern Synod, a second and amended "Licence" was introduced on May 29, empowering the Synod to proceed to Canonical legislation, not limited by the words "present Parliament," but "during the Royal will and pleasure." This York Synod granted subsidies to the King, as had been done in the Southern Province, and they were collected without any parliamentary confirmation, in conformity with the precedent laid down in the 29th year of Queen Elizabeth.

Sovereign: K. Chas. I. 1640.

York Convocation enacts the Seventeen Canons of 1640. Conc. M. B. iv. 553.

Metropolitans: Laud, Neile.

Finally, the Seventeen Canons received from the Canterbury Convocation were unanimously accepted and subscribed in the York Synod, and enacted as obligatory throughout the Northern Province. The last session appears to have been held on June 26, and shortly after this Convocation was dissolved.

The Seventeen Canons thus having received full Synodical authority in both Provinces were confirmed by Letters Patent under the Broad Seal [though it may be fairly doubted whether this was constitutionally necessary] on June 13, and were promulgated on the 30th of that month. Shortly after this was done, a perfect hurricane of outcry arose. But the subsidies granted to the King for securing the safety of the country and repressing the rebellious Scots was the real offence, as may be gathered from the language used. Mr. Pym and Mr. Hampden were the leaders of the malcontents. Some went so far as to say, "that their party was then strong "enough to pull the King's crown from his head, "but the Gospel would not suffer them." It is no Theban puzzle to discover what this meant, nor does it need an Œdipus to divine that the grant of the subsidies by the Convocations was the spark which really kindled this flaming rhetoric.

Vid. sup. pp. 146-7.

Cyp. Ang. ii. 126.

Ibid. p. 123.

Nalson's Coll. i. 562.

Echard's Hist. Eng. iii. 188.

Parliamentary flowers of rhetoric.

Echard's Hist. Eng. iii. 194.

On Nov. 3, 1640, that Long Parliament met to whose account may be set down torrents of fratricidal bloodshed, the murder of an Archbishop, the martyrdom of a King, and the misery of this country lasting for well-nigh twenty years. This Parliament had not long begun its sessions when Mr. Pym, Sir B. Rudyard, Mr. Bagshaw, Sir J. Holland, Lord Digby, Sir J. Culpeper, Mr. Harbottle Grimston, and others of like temper, launched their bolts of invective against the Church and Clergy with nothing short of frenzied fury. The records of the parliamentary speeches of the day must be studied if anyone would gain a true knowledge of the extravagance of language indulged in. It would be impossible here to follow out the frantic rambling of the speakers, or give in any detail an account of the strained flourishes of rhetoric which likened the Pope of Rome to Herod, and Archbishop Laud to Pontius Pilate. Suffice it to say, that these parliamentary orators dashed off numerous figures of speech equally as discreditable as the above to their character for precision in comparisons or skill in expression. In truth, they indulged in the last excesses of coarseness and vituperation, and dealt more profusely in vulgar raillery and pothouse abuse than in accurate learning or persuasive logic. Sir Edward Deering indulged himself in language of all-embracing extension when, in making a frantic attack on the character of Archbishop Laud, he garnished his metaphorical peroration with these graceful words: "Before the year ran out he

Sovereign:
K. Chas. I.
1640.

Nalson's Coll. i. 678.
Collier, Eccl. Hist. viii. 190 seq.

Nalson's Coll. i. 564.

Metropolitans:
Laud.
York vacant.

Echard, Hist. Eng. iii. 198.

"hoped his Grace would either have more grace "or no grace at all, for our manifold griefs do "fill a mighty and vast circumference, yet so "that from every part our lives of sorrow do "lead to him and point to him as the centre "from which our miseries in this Church, and "many of them in the Commonwealth, do flow."

The fairest and sweetest contribution, however, to the garland of parliamentary rhetoric at this time, was made by Mr. Harbottle Grimstone. The delicacy of language and aptness of metaphor acceptable to this House of Commons was exemplified by that gentleman's address when he announced that Archbishop Laud was

Comp. Hist. iii. 107.

"the sty of all pestilential filth"—"the great "and common enemy of all goodness and of all "good men"—"a viper near His Majesty's per-"son to distil poyson into his sacred ears," &c.

Upon consideration, however, it seems that Mr. Grimstone's heat of temper made his language overboil. His first metaphor, however much it may have been approved of by those to whom it was addressed, can no way hold good. A man under certain conditions might possibly be likened opprobriously to the occupant of a sty, without doing any great violence to language; but even the speaker himself on this occasion, though quite worthy of an unsavoury comparison, could by no one, without the vulgarest perversion of thought and word, be likened to the offensive outbuilding which he invoked. In fact, the coarse railleries and vulgar abuse indulged in by the members of this House of Commons have rarely, if ever, been equalled, certainly never surpassed; save by the profane language subsequently delivered to the same assembly by Oliver Cromwell, and the obscene terms by which he thought fit to designate the members, and that, moreover, to their very faces.

<small>Sovereign: K. Chas. I. 1640.</small>

<small>Comp. Hist. iii. 207.</small>

The above niceties, however, of simile, metaphor, and illustration, were applied only individually to the Archbishop. The more noisy explosions of parliamentary rhetoric were reserved for assaulting the Convocations. The " &c." in the Sixth of the Seventeen Canons they had enacted in the previous spring was the special object of attack. And here Lord Digby, Sir John Culpeper, and Mr. Grimstone distinguished themselves remarkably in the field. The " &c." was defined as a " bottomless perjury," as " gross and absurd," as " reaching numberless fathom deep" in mystery, and as containing " neither divinity nor " charity." These were lively sallies; but the heroic champions in parliamentary warfare were not satisfied with vituperation only, they took more practical measures. So an order was made that Mr. Selden, Sir Thomas Widdrington, and Mr. Whistler should procure the formal document under which the Convocations had last spring been continued and had confirmed

<small>Ibid. iii. 112.</small>

<small>Ibid.</small>

Metropolitans:
Laud.
York vacant.

their subsidies to the King after the Parliament had been dissolved. When this subject was resumed, Mr. Bagshaw, Mr. Nathaniel Fiennes, Sir Edward Deering, and some others, took the opportunity to renew their noisy declamations.

All these explosions, however, were nothing but theatrical thunder; these flashes of rhetorical display were no more than the pyrotechnics of a pantomime. No man can believe, after a moment's reflection, that the "&c." as above explained could be any real cause of offence. No; it was the six subsidies of four shillings in the pound, voted in both Convocations and extending over both Provinces, with a promise also of more to the King if possible, that rankled in the patriotic hearts of these parliamentary orators. Those supplies to the Crown threatened to thwart some dark designs now imminent, and very dear to some at least of these rhetoricians. And had it not been for those supplies, it is but likely we might have heard of an earlier mutinous occupation of Hull, of an earlier assumption of parliamentary possession of the arsenal of Portsmouth, of an earlier acquisition of authority over the Royal armoury in the Tower of London. The subsidies were the real offence; not the "&c." And that they were so is proved by the evidence of the House of Commons itself, which, after all this fire and fury, passed this very plain, practical, and ungarnished reso-

lution: "That the several grants of the benevo- *Sovereign:*
"lences or contribution granted to His Most *K. Chas. I.*
"Excellent Majesty by the Clergy of the Pro- *1640.*
"vinces of Canterbury and York, in the several *Comp. Hist.*
"Convocations or Synods holden in London *iii. 112–13.*
"and York, 1640, are contrary to the laws, and
"ought not to bind the Clergy." Now this was
a downright palpable falsehood; but let that pass,
in party heats truth is not always paramount.

This Parliament, moreover, very soon after- *Parlia-*
wards took precautionary measures to prevent *mentary precautions*
any more subsidies to the Crown from being *against subsidies*
hereafter thus voted, at least, while this Parlia- *being voted by the Con-*
ment ruled the destinies of England. Those *vocations.*
measures were certainly of a somewhat stringent,
one may say outrageously cruel character, being
three in number.

(1) The first precaution taken was the com- *Cyp. Ang.*
mittal of Archbishop Laud to the custody of *Lib. V. p. 11.*
Maxwell, Usher of the Black Rod, on Dec. 18,
1640, by order of the House of Commons; and, *Ibid.*
on March 1 following, the prisoner was conveyed *pp. 1 & 57.*
amid the railing of a rabble rout to the Tower.
There he languished in prison nearly four years,
and on the 10th of January, 1645, N.S., was brought
to the scaffold, where he died, a pattern of manly
courage and Christian constancy, a martyr to the
rancorous hostility of this Parliament.

(2) The second parliamentary precaution against
any more subsidies being voted to the Crown by

the Clergy, was taken by "proceeding to a Bill "for punishing and fining the members of the "Convocations of the two Provinces" who had enacted the Seventeen Canons. The proposed fines are reported to have been as follows: The Archbishop of Canterbury, £20,000; the Metropolitan of York, £10,000; Bishop Wren, £10,000; the Bishop of Chester, £3,000; the Dean of Canterbury, £1,000; each Proctor, £1,000, &c. It has been computed that the total of the fines would amount to £200,000, a sufficient burden, one would think, on the Clergy to prevent their ever being in a condition during their natural lives to vote any more money for their Sovereign's needs.

Metropolitans: Laud, Williams.
Walker's Suff. p. 7.

Comp. Hist. iii. 124.

(3) The third precaution taken by the House of Commons for its purpose was the impeachment of thirteen Prelates of the Church, viz. the Bishops of Bangor, Bath and Wells, Bristol, Ely, Exeter, Gloucester, Hereford, Llandaff, Lichfield and Coventry, Peterborough, Rochester, St. Asaph, and Winchester, who were put to their answer Nov. 12, 1641.

This impeachment, however, of thirteen Bishops, and the imprisonment of Archbishop Laud, did not satisfy the ardour of this House of Commons. That assembly soon afterwards committed Williams the new Metropolitan of York and eleven Bishops to the Tower, viz. the Bishops of Bath and Wells, Durham, Ely, Gloucester, Hereford, Lichfield and Coventry,

Ibid. iii. 125.

Llandaff, Norwich, Oxford, Peterborough, and St. Asaph, merely for having signed a petition asserting their constitutional rights. And here it is observable that in this proceeding the House of Commons had at least the acquiescence, and in a measure the actual help, of the House of Lords. Upon which it seems not out of place to remark, that it would be but common prudence on the part of the exalted members in our own times of that august assembly to remember what speedy fate overtook their noble predecessors at the hands of this House of Commons, when its members afterwards discovered that their spleen against their betters had neither been satisfied nor appeased by the imprisonment of two Metropolitans, the execution of one, and the sufferings of eleven Bishops who had groaned in prison by the tyrannical act of that popular assembly. The historical records of January 6, 1649, and of the first week of February in that year, may supply some instructive matter for consideration to noble Lords, before they again join with the House of Commons in dishonouring Bishops of the Church of England.

<small>Sovereign: K. Chas. I. 1641.</small>
<small>Comp. Hist. iii. 124-5.</small>
<small>Ibid. iii. 191-2. Student's Hume, pp. 436-8.</small>

The reader may here fairly pause for a few moments of recollection and reflection. It may reasonably be asked, What can be said for the honesty of men who, with such powers of parliamentary oratory as they possessed, fictitiously represented a perfectly innocent " &c."

Metropolitans: Laud, Williams.

as the subject of their complaint, when the real offence in their hearts was the subsidies to the Crown? What can be said for the justice of men who proposed and proceeded far in a scheme for mulcting the Clergy in a sum certainly approaching, if not amounting to, £200,000, because they had voted subsidies for the needs of their King? What can be said for the loyalty of men who proceeded to impeach thirteen Bishops, because they had been instrumental in promoting a grant of a benevolence to the Sovereign of the Realm? And what can be said for the humanity of men who committed to the walls of a prison a Prelate personally most religious, kept him languishing in that confinement nearly four years, and then consigned him to the axe of the executioner; and who also committed to the Tower another Metropolitan and eleven Bishops, merely for the offence of having signed a petition asserting their constitutional rights?

Monetary transactions between Parliament and the Scotch for the purchase of the king's person.

Not long after the barbarous parliamentary severities above recorded another event occurred, in its sequel not wholly unconnected with the Church, and which is not calculated to exalt the character of this Long Parliament, which first saw light on Nov. 3, 1640, at least in most people's estimation. King Charles the First had invoked the hospitality of the Scotch, and was indeed their guest at Newcastle. And at this juncture a commercial transaction between his hosts and

Comp. Hist. iii. 163.

the English Parliament was floated for the sale of the King to his enemies. The huckstering of the Caledonian Commissioners, whose national caution in monetary affairs did not on this occasion fail them, and the haggling for rebate in price on the part of the English Parliament, is not altogether an edifying study. In truth, an illustration of the sacred rights of hospitality by the disposal of a guest on the part of the sellers, and a wrangle over a future money payment for his delivery to the purchasers on the part of the buyers, are short of being pleasant subjects for contemplation by any one. Nor would the dissatisfaction in perusing such an account be any way lessened, in case the reader were a Briton, by the reflection that the parties to this bargain were Scotch Commissioners and an English Parliament. He need not scrupulously weigh out the proportions of disgrace to be allotted to each, but he may well blush with deepest blood-red shame at the retrospect of such a foul national stain as Clytemnestra's invoked ocean of oblivion can never wash out. He would devoutly hope and pray that the fact may be as far as possible concealed from all civilized peoples in both hemispheres; and further, that it may not hereafter become known to any savage tribes in our Colonial possessions, who, in contrasting the parliamentary progenitors of their new masters with themselves, might most fairly

Sovereign:
K. Chas. I.
1640.

Comp. Hist.
iii. 163.

Metropolitans: Laud, Williams.

and righteously draw a comparison overwhelmingly in their own favour.

The ready-money payment for the bargain above mentioned included some outstanding book debts; and the sum agreed on, after much haggling, was £200,000. This sum was raised by a loan from the City of London, and was placed on deposit at Goldsmiths' Hall on Nov. 27, 1646. It was soon after transmitted to the Scots; but whether in hard cash, by notes, or by a bill payable on demand, or postdated, does not appear. However, the security on which the loan was raised is observable. It was none other than a lien on the credit of the sale of Church lands. But whether the original donors, in a more pious generation, of gifts dedicated to Almighty God, and bestowed to promote the message of "peace on earth" and "good will "towards men," would have approved of this devotion of those benefactions to the purchase of a victim for the axe of the executioner may be gravely questioned; and had they foreseen this application of their offerings, it may well be doubted if ever they would have been made.

Comp. Hist. iii. 163.

This House of Commons did not eventually escape the proverbial fate of evil doers. Surely

"Rarò antecedentem scelestum
"Deseruit pede pœna claudo."
Hor. Car. III. ii. 31-2.

For let it be remembered that this was the very same House of Commons which, after all its magniloquent flourishes of rhetoric and high pretence, was "purged" by the drastic remedies of one of Oliver Cromwell's creatures who had formerly served the menial office of a drayman, but who now, being promoted to the dignity of arbiter of the destinies of these senators, incarcerated 52 of them in a chamber profanely denominated H—l, and drove above 160 more from the House like a rabble rout. This was the House of Commons whose members sat tamely in their seats and submitted there to be railed at in language so profane and obscene that it is impossible to defile these pages by recording it; and that, too, from the lips of a man who, clothing himself in a robe of sanctimonious hypocrisy, usually delivered himself in phrases of religious cant, but yet thought the members of this assembly fit to be addressed in such opprobrious terms as could not be exceeded by the coarsest abuse of a Billingsgate fish fag. These were the men who submitted to see their Speaker's mace carried off for a fool's "bauble," and to be themselves a second time ignominiously thrust out into the street, the doors meanwhile being locked against their possible return. These were the men who, after all their hectoring display and vaulting ambition, instead of standing to their position in some manly form and flashing the last grain of powder in defence,

Sovereign: K. Chas. I. 1640.

Nemesis of fate overtakes this House of Commons.

Student's Hume, p. 435.

Comp. Hist. iii. 207, col. 1.

<small>Metropolitans: Laud, Williams.</small>

<small>Comp. Hist. iii. 207, col. 2.</small>

skulked away in dispersed rout from their posts; and who, after all their airy flights and soaring ambition, crawled contemptibly to their end like insects, and went out in smoke and smoulder. Nor did the ignominy of this House of Commons end with its existence; for this was the House of Commons which, having cumulated all the above dark catalogue of disgraces upon its memory, was eventually stigmatized at its latter end by a base and contemptuous epithet which will perpetually cover its name with ridicule and contumely so long as national records shall last or English history be read.

But enough of these tempestuous times, and so we may hail the advent of a more genial season,

> "Nec fera tempestas toto tamen horret in anno,
> "Et tibi, crede mihi, tempora veris erunt."
>
> Ov. Fast. I. 495–6.

IV.

COMPILATION AND SYNODICAL AUTHORIZATION OF THE PRESENT BOOK OF COMMON PRAYER.

We next approach an event to English Churchmen of this day the most interesting of all those which have been considered. That is, the compilation and authorization of the present Book of Common Prayer.

<small>Sovereign: K.Chas.II. 1649–1685.</small>

Now it must be confessed that the English mind is not wont to investigate causes of things, but is mostly satisfied with effects and results. To this may be ascribed very much of the Gnosticism, Humanitarianism, Scepticism, and, what is more common, the Indifferentism of the present day. Tangible and visible phænomena are scientifically investigated and volubly enough discussed: the causes and originals of things are sadly ignored. This national habit of mind accounts for the fact—and it is a fact indubitable—that if an ordinarily well-disposed Churchman is asked on what authority he accepts the Prayer Book and honours it as a manual of devotion, he will either tell you that he never contemplated the matter, or that he does not know, or that he accepts and

<small>Authority of the present "Book of Common Prayer."</small>

Metropolitans: Juxon, Frewen.

honours the book because he found it in existence, or because his forefathers had accepted and honoured it before him. And this, to my certain personal knowledge is true, that any reasonable answer to the above question could not in any one instance be obtained, though constantly sought from those very persons who above all others ought to be in condition to make reply. Of course, the two first answers to the query above suggested are self-condemnatory. To the two last the plain rejoinder is, How then did it happen that you found it in existence, or that your forefathers accepted and honoured the book? And of these facts as admitted there is but one simple explanation, and it is this—at least in the mind of any reasonable being—because the book was rightly and duly authorized by proper authority, i.e. the Provincial Synods or Convocations of the Church of England. That this was the case shall hereafter be abundantly shewn; and the reader must forgive, on account of the importance of the subject, a somewhat long discussion of it and of its surrounding circumstances.

Republican tender mercies.

During the time which elapsed between the martyrdom of King Charles I. and the return of his son King Charles II., Constitutional government was banished from this country, and the tender mercies of Republican institutions, which are sometimes the reverse of gentle, were sensibly experienced. Respect for the rights of property was exemplified by the expulsion of at least seven thousand of the Clergy, with their families, from their homes, as nominally specified in detail by Walker, in his well-known book, "The "Sufferings of the Clergy." Humane regard for the liberty of person was signified by committing large numbers of the Clergy to prison; and a project indeed was set on foot, with which gentle purpose considerable progress was made, for selling some of the most eminent of them, and some Masters of Colleges, as slaves to the Turks. Furthermore, a very keen sensibility to the claims of liberty of conscience was signalized when their Wisdoms in Parliament enacted a Statute which provided not only that it should be a punishable offence to use the Book of Common Prayer publicly in church, but that if any person should read it in any private house or family within this kingdom of England, penalties should be imposed amounting to five pounds for the first offence, ten pounds for the second, and for the third one year's imprisonment without bail or mainprize. This Republican Parliament had, moreover, a peculiar method of dealing out distributive justice. It voted on one occasion "liberty to tender consciences, by way of indul-"gence;" and within two days, upon mature consideration of the extent of this concession, added a proviso, "that the indulgence as to

Sovereign:
K.Chas.II.
1649–
1685.

Walker's Suff. Pref. xviii.

Ibid. xvii.

Walker's Suff. p. 28.

Metropolitans:
Juxon,
Frewen.

"tender consciences shall not extend to the Book of Common Prayer." Thus was the Common Prayer Book of the Church of England, so far as Republican amenities and parliamentary enactment could go, suppressed.

On the Restoration of the Monarchy in 1660, and the return of King Charles II. to England, the English Clergy who had been with their families expelled from their Cures, into which dissenting preachers had been intruded, were restored to their homes. On some occasions in late years most doleful complaints have been uttered by persons in very high quarters about this proceeding. It has been execrated as an act of exceeding cruelty, and recorded with wailing most dismal. But this is really nothing short of a fantastical display of perverted feeling. It requires a capacity more than commonly improved to discover any cruelty in restoring men to their rightful possessions, of which they had been forcibly and unjustly deprived. The charge of cruelty seems to a common understanding to lie quite the other way, and to be more fairly chargeable on those who had in the first place deprived the Clergy of their property, and had then so long continued to sanction and uphold such confiscations.

Schemes for restoring a Book of Common Prayer.

Several schemes shortly after the Restoration of the Monarchy were set on foot for restoring, but meanwhile remodelling, the Prayer Book, in order that it might be made more acceptable to the Puritan and Presbyterian dissenters, and might become a manual for public worship acceptable to all.

Sovereign: K. Chas. II. 1661.

The first endeavour towards this end was made by assembling the Savoy Conference, so called because this company met at the Bishop of London's lodgings in the Savoy, by the Strand, in London. The scheme was not a hopeful one, nor was the event other than might have been reasonably expected. This assembly met under a Royal Commission issued for the purpose, and bearing date March 25, 1661. The Metropolitan of York [Accepted Frewen], eleven Bishops, and twenty-nine so-called Divines were appointed, nine of the latter being members of the Church of England, and twenty belonging to the Presbyterian or Puritan platform. It would be tedious here to pursue the debates of these Commissioners, through the exceptions taken by one party against the existing Prayer Book and the defences set up for it by the other. And it would be beyond anyone's power, unless he had a remarkably penetrating intellect, and that too uncommonly improved, to unravel the fine-drawn distinctions in which Mr. Richard Baxter entangled the company. Indeed, no one could possibly follow that gentleman with any hope of satisfaction through his misapplication of the rules of logic. Nor would it be any way

First essay at Liturgical Revision. Savoy Conference.

Comp. Hist. iii. 253–4.

instructive to enter now upon an examination of his "Reformed Liturgy," which, though drawn up by his single hand, no sense of decency or modesty prevented him from offering as fit to supersede the Liturgy of the Church of England. It may suffice here to say, that the labours of the Savoy Conference came to a most impotent, not to say absurd result, as in effect expressed in their own report, which assured the King that they were most anxious to comply with His Majesty's wishes, but that the only conclusion they could come to was that they could agree on nothing at all.

The next effort to provide a Prayer Book for the Church of England was made in Parliament, an odd assembly, one would think, to undertake the functions of a National Synod, or at least a Synod of the Exarchate. This Parliament met on May 8, 1661, and on the 11th of that month it was ordered in the House of Commons that "A Committee for Religion should meet every Monday." A committee was accordingly appointed of all the members of that House that were of "the long robe," this being the emphatic and particular direction of the House; and the preparation of a Bill for authorizing a Public Liturgy was especially commended to the care of Mr. Serjeant Keeling.

Certainly it is somewhat puzzling to understand why the duty of providing a Liturgy for the Church of England should be confided exclusively to gentlemen of "the long robe," at least, if we may judge from our later experiences of the theological acquirements of members of the learned profession, and from the performances of the Judicial Committee of Privy Council and of other high legal authorities in our own times. However, after sundry discussions, the result was that on July 9 "A Bill for the Uniformity of "Public Prayers and the Administration of the "Sacraments," having been engrossed, was read a third time in the Commons, and was sent up to the House of Lords on the following day.

<small>Sovereign: K.Chas.II. 1661.</small>

<small>Commons' Journals, viii. 296.</small>

<small>Lords' Journals, xi. 305.</small>

To the Bill sent up from the Commons to the Lords there was attached a book which the "Committee for Religion" proposed should become by Statute the Prayer Book for the Church of England. It would be highly interesting to be informed with absolute certainty what were the exact contents of this parliamentary volume. This, however, is a desire which cannot be absolutely satisfied. The most earnest and diligent search has been made for this liturgical performance of the "members of the House "which were of the long robe," but, unhappily, without any success. Indeed it has been learned from a librarian of the House of Lords that this accession to liturgical literature perished in the fire which destroyed the Houses of Lords and Commons in the year 1834.

<small>Parliamentary Prayer Book.</small>

But, notwithstanding this deplorable loss of the volume itself, some interesting particulars about it may be surely derived from collateral sources which are still accessible. It was certainly a Prayer Book of the edition of 1604, as we learn from the House of Commons' Journals themselves; and, happily, a duplicate of the same edition is now preserved in the British Museum. At the end of the Commination Service, and immediately preceding the Psalter in that volume, there are two "godlie prayers"—one "A Prayer "necessarie for all Persons;" and secondly, "A "Prayer necessarie to be said at all times." Immediately after the Psalter are ten prayers; and following them are the Metrical Psalms, versified by Sternhold and Hopkins, "with tunes." This then we can consequently learn with absolute certainty as to the Prayer Book commended for adoption by "The Committee for Religion"— (1) that a duplicate of the book now existing in the British Museum was the book attached to the Bill; (2) that the reviewers decided that the two prayers "before the reading Psalms" should be excised, to which fact the House of Commons' Journals testify; and also (3) that Sternhold and Hopkins' Metrical Version of the Psalms, "with tunes," should be included in the Liturgy of the Church of England.

This very meagre information as to the liturgical provision proposed for the Church of England by the House of Commons' "Committee for Re-"ligion," composed exclusively of gentlemen "of "the long robe," is no doubt sadly disappointing, as fuller revelations might have supplied some interesting studies for theologians. But two things under these disabling circumstances are yet quite clear. First, that any Committee, which could have been guilty of employing such a vulgar barbarism as "reading Psalms" to describe the divine poetry of the sweet Psalmist of Israel, must have been sadly unfit for the duties committed to its charge. And secondly, that it may be a matter of unmingled thankfulness to all Englishmen that Sternhold and Hopkins' doggrel burlesques, "with tunes," of King David's divine poetry did not become, under the auspices of these gentlemen "of the long robe," part of the liturgical formularies of the Church of England. A learned author, indeed, once expressed a devout hope that Sternhold and Hopkins were "better Christians than they were poets." In this aspiration every humane mind must cordially join; to which also an equally earnest hope may be added, and it is this: that the members of the House of Commons "that were of the long "robe" in the "Committee for Religion" were also better Christians than they were adepts at the proprieties of rubrical language; and further, in more mundane regards, that for the sakes of their clients and themselves, they were better

Sovereign:
K. Chas. II.
1661.

Metropolitans: Juxon, Frewen.

lawyers than they were poetical critics, or judges of Church music.

The Bill and Book, as before said, were sent up from the Commons to the Lords. But this session of Parliament soon coming to an end on July 30 [1661], nothing was done in the Upper House during this summer. Thus the matter, as far as Parliament was concerned, slept till the next session, which began in November following. And during that session we shall learn more both of Bill and Book.

Capacity of "members of the long robe" for theological engagements. A digression.

Now, inasmuch as the wisdom of this House of Commons chose for the revision, or at least the provision of a Liturgy for the Church of England, exclusively those members in that assembly who were "of the long robe;" and inasmuch as a Royal Commission has lately, in 1883, improved on that example by recommending to the Crown that five lawyers, without any necessary reference for advice to spiritual authority, should be constituted as arbiters of faith and doctrine over both Metropolitans, all the Bishops, and the whole Clergy of the Church of England, the reader must here pardon a digression. And the reader must further concede his pardon if that digression should appear long, and have a whole section of that part of the volume in his hand specially devoted to this subject. For it is really a very interesting engagement, and may too prove an instructive one, to enquire somewhat carefully how far our own experiences of the present time commend as salutary this choice of Parliament in 1661, and this recommendation of the Royal Commission in 1883.

Sovereign: K. Chas. II. 1661.

The appointment by the House of Commons of a Committee of gentlemen "of the long "robe" exclusively, with Sergeant Keeling as their Chairman, for liturgical preparation and the introduction of a Prayer Book for the use of the Church of England, as before said, is somewhat surprising. Indeed there is not a more odd episode, if indeed any one so odd as this, in all English history. It transcends the whimsical choice of the name "Defender of the Faith;" which was appended to the styles and titles of that fleshly monarch King Henry VIII. It is more comical than the event which has been historically and graphically represented of that very questionable personage, Lord Howard of Esrick, being pulled heels forward from a chimney in which he had endeavoured to escape from the punishment of his ill-doings.

The gist of the comedy was, that this theological Committee was to be confined exclusively to gentlemen "of the long robe." No one other member of the House of Commons was deemed a sufficiently expert theologian to be included in the composition. But why members of this particular profession should have been

Metropolitans:
Juxon,
Frewen.

exclusively singled out for the purpose is, in these days at least, really a somewhat embarrassing question. Why the wisdom of this House of Commons should not have, with equal if not greater reason, deemed it essential that all members of their "Committee for Religion" should be exclusively medical men, or exclusively agriculturists, or exclusively bankers, or exclusively merchants, or exclusively members of even some meaner craft, is altogether mysterious. Indeed, if we may judge from the experiences of our own days, either one of such restrictions would appear to have been preferable for the purpose in hand.

It is universally supposed that the highest authorities of the law are the best qualified for their engagements. And so, to omit for the present the wearers of stuff, or even of silk gowns, such as were members of this theological Committee, and to pass upwards to the very highest grades of the learned profession, to the wearers of Chancellors' robes and ermine—that is, to Lord Chancellors, to the rank of a Lord Chief Justice, to Justices of the Queen's Bench and Common Pleas, to Barons of the Exchequer, and to the members of the Judicial Committee of Privy Council—What preferential claim could they maintain for discharging the duty of liturgical reformers? Their excursions into the theological region surely have not always proved happy or successful.

Let us then pursue some enquiry on this head, and, confining ourselves strictly to our own times, and not making search one year further back [though I assure the reader that such retrospect would be very helpful for the purpose], some very interesting information may be obtained. *Sovereign: K.Chas. II. 1661.*

It is doubtless needful, in approaching such an enquiry, to be very careful that merely facts should be recorded, and that no opinion on any question of law should be ventured upon for a moment, on any consideration whatever, by one who has not the advantage himself of belonging to the learned profession. Indeed, every word shall be written with a vivid remembrance of Sir E. Coke's warning in this respect, when he affirmed, to use his own words, "that he never "knew a Divine meddle with a matter of law, "but therein he committed some great error."

Now one would not venture for an instant to doubt the truth of this assertion of experiences contributed by an authority generally so precisely accurate. So this wholesome warning shall be most carefully kept in mind. While in all reason it must in the meantime be remembered, on the other hand, that, as regards the coherence of dates and the existence of matters of fact, other people, and even those who may happen to be Divines, do not labour under any greater incapacity for arriving at the truth than

*Metro-
politans:
Juxon,
Frewen.*

those who are so fortunate as to be numbered among the members of the learned profession itself. And one other remark, too, may not be here out of place, in reference to Sir E. Coke's affirmation above quoted, and it is this. If that learned writer had substituted the word "Lawyer" for "Divine," and the words "Ecclesiastical History" for "Law," he would then have made an announcement not one whit less credible than his original assertion. Indeed, Sir E. Coke himself has contributed considerably to its credibility in his own person, when

Coke's Inst. iv. 323.

he wrote of Convocation, that "As there be two "Houses, so there be two Prolocutors: one of "the Bishops of the Higher House, chosen by "that House; another of the Lower House, "and presented to the Bishops for their Pro-"locutor." Beyond all question, to adopt the learned jurist's own expression, certainly "there-"in he committed some great error."

Bearing then in mind the above caution, it shall be carefully observed. Meanwhile, it is moreover to be remembered throughout this enquiry that the most exalted members of the learned profession are generally held to be more fully equipped for the high functions they are called upon to discharge than those of inferior grade. Let us then prosecute this essay by contemplating only the examples of proficiency in Ecclesiastical history and theological learning which have in our own times been commended to notice by the very highest members of the legal profession. And let us never in this enquiry descend below the august rank of Lord Chancellors, Lord Chief Justices, and the Judges of the Superior Courts.

Sovereign: K.Chas.II. 1661.

To begin, then: A very distinguished Lord Chancellor of our own times, in a highly elaborated historical speech, informed an admiring House of Lords that there was no religious ceremony connected with marriage before the Council of Trent, that is to say, before the year of our Lord 1545. That announcement is so surprising that the reader may be inclined to suspect that some error may here be made in representing the speaker's affirmation. So, to remove all doubt on that head, his Lordship's words shall be precisely set down as they stand now stereotyped in those national records, Hansard's Reports. And that authority recites this Lord Chancellor's words as follows:—

A Lord Chancellor.

> "With their Lordships' permission he
> "would advert briefly to the history of the
> "Law of Marriage. Throughout the whole
> "of Christendom there was no religious
> "ceremony connected with marriage till the
> "time of the Council of Trent."

Hansard's Parliamentary Reports: Debates, New Series, Vol. xvii. p. 1419, ll. 30 seq.

From this announcement in the House of Lords it is abundantly clear that this exalted member of the learned profession was sadly

*Metropolitans:
Juxon,
Frewen.*

uninstructed in the records of the religious ceremonies which accompanied marriage in the Early Church and throughout subsequent ages. He could never even have heard of the " arræ " and " arrabones," the earnests of marriage; of the " annulus pronubus," of the " kiss," the " cœlestial veil," the " loosing of the woman's " hair," the "joining of hands," the " frequentia " amicorum," the " presence of God's minister," of " his benediction," or of the final " crown of " myrtle." This Lord Chancellor could further never have cast the most cursory glance over the pages of those authors who have treated on the subject of Christian marriage; among whom may be reckoned Tertullian, Gregory Nazianzen, Ambrose, Chrysostom, Augustine, Optatus, Gothofred. Nor could his Lordship ever have paid the smallest attention even to the writings of his own fellow-countryman, Mr. Selden, on marriage. And indeed, even further still, within his own sphere of learning, this highest authority in English judicature could never have troubled himself to consult on this subject the laws of the Emperor Leo the Wise in the East, or of Charles the Great in the West.

That a Lord Chancellor should labour under these disqualifications for deciding on the law of Christian marriage is perhaps in itself no great marvel. But it is marvellous in the highest degree that anyone so miserably ill-informed in the matter should venture to dogmatize upon it before such an august assembly as a British House of Peers. Nor is it credible that anyone unconnected with the learned profession would venture under the like disabling conditions to undertake such an enterprize before any audience whatsoever. However, as we proceed we shall see like performances frequently repeated under equally disqualifying conditions.

Sovereign:
K. Chas. II.
1661.

Another notorious Lord Chancellor, sitting in one of the two highest tribunals in the land, from which unfortunately there is no appeal, announced [without any intentional profanity, at least on this occasion] that two Prelates were

Other Lord Chancellors.

"created Bishops by the Queen, in the exercise
"of her authority as Sovereign of this Realm
"and Head of the Established Church."

Judgment,
Jud. Com.
Privy Council, March 20, 1865.

In preparing this allocution, this Lord Chancellor had the valuable help of another Lord Chancellor, of an associated noble Lord high in the learned profession, thirdly of a Master of the Rolls, and fourthly of an assisting learned Judge. So this announcement was delivered with the highest accumulated legal authority. However, being unfortunately inexhaustive in its terms, it failed to inform the world whether the Sovereign of this Realm has power to "create" Priests and Deacons, as well as Bishops; and omitted moreover to state that the style and title "Head of the Church," as applied to the Sovereign, had

Metropolitans: Juxon, Frewen.

Justices of the Court of Queen's Bench.

been for well-nigh three centuries abolished by Statute and by Royal declaration conjoined.

Still strictly adhering to records of judicial announcements occurring in our own times on Ecclesiastical subjects, we must now descend from the august authority of three Lord Chancellors to the ermined presence of a Lord Chief Justice and the Court of Queen's Bench. From the chief seat in that tribunal a Lord Chief Justice, assisted by his learned brethren, on the 25th of April, 1850, when treating of Ecclesiastical matters, and specially of Ecclesiastical history, imparted to an amazed auditory some very startling information.

Queen's Bench Judgment, April 25, 1850.

That high legal authority assured the Court and the audience there present, that the venerable Sir Thomas More was Lord Chancellor when most certainly he was not; that the pliant Audley was not Lord Chancellor when as certainly he was; and that King Henry VIII. and Queen Anne Boleyn were unmarried when their daughter Queen Elizabeth was at least five months old. And all this was embellished with other "picturesque" fancies which it would be tedious here to recite. In short, facts, dates, history, and truth were trampled down into a mass of inextricable confusion; and, as one may say, their mangled remains were pelted out of Court with supercilious contempt. Nor can one fail to observe that by this judicial performance a sweeping and far-reaching judgment was passed on the Crown of England. For I have been told that it is held in the learned profession as an inexorable rule, that judgments of Courts, until reversed by a higher tribunal, must unhesitatingly be held as governing precedents for all lower jurisdictions. Now beyond dispute the Crown was by this judgment bastardized in the person of our renowned Sovereign Queen Elizabeth. This certainly was a lively performance for the Court of Queen's Bench of all places in the world. And one hopes, for the sake of the nation's credit, though this judgment never has been reversed, yet that in this instance at least some exception may be made to the stern professional rule of faith above referred to. Indeed, so far as the outer world is concerned, the truth must be confessed that the recital of this judgment was afterwards in another Court irreverently greeted with explosive outbursts of irrepressible laughter.

Sovereign: K.Chas.II. 1661.

Court of Common Pleas, May 2, 1850.

Still adhering to our own times, and taking leave of the august wearer of the S.S. chain, we arrive in order at the Justices of the Court of Common Pleas. But as their excursions into the Ecclesiastical domain have been twice before recorded, the reader is referred to the margin. And as it is not needful again here to advert to their researches, we will listen to the deliverances of the learned Barons of the Court of Exchequer when engaged in an Ecclesiastical enquiry.

Justices of the Court of Common Pleas.

Supra, pp. 35, 76.

<small>Metropolitans: Juxon, Frewen.</small>

<small>Barons of the Court of Exchequer.</small>

<small>25 Hen. VIII. 19.</small>

<small>Court of Exchequer Judgment, July 8, 1850.</small>

Now, still confining ourselves strictly to matters which have occurred in our own times, we find that those learned Barons, on the 8th of July, 1850, when approaching the Ecclesiastical region, lost themselves hopelessly in a very wilderness of error, and that, too, in a matter peculiarly within their own province. In discoursing on the effects of the Statute which gave all final Ecclesiastical appeals to the King in this country, their exact words were as follows, for one fears lest any misrepresentation might creep into a paraphrase. This Act, they said, "did but restore the ancient law of the "land, as settled on this point by the Con-"stitutions of Clarendon in the reign of "Henry II., Anno Domini 1164."

Now here, in these few words, are contained two several deceptive phantoms as false as ever emerged from the ivory gate. As to the first, respecting the ancient law of the land, if the learned Barons had given the most cursory attention to the very first Constitution of one of the earliest Councils recorded

<small>Spel. Conc. i. 194.</small>

<small>Ibid. pp. 205, 242.</small>

<small>Leges Edg. v. Conc. M. B. i. 246.</small>

<small>Spel. Cod. p. 310.</small>

in this country's history, the Council of Brasted, A.D. 696; to the records of the Council of Cliff-at-Hoo, A.D. 747; or of the Wittenagemote at Grately, A.D. 928; to the laws of King Edgar, or to that King's declaration to Archbishop Dunstan; to King William the Ist's Great Charter, A.D. 1085; or to the oath of King Stephen, they never could have delivered from the Bench this astounding announcement, that in Ecclesi- *Sovereign:* astical causes an appeal lay to the King, "and no *K.Chas.II.* "further," "by the ancient law of the land." The *1661.* statement is absolutely false. As to the second affirmation, that such was an effect of the Constitutions of Clarendon, it can only be said that what the VIIIth Constitution—the only one of the sixteen *Matt. Par.* Articles ratified at Clarendon which touches this *Conc. M.'B.* subject—did settle was this: that all Ecclesiasti- *Coll. Eccl.* cal controversies within the Realm "should be *Hist. ii.* "finally decided in the Archbishop's Court." And *272-6.* that is directly contradictory to the learned Baron's solemn and deliberate affirmation. For the sake of their own credit it was a great pity that they did not strike a light, and, proceeding by way of regular discovery, consult authentic copies of these Constitutions of Clarendon, which they might have found in "Matthew Paris" and the "Concilia Magnæ Britanniæ." However, by neglecting such obvious precautions, and by rambling about in the dark, they unfortunately stumbled over a mutilated extract given in Mr. Justice Blackstone's Commentaries fortuitously lying *Comm. iii.* in their way, and so plunged themselves into a *66.* hopeless pitfall of error, and became an easy prey to a Chimæra from which no Pegasus can possibly devise for them any means of escape.

But all these Ecclesiastical performances by *Judicial* the exalted members of the learned profes- *Committee of Privy* sion, in Parliament, and in what must now be *Council.*

termed the several divisions of the High Court of Justice, are outshone by the exhibitions presented to view in the Whitehall Chamber of the Judicial Committee of Privy Council. To schedule in brief the interminable self-contradictions, historical misstatements, and flagrant inconsistencies of that ill-starred tribunal would swell a list intolerably tiresome to peruse. The proceedings of that Court have been sufficiently exposed, and indeed somewhat cruelly submitted to reproach by the contents of the very first page of the Royal Commission on Ecclesiastical Courts in 1883. It may therefore be enough to say here, that there now lie before me seven and a-half closely-printed octavo pages containing specific records of the mishaps of the Judicial Committee, and consisting of one hundred and fifty-seven items. The natural consequence of all this is that the tribunal has become a "lu-"dibrium pagi." The world is not so polite as the Roman, who seems to have endeavoured at least to conceal any outburst of laughter—

"........ Varius mappâ compescere risum
"Vix poterat."

However, two of its odd performances, one a very early one, and the other its very last essay in Ecclesiastical regards, shall be here recorded merely by way of specimens. The early exploit was this: In an Allocution [for as this tribunal assumes to be an Ecclesiastical

Court, I am fain to use Ecclesiastical termi- *Sovereign:* nology] pronounced on March 21, 1857, in the *K.Chas. II. 1661.* Privy Council Chamber in Whitehall, and which also, by the way, had the aid of a Lord Chancellor in compilation, a surprising piece of liturgical information was imparted to the world. This Allocution pronounced that there was no "Conse-"cration Prayer" in the Second Reformed Prayer Book published in King Edward the VIth's reign. But this is directly contradictory to matter of fact. For the "Consecration Prayer" in that book is all but identical word for word with the Consecration Prayer as existing in the present Book of Common Prayer of the Church of England. In later reprints of this Allocution the passage has been mutilated; so that, to use Ecclesiastical language again in reference to an Ecclesiastical proceeding, what now appears in the Conciliar Acts of Whitehall is a "False Decretal."

The last essay of the Judicial Committee in Ecclesiastical regards has been to promulge its latest dogma, which is this: that its judgments are

"STANDARDS OF FAITH AND DOCTRINE ADOPTED BY THE CHURCH OF ENGLAND." *Merriman v. Williams. Judgment, Privy Council Chamber.*

And with this dogmatic announcement we may take leave of this tribunal. Only I commend to the reader's notice, and, if he is an

<small>Metropolitans: Juxon, Frewen.</small>

English Churchman, request his earnest attention to the "Standards of Faith and Doc-"trine" which the Judicial Committee of Privy Council solemnly declares to be imposed on his conscience. And here our enquiry ends.

To write the plain truth without disguise, it does seem as though the atmosphere of the Ecclesiastical region was fatal to the healthy exercise of the legal brain; and so long as it remains exposed to those influences it appears doubtful whether all the remedies contributed by both Anticyras could give relief to the ailment.

If the densest Cleric in either Province of Canterbury or York were to address one of the divisions of the High Court of Justice on an intricate question of barred remainders, or to deliver himself before a Scientific Society on the comparative potency of physical force, as contrasted with natural force acting inversely as the square of the distance, he could not display more melancholy incapacity for handling the subjects he approached than the legal authorities above recorded have revealed when dogmatizing on theology and dealing with Ecclesiastical history. For at the very worst he could do no worse than affirm as fact what is demonstrably false. And yet, forsooth, in face of all this, a Royal Commission has lately recommended to the Crown that, as was before said, five judges, selected in rotation from the

Bench, without any reasonable regard either to qualification or character suitable for the purpose, or any necessary reference to spiritual authority, should be constituted as arbiters of faith and doctrine over the two Metropolitans, the Bishops of both Provinces, and the whole Clergy of the Church of England. "Quousque "tandem" may be well exclaimed by all her true and faithful children,

Sovereign: K.Chas.II. 1661.

"Di talem terris avertite pestem."

But what makes the matter more alarming is this: It is held as an inexorable rule by the legal profession, that the judgment of a superior Court is absolutely binding on inferior tribunals where a like case subsequently arises. And it may be observed that this professional etiquette—for it can rightly be described by no other words—being wholly insular, unknown to Roman law, unknown to foreign law, unrecognized by Statute law, and confined exclusively to our Imperial Bench and Bar, is capable of introducing abuses intolerable into Ecclesiastical Jurisprudence, and may hereafter prove disastrous to the best interests of the Church of England. From the Judicial Committee of Privy Council there is no appeal; nor would there be any from the tribunal proposed by the Royal Commission. And if Ecclesiastical Judges, both in Provincial Courts and in all the Consistory Courts throughout England, are to be bound

Metropolitans: Juxon, Frewen.

by the antecedent judgments of such tribunals as the Judicial Committee, or the Court proposed by the Royal Commission of 1883, it is impossible to say what contradictions of facts or what heresies in doctrine may be the governing rules for judgments. And even though the Church's Courts are not in the same "Ordo "Judiciorum," the Judicial Committee being a Civil Court, the Ecclesiastical Courts being Spiritual Tribunals, yet still we know from experience that the etiquette above mentioned is even in them, though without just reason, to be retained—at least for the present—inviolable.

How dear this worship of insular etiquette has become to the legal mind of this country may be gathered from the following facts. I enquired personally of a renowned Professor of Law in our elder University whether, if he were a Vice-Chancellor, he should feel himself personally bound, supposing a Lord Chancellor had delivered a judgment when both mad and drunk, to follow such judgment in every like case in any future litigation. And I received a most emphatic affirmative reply. I enquired of an Attorney-General whether an inferior tribunal was absolutely and inexorably bound in every subsequent case to follow the judgment of a superior Court, however wrong, until reversed. The same affirmative reply, without doubt, hesitation, or qualification, was returned. The like information has been also received from less exalted legal authority. And more than this, there have been several announcements in very recent times indeed, from the Judicial Bench, that the judges, though entirely dissenting from previous rulings, still felt themselves bound to abide by them in new cases coming before them. On all this it can only be remarked, that to argue that because injustice has been done to a suitor in the past, therefore all future generations of suitors are to suffer injury, seems a very questionable philosophy. And it would further seem that such a principle is no very attractive encouragement to a conscientious man to accept the high office of a judge, or even to enrol himself in a profession which would subject him to such immoral slavery if the highest object of his ambition were attained.

Sovereign: K.Chas. II. 1661.

There is, however, one comforting reflection, and it is this: that the late Sir G. Jessel, thought by many to have been one of the most acute and learned lawyers of this century, publicly gave the world very unmistakeable assurance that he would never consent to be bound in such ignominious bonds. And further, it may be justly deplored and very deeply regretted that he did not live to give the world some practical and incisive assurance that he could be as good as his word; and that, too, for the credit of our country's common sense.

Metropolitans: Juxon, Frewen.

However, as matters now stand, what will be the judgments of Ecclesiastical Judges with such precedents to guide their decisions as the Judicial Committee has contributed, so long as the above-mentioned professional etiquette of Secular Courts prevails in Ecclesiastical Tribunals?

And now to return to our special subject from this long digression. The superiority of Lord Chancellors, Lord Chief Justices, and the highest judges of the land, to the common rank and file of the profession, is esteemed great. But if, meanwhile, the first-named highest authorities manifest, as we have just seen, such hopeless incapacity when they approach Ecclesiastical subjects: what can be thought of the wisdom of the House of Commons of 1661, which entrusted the provision of a Liturgy exclusively to gentlemen "of the long robe;" and those too who, from the fact of their presence in that House, certainly were not Lord Chancellors nor Chief Justices, nor even Puisne Judges, and who were moreover to be presided over in their deliberations not even by a King's Counsel, but only by a Sergeant-at-law? Truly, a more ridiculous farce was never conceived by the funniest of comic writers.

King Charles the IInd's method with his Parliament, in reference to their proposed Prayer Book, was something milder than that of our *Supra, pp. 138–140.* heroic Queen, recorded in a former part of this volume, but was nevertheless eminently successful. And we must now turn to the part taken by King Charles II. and by the Convocations in the matter of compiling and authorizing the present Prayer Book of the Church of England.

Sovereign:
K. Chas. II.
1661.

A dislike of the expedient of the Savoy Conference, which, as we have seen, proved abortive, and a fear of the parliamentary essays at liturgical composition, seem greatly to have disturbed the mind, among others, of the learned Dr. Peter Heylin, who directed a well-timed letter at this time to one of His Majesty's principal Secretaries of State on this matter. After the introduction of his subject, Dr. Heylin gave his correspondent to understand that if Synodical authority should be overlooked, the rights entailed by Magna Charta would be disregarded; and that, if Parliament should be called without its concurrent Synod, an innovation on the Constitution would be inaugurated. And this he maintained by sufficient examples. "If it be objected," to use the Doctor's own words, "that the Commission now "on foot" [meaning the Savoy Conference] "for "altering and explaining certain passages in the "public Liturgy may either pass instead of a "Convocation or else be thought to be neither "compatible nor consistent with it; I hope far "better for the one, and must profess that I can "see no reason in the other. For first, I hope "that the selecting some few Bishops and other

Dr. Peter Heylin's letter.

Comp. Hist. iii. 251.

Metropolitans: Juxon, Frewen.

"learned men of the lower Clergy to debate on
"certain points contained in the Common Prayer
"Book is not intended for a representation of
"the Church of England, which is a body more
"diffused, and cannot legally stand bound by
"their acts and counsels. And if this Confer-
"ence be for no other purpose, but only to pre-
"pare matters for a Convocation [as some say it
"is not], why may not such a Convocation and
"Conference be held at once? For neither the
"selecting of some learned men out of both
"Orders for the composing and reviewing of
"both Liturgies digested in the reign of King
"Edward VI. proved any hindrance in the call-
"ing of those Convocations which were held
"both in the second and third and in the fifth
"and sixth of the said King's reign; nor was
"it found that the holding of a Convocation
"together with the first Parliament under Queen
"Elizabeth proved any hindrance to that con-
"ference or disputation which was designed
"between the Bishops and some learned men
"of the opposite parties. All which considered,
"I do most humbly beg your Lordship to put
"His Majesty in mind of sending out his man-
"dates to the two Archbishops for summoning
"a Convocation [according to the usual form] in
"their several Provinces, that this poor Church
"may be held with some degree of veneration
"both at home and abroad." After this reason-

able application the learned writer craves pardon for his presumption, lamenting that no one of higher figure and worth than himself had undertaken to press the matter; and at the same time assuring the noble Secretary that nothing but a zeal of God's glory, and an affection for the Church, would have forced the present letter from its author.

Sovereign: K.Chas. II. 1661.

Whether it was in consequence of this letter it is impossible now to say, but certainly shortly after this very seasonable and well-supported application the necessary measures were taken for convening the two Convocations. These assemblies had not met for nearly twenty-one years, having been silenced since the year 1640 by those rebellious commotions which made havoc of our national institutions both in Church and State. During part of that period the Convocations had been superseded by that amphibious apparition the Westminster Assembly, which, pretending to usurp no less than the functions of a National Synod, exhibited to the world a spectacle of impotence and absurdity which is calculated only to excite contemptuous ridicule. Its parent was the Parliament; and the Parliament cruelly strangled its own offspring, as in that day was likely enough. However, as this nation had now recovered some measures of common reason, one of the most ancient of her institutions was restored and the Convocations were convened.

Coll. Eccl. Hist. viii. 253.

Comp. Hist. iii. 146–7.

Hist. Later Puritans, pp. 146–7.

Metropolitans: Juxon, Frewen.

Canterbury Convocation, May, 1661.
Conc. M.B. iv. 565.
Syn. Ang. ii. 57.

On the 8th of May, 1661, concurrently with the meeting of Parliament, whose proceedings have been before described, the Synod of Canterbury assembled at St. Paul's Cathedral. The Bishop of London [Sheldon] presided, Juxon, the Archbishop, being in weak health. After the Te Deum had been sung, prayers offered up, and an anthem sung, a polished and eloquent discourse was delivered in Latin by Dr. Thomas Pierce, on the text, "For it seemed good to the Holy "Ghost, and to us, to lay upon you no greater "burden than these necessary things" [Acts xv. 28]. The assembly, after service, adjourned to the building then used as a Chapter House, the goodly old house having been rendered unfit for occupation by the impious barbarities of some of Oliver Cromwell's troopers. And there the usual formalities having been gone through, Dr. Fern, Dean of Ely, was elected as Prolocutor of the Lower House. Subsequent sessions were held in King Henry VIIth's Chapel in Westminster Abbey. In these sessions measures were taken for providing a service for the anniversary of the martyrdom of King Charles I., another for the restoration of the present Sovereign, and another for a day of public humiliation. The Canons and Constitutions were also reviewed, with an intention of publishing a new Code, an intention which unfortunately has never been carried out, and which, it is said, at that time was obstructed by one or two persons on whom the matter depended. And so those who should have been most forward in promoting and defending religion were the chief impediments in the way of its advancement. Finally, this group of sessions having completed, on July 27, the business of a benevolence voted to the King, was brought to a close on July 31, and prorogued to the 21st of November next following [1661].

Sovereign:
K. Chas. II.
1661.

Concurrently with the above, the York Synod assembled on May 8, 1661. This Synod was opened under the presidency of Dr. Richard Marsh, Dean of York, Archdeacon John Neil, D.D., and Dr. Anthony Elcocke, as Commissioners for their Metropolitan Accepted Frewen, who was absent. After service in the Cathedral, the singing of the hymn "Veni Creator," and the delivery of a sermon, the members adjourned to the Chapter House. There, after some formal business had been transacted, and the Clergy præconized, the President, having said the Lord's Prayer, offered up a Latin prayer, imploring a blessing upon the Synod. And it is here remarkable, that this prayer, which was of some length, was almost identical, word for word, with a prayer which was used at Synods in the Anglo-Saxon Church. Thus was commended to notice by this York example the connexion between the earlier and later Church of this land. And thus it is

York Convocation, May, 1661.
Conc. M.B. iv. 567.

Vide MSS. Cotton, Cleop. viii. fol. 35; and Conc. M.B. iv. App. 784.

Metropolitans: Juxon, Frewen.

quite clear that at this time some authority in the York Synod was not unacquainted with the ancient Ecclesiastical records of his country. By the unanimous choice of the Clergy, Archdeacon Neil, D.D., was elected Prolocutor, and so the Synod was put into a condition for proceeding to active business.

This Synod held a group of six sessions; and meanwhile a Royal Licence, dated July 23, was sent down to it, authorizing the enactment of Canons. This measure was adopted by the Crown in conformity with the course pursued at this time relating to the Southern Province, where, as we have seen above, a project for reform of the Ecclesiastical laws had been promoted. This York Synod, shortly after the arrival of this Licence, was continued, on the 8th of August [1661], to Nov. 21 next ensuing, the same day as that to which the Canterbury Synod had been continued.

The Canterbury and York Convocations, Nov. 1661.

The two Synods next assembled on the same day, Nov. 21 [1661]. These were the most important in their results—namely, the establishment of the present Prayer Book of the Church of England—of any Synods which ever met in this country, save perchance those of the year 1534, which synodically discharged the Papal Supremacy over this Church, as before recorded.

Supra, p. 78.

York Convocation, Nov. 1661.

It will be convenient on this occasion to trace in the first place the Acts of the York Convocation, and then to turn in the second place to those of the Convocation of Canterbury.

On the day above specified [Nov. 21, 1661] the York Convocation assembled, and was continued to the 30th of that month. But before the last-named day arrived, some important communications were made to the officers of the Synod. For on the 22nd of November, the day after the Synod met, a "Letter of Business" from the King was directed to the York Metropolitan [Accepted Frewen], requesting that his Provincial Synod should "review the Book of "Common Prayer and the Ordinal;" and a further instruction was contained in the letter, that the Synod should "make such additions "or alterations in the said books, respectively, as "to them shall seem meet and expedient."

At the time of the receipt of this "Letter of "Business," the Metropolitan of York, with his three Suffragans, the Bishops of Durham [John Cosin], Chester [Bryan Walton], and Carlisle [Richard Sterne], were in London; and measures were immediately taken for transmitting this instrument to the York Synod, which had now assembled. Together with the Royal letter of business those Prelates sent a letter of their own to York, directed to Dr. John Neil, Prolocutor of that Convocation. The contents of that letter were to the effect that the authors of it were joining in consultation with the Bishops of the Southern

Sovereign:
K. Chas. II.
1661.

Conc. M.B. iv. 567.

Wake's State, Append. No. 158.

Appointment of Proxies by York to appear in the Canterbury Synod.

Conc. M.B. iv. 568.

<small>Metropolitans: Juxon, Frewen.</small>

Province on the business referred to; that the time available for settling the matter was brief; and that inconvenient delay would arise if the ordinary course was pursued of transmitting for concurrence documents from the Southern to the Northern Synod. Under these circumstances they desired the York Convocation to appoint proxies, who should be empowered to assent and consent to the acts of the Canterbury Convocation at Westminster, so far as they related to the business under hand. Urging expedition, the Northern Prelates committed their correspondents to God's protection, and appended their signatures—Accept. Ebor, Jo. Duresme, Rich. Carliol, Bri. Cestrien.

<small>Wake's State, Append. No. 158.</small>

In addition to the "Letter of Business" and that of the four Prelates just mentioned, the Northern Metropolitan enclosed a note of his own also, dated Nov. 23, to Mr. George Aisleby, the Registrar of the York Convocation. In this communication his Grace requested that the business referred to might be hastened with the greatest despatch, as being of " great and general concern-" ment; " and he also took notice that in case delays should occur the rights and privileges of the York Synod might be endangered.

<small>Conc. M.B. iv. 568–9. Kennett's Register, p. 565.</small>

On the 30th of November, the day to which the York Convocation, as before stated, had been continued, an earnest debate took place on the matters above mentioned. After careful deliberation, an instrument of proxy was, by unanimous consent, drawn up, deputing the following persons as delegates on behalf of the Convocation of York to act in that of Canterbury, viz.:—

Sovereign: K. Chas. II. 1661.

Dr. John Barwick, Dean of St. Paul's.
Dr. John Earles, Dean of Westminster.
Dr. Henry Fern, Dean of Ely, Prolocutor [Canterbury].
Henry Bridgeman, Dean of Chester.
Robert Hitch, Archdeacon of Leicester.
Matthew Smalwood, Proctor for the Archdeaconry of Chester and Richmond.
Andrew Sandeland, Proctor for the East Riding.
Humphrey Floyd [? Lloyd], Proctor for the York Chapter.

It will, however, appear hereafter that only six of the above afterwards signed the Synodical Act confirming the Prayer Book—the names of Dr. John Earles and Henry Bridgeman, from some cause unexplained, not appearing.

The above-named eight persons were intrusted with very large powers by the instrument of proxy. They were authorized to assent and consent, or to dissent and oppose, on behalf of the Lower House of York, in regard to all propositions which might be made. A general power was given to transact all such business as might be executed by the members of the York Lower House if personally present in London.

Conc. M. B. iv. 568-9. Kennett's Register, p. 565.

**Metropolitans:
Juxon,
Frewen.**

A formal reservation was added of the liberties and customs of their Province, as well as of the dignity and honour of their Cathedral Church. The House also finally bound itself to the acts of its proxies, under recognizances reaching to the value of their goods and chattels. And the Chapter Seal of the Cathedral Church of York having been appended to the document, this business came to an end on the 30th of November, 1661.

However, notwithstanding these very large powers conceded to their proxies, the Lower House of York did not deem itself precluded from entering, during some subsequent sessions, upon deliberations and discussions on the subject of the review of the National Liturgy. Six propositions were brought forward by Dr. Samways, a Proctor for the Clergy of Chester and Richmond, and colleague of one of the deputed proxies above mentioned. Dr. Samways' propositions were certainly conceived with much wisdom, and drawn up with considerable dexterity. Indeed, they so far commended themselves to that part of the Synod sitting at York that an order was made that they should be transmitted to their Metropolitan and his Suffragans in London, with the view of their being commended [if it should so seem fit to the Northern Prelates] to the consideration of the joint Canterbury Synod.

Conc. M. B. iv. 569.

Such were the proceedings in the Northern Convocation with regard to the review of the Book of Common Prayer and the Ordinal. We must now return to a consideration of the Acts of the Canterbury Convocation, fortified as it was by the presence of Prelates of the Upper House and delegates from the Lower House of the Northern Province.

The Canterbury Convocation met on the same day with that of York last mentioned, on November 21, 1661; and to the Synod at this time convened the Church of England is indebted for her Book of Common Prayer. The measures taken for a review of the Liturgy and Ordinal were as follows. A Book of Common Prayer printed in the year 1636 was used, which has lately been photozincographed by Major-General Sir H. James, R.E., under the authority of the Lords of Her Majesty's Treasury, and is now published.

In the volume interlineations were made, according to the alterations and the additions agreed upon in Synod. Several books and papers were made use of in prosecuting the work. The first of these were some MS. notes in an interleaved Common Prayer Book belonging to the Bishop of Durham's library, and which were believed to have been extracted from the collections of the learned Bishop Overall. The second were some MS.

Sovereign: K.Chas.II. 1661.

Canterbury Convocation, Nov. 1661.

Kennett's Register, p. 565.

Methods adopted in compiling the present "Book of Common Prayer."

Metropolitans: Juxon, Frewen.

notes in another Prayer Book, collected by Bishop Cosin himself, than whom no man ever was in a condition to render on the subject in hand more wholesome advice. The third were some supplementary Latin notes of the same Prelate, written in his own hand, and belonging to the Rev. C. Neil, Rector of North Allerton. The fourth were MS. notes of Bishop Andrews, of revered memory, partly borrowed from the Bishop of Durham's library, and partly from the collections of Mr. Neil, before mentioned.

Syn. Ang. ii. 84.

A Committee of Bishops was appointed by the Upper House to prosecute the work; these were in number eight, namely:—

1. Bishop of Durham (Cosin).
2. Bishop of Ely (Wren).
3. Bishop of Gloucester (Nicholson).
4. Bishop of Lincoln (Sanderson).
5. Bishop of Oxford (Skinner).
6. Bishop of Rochester (Warner).
7. Bishop of Sarum (Henchman).
8. Bishop of Worcester (Morley).

It was arranged that these Prelates should meet daily, except Sundays, at 5 o'clock p.m., at the Bishop of Ely's house, until their labours should be completed. And it appears that this Committee were assisted in their work by aid supplied from time to time by sessions of the Upper House. When portions of the book were there agreed to, they were delivered to the Prolocutor with directions that the Lower House should revise and amend the matter sent down as might seem needful. Matters progressed speedily as regarded the body of the work, and on the 2nd of December they were so far advanced that the Preface [a production which, though standing in the forefront of a book, is usually written last], which had been composed by Sanderson, and from the contents of which we learn that many frivolous and vain alterations in the Liturgy had been suggested during the revision, was committed to the Bishops of Ely, Oxford, Sarum, and St. Asaph, that it might receive the final touches of their hands. The reformation of the Calendar was mainly the work of one Mr. Pell, associated with Dr. Sancroft, who afterwards became Archbishop of Canterbury, and has left a name to be honoured by all posterity, as having sacrificed all worldly interests to the dictates of his conscience, and as having, with the saintly Ken, accompanied by four other Bishops, preferred deposition from earthly honours by our Dutch Monarch to a breach of his sacred obligations to another Sovereign.

Sovereign:
K. Chas. II.
1661.

Lathbury, Hist. Conv. p. 301.

Syn. Ang. ii. 88–90.

Kennett's Register, p. 574.

The Mr. Pell above mentioned was wisely chosen to make the calculations required for a reformation of the Calendar, as he was a most acute and accomplished mathematician. He must have been a man of penetrating genius, diligence, and great learning, as he was acquainted with nine languages besides his own. His advancements in learning, however, appear to have been more remarkable than his providence for his own worldly needs. For he was more than once in prison [presumably for debt], wanted the commonest necessaries of life—at least, the life of a scholar—even pens and ink, and was at last buried by the charity of his friends.

Metropolitans: Juxon, Frewen.
Kennett's Register, p. 575.

On December 9, Forms of Prayer to be used at Sea, Emendations in the Commination and Churching Services, and in the Office for Burials at Sea, were introduced.

Syn. Ang. ii. 89–90.

By the 13th of December the work of revision had so far proceeded that the Prayer Book of 1636, above mentioned, in which the interlineations and emendations had been made, had been fairly transcribed into a MS. copy, which was committed for final revision to a joint Committee of both Houses. This Committee consisted of the Bishops of Carlisle, Gloucester, Salisbury, and St. Asaph, associated with Drs. Robert Pory, John Pearson, and Anthony Sparrow. By this Committee the last touches appear to have been accorded to the work, some small emendations being made in the Preface, some few Collects revised, it is said, by Sanderson, and the General Thanksgiving added, which

Ibid. p. 93.

was composed by Reynolds, Bishop of Norwich.

Matters being now ripe for a conclusion of the whole business, a form of subscription by the members of the Synod had to be prepared. This was a matter of importance and delicacy; and so the careful preparation of an instrument for the purpose was committed, on the 19th of December, to the hands of Drs. Cosin and Henchman respectively, Bishops of Durham and Salisbury. These Prelates were to be assisted in their work by Dr. Chaworth, Vicar-General of the Bishop of London, and Dr. Burrell, who held that office in the Diocese of Durham. They met on the afternoon of the day on which the business was committed to them, at the office of the principal Registrar of the Archbishop of Canterbury; and there, after inspecting some ancient documents preserved in the archives, unanimously agreed to a form of subscription suitable for the purpose under hand. This consultation took place in the presence of two public notaries, Mr. William Fisher and Mr. Francis Mundy, so that no pains were spared for securing an unexceptionable instrument.

The following day, Dec. 20, 1661, is a day certainly memorable in the annals of the Church of England, even though it may be little commemorated. On that day her two Convocations or Provincial Synods [the Northern Synod united

Sovereign:
K.Chas.II.
1661.

Syn. Ang. ii. 93–95.
Kennett's Register p. 579.

Instruments of ratification.

Metropolitans: Juxon, Frewen.

Conc. M. B. iv. 566.

by delegation with the Southern] adopted and authorized her Book of Common Prayer. But while her faithful children value that manual of devotion they very scantily acknowledge the source to which they are indebted for the blessing. Copies of the instruments of subscription, and a list of the names of the members of the two Provincial Synods who signed them, are here appended in full, as they are attached to the original document from which all our Common Prayer Books have been printed. The document itself is a MS. consisting of 544 pages, copied from the book of the edition of 1636, in which the interlineations and additions were made, as above described; and the instruments of subscription run as follows.

Canterbury.

Nicholl's Common Prayer, Pref. 10–12. Fourth Rep. Ritual Com. pp. 39, 40 bis.

LIBRUM PRECUM PUBLICARUM, Administrationis Sacramentorum aliorumque Rituum Ecclesiæ Anglicanæ, vnà cum formâ, et modo ordinandi, et consecrandi EPISCOPOS, Presbyteros, et Diaconos, iuxta Literas Regiæ Majestatis nobis in hâc parte directas REVISUM, et quingentas, quadraginta, et quatuor paginas continentem, NOS GULIELMUS providentiâ Divinâ Cantuariensis Archiëpus, totius Angliæ Primas et Metropönus, et NOS Episcopi ejusdem Provinciæ in Sacrâ provinciali Synodo legitimè congregati, unanimi assensu et Consensu in hanc formam redegimus, recepimus, et approbavimus, eidemque subscripsimus,

Vicesimo die mensis Decembris Anno Dni Millesimo sexcentesimo sexagesimo primo.

Sovereign: K.Chas. II. 1661.

W. CANT:

GILB: LONDON.	GEORGIUS VIGORNIENSIS
GULIELMUS BATH. ET WELLENS. p. ꝑcuratorem suū Ro. Oxoñ.	GEORGIUS ASAPHENSIS. GULIEL: MENEVENSIS. RO: LINCOLN.
MATTHÆUS ELIEN.	B: PETRIB
RO. OXOÑ.	HUGO LANDAVENSIS
GUIL. BANGOR:	IOHᵉ EXONIENSIS.
JO: ROFFENS.	GILB BRISTOLIENSIS
HEN: CICESTRENSIS.	GUIL. GLOUCESTRENSIS
HUMPHREDUS SARUM.	ED: NORVIC:

Nos ETIAM Universus Clerus inferioris Domus ejusdem Provinciæ Synodicé congregat dicto Libro publicarum precum, Sacramentorum et Rituum, unà cum forma et modo ordinandi et consecrandi Episcopos Presbyteros, et Diaconos unanimiter consensimus et subscripsimus Die et Anno prædictis.

Henr. Fern Decan. Eliens. et Prolocutor.
Guil: Brough. Decan. Glouc\.
Tho: Warmstry Decanus Wigorn:
Io. Barwick S. Pauli London Decan.
Io. Earles Dec. Westmonasterii.
Alex: Hyde Dec: Winton:
Herbert Croft Dec: Hereford:
Jo. Croftes Dec: Norvicensis:
Michael Honywood. Decan. Lincoln.

Metropolitans:
Juxon,
Frewen.

Edv: Rainbowe: Dec: Petriburgensis.
Guilielmus Paul. Decan. Lichfield.
Nath: Hardy Decan. Roff:
Seth Ward: Decan. Exon.
Griff: Ossoriensis Decanus Bangor.
Johan: Fell Decan: Æd: Christi Oxoñ.
Guil: Thomas Præcentor Menevensis.
Geo: Hall Archidiac Cantuar.
Thomas Paske Archidiac. Londin. per Procuratorem suum Petrum Gunning.
Robertus Pory Archidiac. Middles.
Johes Hansley Archidiac: Colcest:
Marcus Franck. Archidiac S. Alban.
Iohannes Sudbury Procurator Capituli Eccles. Westmonaster
Tho: Gorges Archidiac Winton.
Bernardus Hale Archidiac: Eliensis.
Grindallus Sheafe Archidiac. Wellensis.
Iohes Selleck Archus Bathon.
Ioannes Pearson Archidiaconus Surriensis.
Gulielmus Pierce Archidiaconus Tanton per Procuratorem suum Ri: Busby.
Gulielmus Creede Archidiaconus Wilts.
Io: Ryves Archidiaconus Berks
Tho: Lamplugh Archidiaconus Oxoñ
Gulielmus Hodges Archidiaconus Wigorn.
Franc. Coke Archidiaconus Staffordiæ.
Edvardus Young Archidiaconus Exoniensis
Raphæl Throckmorton, Archidiaconus Lincoln.
Iasper Mayne Archidiaconus Cicestrensis.

Geo. Benson; Archidiac; Heref: Sovereign:
Antonius Sparrow Archidiaconus Sudburiensis.   K.Chas. II. 1661.
Robertus Hitch Archidiaconus Lecestrensis.
Guil: Iones Archidiaconus Carmarthen.
Edvardus Vaughan Archid: Cardigan. p̃ Procuratorem suum Guil: Iones.
Guilielmus Gery Archidiaconus Norvicensis.
Guilielmus Fane Procurator Dioeceseos Bathon. & Wellens:
Gualterus Ffoster Procurator Dioeceseos Bathon. & Wellens.
Petrus Mews Archidiaconus Huntingdon
Nicolaus Preston Procurator Capituli Wintoniensis.
Iosephus Loveland Procurator Capituli Nordovicens:
Henricus Sutton Procurator Vigorn. Dioeces:
Ričus Harwood Procurator Dioeces. Glocestrens.
Franciscus Davis Archīnus Ladaven:
Rob'tus Morgan Archidiac: Merion.
Mich: Evans Capituli Bangor P'curator.
Rodol. Bridcooke Dioeces. Oxoñ. Procurator.
Joh: Priaulx Procurator Capituli Sarisbur:
Guilielmus Mostyn Archidiaconus Bangor.
Edoardus Wynne Dioeces. Bangor Procurator.
Edoardus Martin Procurator Cleri Eliensis
Herbertus Thorndike Procurator Cleri Dioec. Londinensis
Johannes Dolben Capit: Eccl: Cath. Christ. Oxon. Procurator

<small>Metropolitans: Juxon, Frewen.</small>

Guilielmus Haywood Cleri Diœc. Londinensis Procurator.

Ri: Busby Capit. Ecclesiæ. Wellens Procurator

Edvardus Cotton Archidiaconus Cornubiens. per Procuratorem suum Ri: Busby.

Gulielmus Dowdeswell Procurator Capituli Wigorniensis

Josephus Crowther Procurator Cleri Wigorn

Rad. Ironside Procurator Diœces. Bristoll

Ed: Hitchman Proc: Cleri Glocest:

Iohannes Howorth Procurator Capit: Eccles. Petrob:

Thomas Good Procurat. Diœces. Hereford.

Gualt: Jones Procurator Capit: Eccles. Cathed: Cicestrensis.

Petrus Gunning Procurator Diœcesis Petriburgensis

Jacobus Ffletwood Capituli Co: et Lich. Procurat:

Gualterus Blandford Capituli Glocestr: Procurator

Henricus Glemham Decanus Bristol per procuratorem suum Gualt Jones.

Gulielmus Herbert Procurator Cleri Suffolciensis

Iosephus Maynard Procurator Cleri Diœceseos Exoniensis.

Iohan: Pulleyn Procurator Capituli Lincolniensis

Richardus Ball Procurator Capituli Eliensis: *Sovereign:*
Basilius Beridge Procurator Diœces. Lincolni-   *K.Chas. II.*
ensis.   *1661.*
Georgius Stradling Cleri Dioces. Landavensis Procurator.
Humphredus Lloyd Procurator Cleri Diœces: Asaphensis:
Timotheus Halton Capituli Ecclesiæ Cathedralis Menevensis Procurator.
Egidius Aleyn Procurator Cleri Diœces Lincoln:
Guil. Foulkes Capituli Asaphensis Procurator.
Richardus Clayton Cleri Diœces. Sarisburiensis Procurator.
Iosephus Goulston Cleri Diœces: Wintoñ: Procurator.
Guil. Rawley Cleri Eliens. Procurator.

LIBRUM PRECUM PUBLICARUM Administrationis   *York.*
Sacramentorum, aliorumque Rituum Ecclesiæ Anglicanæ, unà cum forma, et modo ordinandi, et consecrandi Episcopos, Presbyteros, et Diaconos, iuxta Literas Regiæ Majestatis nobis in hâc parte directas, REVISUM, et quingentas quadraginta et quatuor paginas continentem, NOS ACCEPTUS Providentiâ divina Eborũm Archiĕpus Angliæ Primas, et Metropōnus, et NOS EPISCOPI ejusdem Provinciæ in sacra provinciali Synodo legitimé congregati, unanimi Assensu et Consensu in hanc formam redegimus, recepimus et approbavimus,

Metropolitans:
Juxon,
Frewen.

eidemque subscripsimus, vicesimo die Mensis Decembris Anno Dñi millesimo sexcentesimo sexagesimo primo.

ACC: EBOR.

Io: Dunelmensis.   Rich. Carliol.

Nos etiam Vniversus Clerus inferioris Domus ejusdem Provinciæ Ebor Synodicè congregati per ñtros respectivè Procuratores sufficienter et legitimé constitut et substitut dicto Libro Publicarum Precum, Administrationis Sacramentorum et Rituum, unà cum forma et modo ordinandi et consecrandi Episcopos, Presbyteros et Diaconos unanimiter consensimus et subscripsimus die et Anno prædictis.

      Henr. Fern
      Io Barwick.
      Rob: Hitch.
      Matt. Smalwood
      Humphredus Lloyd
      And. Sandeland

It is observable that this Synodical authorization of the Prayer Book was signed by two Metropolitans and by twenty Bishops from the two English Provinces, by eighty-six members of the Lower House of Canterbury, under their own hands or by proxy, and by six delegates for the Lower House of York. In truth, nothing could be more complete than the Synodical authorization of the Book on Dec. 20, 1661.

It may here be added that while the Bill for Uniformity was passing subsequently through Parliament for authorizing this Book of Common Prayer, some verbal corrections in the Book were committed by the Upper House of Convocation for consideration to the Bishops of St. Asaph, Carlisle, and Chester. Their revisions were sent down to the Lower House, where the members unanimously agreed to the corrections of the Prelates aforesaid. The superintendence of the press was placed in the hands of Dr. Sancroft, Mr. Scattergood, and Mr. Dillingham. Order was taken for a clerical alteration, by which the word "children" was inserted in the place of "persons" [not baptized]; for the printing of the book before the 24th of August, 1662; and for supplying the work, when completed, to the parochial churches in the several Dioceses under the inspection of the respective Bishops. The Forms of Prayer for the 5th of November, the 30th of January, and the 29th of May were introduced into the Synod, publicly read, and unanimously approved; and for translating the whole work into Latin, Dr. John Earles, Dean of Westminster, and Dr. Thomas Peirson were appointed by the Upper House.

In the prosecution of this whole business the labours of the Synod gave so much satisfaction

Sovereign:
K. Chas. II.
1662.

13 & 14 Car. II. 4.

Syn. Ang. ii. 103.

Ibid. p. 105.

Ibid. p. 110.

> Metropolitans: Juxon, Frewen.
> Lords' Journals, xi. 408.

that Bishop Sheldon, as President, intimated to the assembled members the gratitude with which the Upper House of the Imperial Legislature had received the Prayer Book. He also added that the Lord Chancellor, in his own name, as well as in the names of the Peers in Parliament assembled, had given thanks to the Archbishops and Bishops of both Provinces for the care and industry which they had displayed in the revision of the Liturgy. Bishop Sheldon was, moreover, charged with a message from the Lord Chancellor to the Lower House of the Synod, declaring the sense of gratitude felt by the House of Lords, not only towards the English Prelates, but towards the Lower Clergy also, for the zeal displayed by them in prosecuting the important work on which they had been engaged.

> Syn. Ang. ii. 106.

And here any reader who is a faithful member of the Church of England may well pause to look back upon the 20th of December, 1661, as a memorable era, and to reflect on the debt of gratitude due from him to the Convocations or Provincial Synods of the Church of England, for having provided him with that inestimable blessing, the "Book of Common Prayer."

> Civil sanction accorded to the Book of Common Prayer.

At the same time with the sessions of the Synods just recorded, Parliament assembled on Nov. 20, 1661. And shortly after the subject of the rival parliamentary Book of Common Prayer before described, as prepared by the House of

Commons' "Committee for Religion," which was composed exclusively of gentlemen "who were of "the long robe," was brought before the notice of the House of Lords. A message was sent from the Commons on Jan. 28, 1662, to put their Lordships in mind of "the Bill." On Feb. 13, the Earl of Dorset, seemingly in a doubtful mood, asked whether the Upper House desired to proceed on the book embodying Sternhold and Hopkins' poetry, "with tunes," which was sent up from the House of Commons, "or stay until the other book be brought in." By "the other book" his Lordship meant our present Prayer Book, which had been synodically ratified by the authority of both Convocations on the preceding 20th of December, as has been above abundantly shewn. To the House of Lords, upon this question being asked, the Bishop of London [Sheldon] signified that "the book" [i.e. the Convocations' book] "will very shortly be brought "in." That book was brought in on February 25, with a message from the King reciting that it had been reviewed by the Presidents, Bishops, and Clergy of both Provinces, and commending it for adoption. Parliament took His Majesty's prudent advice, and shewed its wisdom, at least on this occasion, by giving Civil sanction to the Convocations' book—i.e. the MS. before described, consisting of 544 pages, with its Synodical ratification—which was adopted

Sovereign: K.Chas. II. 1662.

Commons' Journals, viii. 352.

Lords' Journals, xi. 388.

Lords' Journals, xi. 393.

both by Lords and Commons and attached to the Act of Uniformity.

<small>Metropolitans: Juxon, Frewen.</small>

As we have seen, the endeavours of the Savoy Conference to construct a Liturgy for the Church of England came to an absurd and impotent conclusion. The same fate befell the Book provided by the House of Commons' "Com-"mittee for Religion," consisting exclusively of gentlemen that "were of the long robe." And the present Book of Common Prayer of the Church of England, compiled and authorized synodically by her Convocations, was happily established by the Civil power as the Manual of National Public Devotion, on May 19, 1662, when the Act of Uniformity [13 & 14 Car. II. 4] received Royal assent, and provided that the Book should be used on and after St. Bartholomew's Day, August 24th, then next ensuing.

<small>13 & 14 Car. II. 4.</small>

A curious fact connected with the original MS. copy of the Prayer Book, which was attached to the Act of Uniformity, may here be mentioned. On search being made for it some few years since among the records of the House of Lords, it could not be found. In fact, it had mysteriously disappeared; and as mysteriously again appeared on another search being made. Nor do I believe that the mystery has ever been cleared up. Use of this MS. Book was made in 1870 by the Royal Commissioners appointed to enquire into the Rubrics, who have published, in their fourth report, its Synodical authorization with the signatures of the Metropolitans, Bishops, and Presbyters appended in full.

Sovereign: K. Chas. II. 1662.
Fourth Report, pp. 39–40, bis.

V.

REJECTION OF THE "COMPREHENSION" LITURGY.

The next memorable event connected with the Convocations during the time now under view was the rejection of the "Comprehension Liturgy."

Sovereign: K. William III. 1689.

Soon after that balmy breeze so pathetically recorded by Burnet had wafted, in 1688, our Dutch Sovereign King William III. from the dull flats of Holland into Torbay, a scheme was set on foot for propitiating the Dissenters of various denominations. This propitiation was to be effected by the mutilation of the Book of Common Prayer which we now happily possess, and by substituting in its place other forms of Divine Offices. A Company was consequently appointed by Royal Commission, composed of nine Bishops and twenty Divines, with Lamplugh, Metropolitan of York, at their head, to prepare a scheme. Burnet, Tillotson, and Tenison were moving spirits; and among chief advisers for the dissenting interest was Mr. Richard Baxter, that same gentleman who at the Savoy Con-

A "Comprehension" Liturgy proposed. Lathbury, Hist. Conv. p. 318, notes.

Comp. Hist. iii. 588–90.

ference had the assurance to commend for adoption a Liturgy of his own private composition for the use of the Church of England. It would take up here too much space to specify all the so-called improvements which it was proposed by this Company to make in the Prayer Book. A few will serve as specimens of the whole. These were, in effect, that the Calendar should be purified by omitting the legendary Saints' Days—that the use of the surplice should be left to the discretion of the Bishop, who should have regard in that matter to "the desires of the people"—that children should be baptized without sponsors, if the parents so desired—that the signing with the Cross in Baptism should be only recommended, not commanded—that the Communion should be administered to persons not kneeling, if they objected to do so, and "in their pews"—that the word "Priest" in the rubric before the Absolution should be changed to "Minister"—that the words "remission of sins" should be left out of the Absolution, "as not very "intelligible"—that most of the Collects should be changed and enlarged for forms "more "sensible and affecting"—that chanting in Cathedrals should be discontinued. These, with others, were the professed improvements in the Prayer Book of the Church of England to be recommended.

Metropolitans: Sancroft, Lamplugh.

Lathbury, Hist. Conv. pp. 323-4.

It was thought in many quarters that this method of altering the Prayer Book by a Royal Commission would fall short of satisfaction, and indeed this conviction prevailed in both Houses of Parliament. For on a "Comprehen-"sion" Bill being introduced for bringing Dissenters within the Church of England, both Houses of the Legislature demurred, and addressed the Crown thus: "That, according to the an-"cient practice and usage of this kingdom in time "of Parliament, His Majesty would be graciously "pleased to issue forth his Writs, as soon as "conveniently might be, for calling a Convo-"cation of the Clergy of this kingdom, to be "advised with on Ecclesiastical matters." The Canterbury Convocation was accordingly convened in 1689, and immediately on its assembly there was foreshadowed an augury of the reception which would there be given to a proposition for mutilating the English Prayer Book. That augury was the selection of their Prolocutor by the Lower House.

Sovereign: K. William III. 1689.

Comp. Hist. iii. 589. Lathbury, Hist. Conv. p. 321.

Sancroft was under suspension by King William III. from the Archbishopric of Canterbury when this Convocation met. Sancroft is a name which can never be mentioned without reverential honour, as being that of a man who was content to be deprived of the worldly emoluments of his Fellowship at Emmanuel College, Cambridge, because he would not conform to the

Canterbury Convocation meets, Nov. 1689.

Republican standards of doctrine in 1649, and of those of his See of Canterbury in 1691 [whether he could thus be deprived of his spiritual office is quite another question], because he would not abjure allegiance to the very Sovereign who had previously committed him to the Tower for refusing to abandon his proper duty. Five other Bishops, too, are worthy of the same honourable mention, and on the same account. These were five out of those six formerly imprisoned by King James II., namely, Ken, Bishop of Bath and Wells; Lake, Bishop of Chichester; Lloyd, Bishop of St. Asaph; Trelawny, Bishop of Bristol; Turner, Bishop of Ely; and White, Bishop of Peterborough. These men are indeed worthy of all honour, who, having been formerly imprisoned by King James II. for adhering to their duty, were now suspended by King William III. because they would not abjure the allegiance they had sworn to the very man who had so barbarously treated them. A noble example this of conscientious principles paramount!

However, Archbishop Sancroft being, as above said, under suspension when the Canterbury Convocation met, Nov. 21, 1689, Compton, Bishop of London, who had crowned William III. on the refusal of Sancroft to do so, presided in his place.

Great endeavours, it is said, were made by the Court party to secure the election of a Prolocutor suitable to their views and favourable to the "Comprehension Liturgy." Now, if there is an assembly in the world where such back-stairs influences would be futile, and indeed indignantly resented, that assembly is the Lower House of the Canterbury Convocation—

> "...... domus hâc nec purior ulla est
> "Nec magis his aliena malis."......
> HOR. Sat. I. ix. 49, 50.

Sovereign: K. William III. 1689.

Tillotson, one of the King's Chaplains, and Clerk of the Closet, was the Court favourite. But all the influences brought to bear in his behalf were wholly impotent. The choice of the Clergy, by a very large majority, as was likely enough, fell on a man of very different stamp. This was Dr. Jane, Regius Professor of Divinity in the University of Oxford. This champion of the old Liturgy, on being presented for approbation to the President, Compton, Bishop of London, on Nov. 25th, made the usual Latin speech, in which he extolled the Church of England; and, implying that no alterations were needed in her Liturgy, wound up his oration with the words of historical fame addressed by the Barons to King Henry III., "Nolumus "leges Angliæ mutari." Bishop Compton in reply told the Clergy, among other things, that they should shew "some indulgence and charity to "the Dissenters under King William;" thus, by the way, not unreasonably, though perhaps unin-

Comp. Hist. iii. 591.

tentionally, designating that Sovereign himself as a proper object of charitable indulgence.

Metropolitans: Sancroft, Lamplugh. 1689.

At the next meeting the Bishop of London, becoming sensibly aware that the Lower House would not consent to the mutilation of the Liturgy, for the avowed purpose of pacifying dissenting cavils, made an excuse for proroguing the Synod. Subsequently, on the 4th of December, both Houses sitting in united Synod, in Henry VIIth's Chapel in Westminster Abbey, the Earl of Nottingham brought down a Royal Licence, and also a message from His Majesty. In the latter document, King William III. assured the Convocation that he doubted not that they would "assist him in promoting the welfare "of" the Church of England, and in effect commended to them the adoption of the "Compre-" "hension" scheme.

Comp. Hist. iii. 592.

Vain attempt to impose the title "Protestant" on the Church of England.

Immediately there arose some clashing between the Bishops and the Lower House as to the address to be presented to the Crown, the former desiring to append the designation "Protestant" to the Church of England, to which the Lower House demurred, and finally succeeded in expunging that misnomer so far as this Church was concerned. For the word "Protestant" is only rightly applied to such as protested against the Diet of Spires, the Diet of Spires having repudiated the "Augsburg Confession." But happily, the Church of England having no way con-

Comp. Hist. iii. 594.

cerned herself with either Augsburg or Spires, the Lower House was unwilling that a flourish of nomenclature wholly inapplicable, and moreover very absurd in this connexion, should be appended to her time-honoured name. For how can the Church, as teacher of a definite faith, discharge her duty by contradictions? Protesting at best signifies but bald negation. To protest against all the false beliefs which have ever pestered the world, from Confucius to Calvin, from the Vedas and Zendavesta to the latest Mormon apostacy, may be the negation of a vast bulk of error, but can never mount to the assertion of one single simply-defined truth.

Sovereign: K. William III. 1689.

As regards the "Comprehension" Liturgy, after sundry sessions the counsels of the Lower House of Convocation prevailed, and the Comprehension scheme was abandoned, having proved a hopeless failure, notwithstanding its Royal and courtier parentage. Had it not been for the determination of the Lower House of the Canterbury Convocation on this occasion, the English Prayer Book would have been mutilated beyond recovery. That assembly deserves the sincere gratitude of all English Churchmen. The members stood to their position like men, defended their citadel with courage and constancy, and left a worthy example which assuredly their successors will imitate, and resist

"Comprehension" Liturgy abandoned. Comp. Hist. iii. 595.

K K

250   ACTS OF THE CHURCH.   [Part III. 5.

Metropolitans: Tillotson, Tenison, Lamplugh, Blackburne.

attacks, from whatever quarter they may be directed, against the integrity of the Prayer Book of the Church of England.

Synodical action suspended.

During the years which elapsed between the date of the rejection of the "Comprehension "Liturgy" and the date of the suspension of Synodical action in this country, many events of interest connected with the Convocations occurred, such as the condemnation of Whiston's writings, and other matters connected with the privileges of the two Houses, respectively. It is not, however, needful for the present purpose to call special attention to these. It shall here suffice to write,

Lathbury, Hist. Conv. pp.451-460.

that in the year 1716, Hoadly, Bishop of Bangor, published a book entitled, "The Preservative," &c. He was also author of another book, on "The "Kingdom of Christ;" and in the year 1717 he preached a sermon before King George I. at St. James's. Both books and the sermon were accused of false doctrine, and so were delated before the Canterbury Synod in 1717. A warm controversy, known as the Bangorian controversy, was kindled, and the Whig Government of the day, being friendly to Hoadly's principles, was induced for the time to suspend Convocational

Ibid. p. 463.

action by prorogation on the 14th Feb., 1718. From that date Synodical action of any importance was suspended down to the year 1852. For though Convocations met and transacted some business in 1728 and 1741, yet their meet-

SUSPENSION OF SYNODICAL ACTION. 251

ings were generally, in the interval above named, merely *pro formâ*. They did indeed assemble contemporaneously with the meeting of every Parliament, solemnly opened their sessions, formed a Lower House, elected a Prolocutor, and were then dismissed, being continued from time to time by prorogations of the Metropolitans. The blame, however, of this suspension of action must not be laid to the Civil power, as is sometimes done, but to the Metropolitans, Bishops, and Clergy themselves. For by the Royal Writs always issued acourse with the Writs for Parliament, the Convocations were uninterruptedly placed in a condition to proceed to business without let or hindrance, so far as Civil authority was concerned.

Before the year 1664 it was impossible that the Convocations after assembly should separate without proceeding to active work, because until that year they taxed themselves in their Convocations and were not generally amenable to parliamentary taxation. In Saxon times the lands of all Clergy were held by frankalmoigne, that is, were free from all other taxation except for the support of castles, bridges, and expeditions. William the Conqueror turned the frankalmoigne tenures of the Bishops into baronies, which became thenceforward subject to escuage, a money payment in lieu of supplying soldiers. But the lower Clergy not possessing baronies,

1718–1852.

1718-1852.

still held their lands in frankalmoigne, and were in a great measure exempt from the charges which fell on other subjects. It was consequently deemed right that they should contribute more equitably to the public burdens; and after several methods for this purpose had been tried, the practice at last obtained that they should tax themselves in their Convocations and there vote "subsidies" or "benevolences" to the Crown.

Comp. Hist. iii. 274-5.

This practice continued, as above said, to the year 1664, when by a private agreement between Archbishop Sheldon, the Lord Chancellor Clarendon, and some other of King Charles II.'s ministers, it was concluded that the Clergy should waive the privilege of taxing their own body, and should permit themselves to be included in the money bills prepared by the House of Commons. So great a constitutional change has perhaps never before or since been effected by a private arrangement. Jeremy Collier prophesied that after the Clergy ceased to tax themselves, their opinions and interests would be more slenderly regarded. And he seems to have been, from subsequent experiences, no false prophet.

VI.

SUSPENSION OF SYNODICAL ACTION IN THE CHURCH OF ENGLAND.

After the prorogation of the Canterbury Convocation as above mentioned, in 1718, the necessity for the active work of our Provincial Synods in reference to subsidies having ceased, it seems that the Metropolitans and Bishops came to the unwarrantable conclusion that there was consequently no necessity for active work in maintaining the fair fabric of the Church and repairing breaches in her spiritual outworks. Thus they paid slender heed to a very wise man's deliberate conviction and declaration, that as material castles and bridges require repairs and renovations, no other is the case with the edifice of the Church. And so, by the neglect of her own master builders, the active operations of her Synods remained in abeyance.

1718–1852.

Bacon, Works, Vol. II. p. 510. Ed. Lond. 1826.

No misapprehension more groundless can exist, no historical misstatement more transparently false can be made, than that the long abeyance of Synodical action in the Church of England is due to the interference of secular authority, or even to any neglect of constitutional

Suspension of Synodical action not justly chargeable on the Civil power.

duty on the part of the Crown. No doubt the Convocation of Canterbury was prorogued by Royal authority in May, 1717, and Feb., 1718, on account of the "representation" made by the Lower House to the Upper, complaining of the doctrines taught by Dr. Benjamin Hoadly in his books entitled "The Nature of the Kingdom of "Christ," and "The Preservative against the "Principles and Practices of the Non-jurors"—that Bishop being a favourite of the Whig Ministry of the day. But those prorogations were but ephemeral acts. They were only ebullitions of political partizanship of the hour. They were merely the invocations of regal power by a Cabinet, to shelter, under the provisions of the "Submission Act," a Prelate acceptable to the Ministry of the day. These prorogations could have no reference, and had none, to subsequent reigns; nor had they any effect on succeeding practice as adopted by the Crown.

As a fact, the Royal Writs for convening the Convocations have always, since King George I.'s time, issued a course with the Writs for summoning Parliament. Nothing could be more true to the Constitution in this respect than our Sovereigns have ever been, in each succeeding reign. These have been one and all, since the time above specified, uninterruptedly mindful in this respect of their Coronation Oath, and jealously regardful of their princely duty to seek the counsels of the

Convocations for the welfare of this Church and Realm. There certainly has been no omission of Royal duty in this matter since the political interventions of Whig advisers. It is a perversion of historical fact, it is an absolute contradiction of truth, to cast on the memory of our English Monarchs the reproach of the long abeyance of Synodical action in the Church of England. On the contrary, that long discontinuance has been in absolute contravention of successive Sovereigns' direct and emphatic requests.

1718–1852.

To what causes, then, is that abeyance to be ascribed? I do not think a question more difficult of solution could be asked in reference either to the Ecclesiastical or Secular history of this nation; nor does it seem that any perfectly satisfactory answer can be given. Any answer must appear inadequate. That a Church, consisting of Dioceses and Provinces, in fact an Exarchate in the Christian world, meanwhile wholly autocephalous, wholly independent of any external authority or even influence [short of an Œcumenical Council], should continue for more than a century and a quarter without any active Synodical or corporate action, is a phenomenon well-nigh inexplicable. It seems contrary to the experience derived from the previous history of all ages of Christianity.

Real causes of the suspension of Synodical action.

However, without for a moment pretending

that a fully satisfactory answer can be given to this question, some considerations shall be suggested, which, if not removing, may somewhat tend to soften, the difficulty of reply.

1718-1852.

St. Ignatius, in his Epistle to the Ephesians, thus writes: "The Presbytery, worthy of all "honour and of their heavenly calling, are "attached to their Bishop even as cords to a "lyre. Thus, by blended concord and sweet "harmony, the honour of Jesus Christ is cele-"brated," &c. That this concord and harmony was much marred in the first half of the last century—and this is written with shame and sorrow—must, I fear, be put down as one probable cause for the discontinuance then of active Synodical action. The reasons for that lack of concord, however, are patent, and must rather be ascribed to political statecraft, exercised by other interested and somewhat unscrupulous people, than to any natural infirmities inherent in the Clergy themselves.

Lack of harmony between Bishops and Presbyters. Ed. Jacobson, p. 268.

When King William III. ejected from the See of Canterbury the heroic Sancroft [that Christian exemplar of forgiveness of injury], and thrust into his place the pliant Court Chaplain Tillotson, it is not likely that the Clergy of the Southern Province would feel themselves in harmonious relations with the intruded Metropolitan. When that same monarch substituted such a man as Kidder for the saintly Ken, in the Diocese of

Bath and Wells, it is no wonder that the concord between the Clergy and Bishop of that Diocese should be marred. And further, as five Diocesan Bishops were at this time extruded, and successors more acceptable to Dutch proclivities thrust into their Sees, it would be marvellous if harmony throughout this Church had been promoted. Hence the introduction of some discords.

But this is not all. At the several changes in the succession to the Crown in those times, there was further reason for lack of harmony between the Bishops and their Clergy. The former were more than once for the most part complaisant enough, and more than complaisant, apparently welcoming with much gladness the rising dawns of new eras in our country's history. But quite the reverse was the case generally with the lower Clergy. There was then sad havoc among the most learned and most prominent of their ranks who misliked the prospects. The portentous learning of Collier, the deep and solid counsels of the golden-penned Brett, and a roll of such men as Johnson and Kettlewell, whose names are too numerous to write down here, were lost to the brotherhood of the Clergy, and that, too, on grounds of conscience. And if some Bishops did not mourn over the loss of their spiritual sons, but rather the reverse, the Presbyters did bewail the loss of their spiritual brothers. The lack of concord between Bishops and Clergy hence engendered was as sad as it was natural. Indeed, the discords arising, and the secret methods of spying investigations consequently adopted in the very highest Ecclesiastical quarters to detect the Clergy's incompliance with Archiepiscopal proclivities, are abundantly testified by the Wake MSS. in the Christ Church Library, Oxford; never yet, I believe, given to the world, but which I have had the advantage of seeing by the extreme courtesy and kindness of a former Canon of that house, the late learned Bishop of Chester, Dr. Jacobson. And this havoc made among the most esteemed of the ranks of the Clergy, certainly with no disapprobation of some Bishops at least, did not promote harmony, but alas! rather discord, between the chief Pastors of the Church and their Presbyters.

Some minor, more personal matters may be added on this subject. Archbishop Tenison, of whom the Jesuit Pelton said—it seems not without reason—that he was like a certain artisan's goose, "at once hot and heavy," helped to increase discord, for he treated the Clergy in Convocation with considerable contempt, and their Prolocutor, Dr. Hooper, with marked rudeness. Nor did Bishop Burnet promote concord between the Bishops and Clergy, either by his treatment of his own Clergy of Sarum, or by his unseemly language addressed to the Canterbury Prolocutor, or by the language of one of his Visitation Charges, in which he insinuated, if he did not categorically affirm, that the members of the Lower House of the Canterbury Convocation were "enemies to the Bishops, the Queen, and "the country."

1718-1852.

It is not here intended to defend all the proceedings of the Lower Clergy in the Canterbury Convocation at this time, who certainly did on occasion arrogate privileges too expansive for the Lower House. But the above-recorded facts will shew that at this period of our history there was unfortunately engendered a spirit very different from that recorded by St. Ignatius, and arising from various and very dissimilar causes, which would render the assembly of Bishops and Presbyters for common deliberation distasteful to themselves, and perhaps the reverse of beneficial to the interests of the Church. And it may have been that for a time this discord was responsible for the discontinuance of Synodical action in England.

Another fact did most likely help to perpetuate abeyance of Synodical action, after the first immediate cause above mentioned had passed away. This fact also is a sad one to recount, but unhappily too patent. During the last half of the last century there was a lethargy throughout the Church of England, and that

General lethargy in the Church.

perhaps the natural effect of the lack of concord between Bishops and Clergy above mentioned. Cathedral services had fallen to the lowest standard, the services in Parish Churches were scanty in number and meanly performed, the Church fabrics were in a melancholy state of disrepair, and the Churchyards perfect scandals for slovenliness and disorder, thoroughly unworthy the name of "God's acre." It was not until some years of the present century had passed away that a general improvement in these respects took place. It must be in the memory of many now alive, that the inheritance of negligence handed down to the first generation of this century was in the matters above recorded a miserable one indeed. And as the outward manifestations of worship and the material accessories of religion were neglected, it is perhaps no great wonder that the Ecclesiastical fabric of the Church's Constitution should have been neglected too.

Unreasonable exaltation of personal authority.

And, once again, one other cause may be suggested as having contributed to the abeyance of Synodical action. Men of the character of Wesley and Whitfield—to whom all honour is due for their labours in stirring up the careless to a sense of personal religion and the practice of Christian virtues—were not the most likely to encourage any return to corporate action in the Church, nor was the spirit of their teaching. It was wholly personal, and they had vast influence over some of the most religiously-disposed minds in this country. But that influence would certainly not be exerted to recommend the revival of Synods. Quite the reverse: individual personal influence, by the appliances of pulpit rhetoric and the unlimited exercise of private judgment, were far more congenial to their natures, and much more likely to be commended by them to others than any dogmatic teaching enunciated by the quiet but authoritative voice of the Church's Councils.

It is again here repeated that I do not think all the above causes united are sufficient to account adequately for the phenomenon—for it is nothing less—that all Synodical and corporate action in this Church of England was suspended for well-nigh a century and a-half. The matters, however, above stated may go a little way towards solving the mystery, which, if it can in any measure be accounted for, must be primarily set to the account of political complications not over creditable to those concerned in them.

Seeing, however, that this suspension is a matter of fact, it may perhaps occur to some minds that, however unaccountable it is, it may have been ordered in God's providence for this Church's good. Had the Church's Synods been actively engaged in the latter part of the last century there were then political principles prevalent, infidel doctrines propagated in quarters not on the score of intellect to be despised, a disregard of Church ordinances abounding, and a general laxity as regards religion pervading the nation, which might have found some reflection in the Church's counsels, and entailed consequences most disastrous. And of these not the least might have been a stamp of Erastianism—that very pestiferous and at the same time silliest of all hallucinations—impressed upon the Church of England, fatal to her integrity as a Spiritual Kingdom founded on a commission higher than any which the powers of this world can give or take away.

PART IV.

SURVEY OF THE HISTORY OF THE CONVOCATIONS AFTER THE REVIVAL OF SYNODICAL ACTION.
1852—1885.

I.

REVIVAL OF SYNODICAL ACTION.

It is recorded of Dr. Johnson that his respect for churches was so great that he never passed one without taking off his hat; but it is at the same time affirmed that it was not a habit of his to take it off when entering one. The paradox, however, may be accounted for by the fact that it was not his practice to attend public worship. But, however negligent he may have been in respect of personal religious duty, he professed a high regard for the Church as an institution of the country, and as a proof of that regard this unromantic lexicographer affirmed that he would "face a battery of cannon" to see Convocations restored. However, if such was his devotion to the cause when Parliament, which affected to legislate for the Church, was composed of her professing members, how vastly would that devo-

Sovereign:
Q. Victoria.
1852.

Metropolitans: Sumner, Musgrave.

tion have been intensified had he lived to see the doors of our secular legislative assembly opened so widely as to admit professors of all religions and of none!

Measures taken for the revival of Synodical action.

After the admission of Jews and other aliens from the Church's faith into Parliament, a feeling began to prevail generally among Churchmen, and indeed among all reasonable people, and rapidly spread, that that assembly was not a fitting or seemly arena for the discussion at least of spiritual matters affecting the Church. It was most deeply felt that the Church should herself speak on such matters, and that her voice could only be rightly heard through her Provincial Synods or Convocations. Consequently, as the first half of this century approached completion strenuous efforts were made for the revival of their active functions. Among the most active promoters of this object were the late Dr. Samuel Wilberforce, then Bishop of Oxford, the late Mr. Henry Hoare, and a society established for this special purpose. Although our two Metropolitans at that time, Dr. Sumner and Dr. Musgrave, were not favourable to the movement, still the general feeling in the Church finally prevailed, and from the year 1852 Convocations have resumed their active and proper functions. They now meet acourse with every session of Parliament, and usually each Provincial Synod holds two or three groups of sessions in every year during the parliamentary session. *Sovereign: Q. Victoria. 1851-2.*

However, the first efforts for the revival of Synodical action were not immediately successful, mainly on account of the opposition of the two Metropolitans. *Resistance of the two Metropolitans.*

At the formal opening of the Canterbury Convocation, on Feb. 5, 1851, endeavours were made by some of the members to enter upon active business after the usual preliminaries were completed, but Archbishop Sumner at once repressed those endeavours by ordering his Registrar, Mr. Dyke, to read a schedule of prorogation. *Canterbury. Private Collections, MSS., &c.*

On Feb. 4, in the following year, 1852, the like endeavours were made, many of the Bishops of the Southern Province being favourable to the revival of the action of their Provincial Synod, and many petitions from all parts of the Province being presented with like intention. Still, again Archbishop Sumner brought all business to an abrupt close by ordering his schedule of prorogation to be read. *Ibid.*

In the Province of York, at the times last mentioned, the Metropolitan, Dr. Musgrave, did not even attend, nor were the members who assembled allowed to enter the Chapter House. Some of them, however, sent a representation to their Metropolitan on the subject. His Grace curtly replied by letter that, in the absence of a "Licence" from the Crown no active business *York. Private Collections, MSS., &c.*

would be entered on. By which reply this Metropolitan seems to have been insensible to two facts. The first being that he had already received a "Royal Writ," requiring him to convene his Synod in order to consult for the "defence of the Church and peace of the king-"dom," a Writ which he disobeyed in his own person. The second fact being, that such an instrument as a "Royal Licence" is never required save for enacting Canons, a process at this time by no one contemplated.

Metropolitans: Sumner, Musgrave.

In the same year, 1852, there was a new Parliament, and consequently new Convocations, and from this time we may date the real revival, after an interval of 134 years, of Synodical action in the Church of England.

II.

SUMMARY OF THE MOST MEMORABLE ACTS OF THE CONVOCATIONS SINCE THE REVIVAL OF SYNODICAL ACTION.

Summary of Acts.

The most prominent Acts of the Convocations since the revival of their active functions have been—the promulgation of a Harvest Service; the Synodical condemnation of Dr. Colenso's volume on the Pentateuch and the Book of Joshua; the Synodical condemnation of the volume entitled "Essays and Reviews;" the remodelling and re-enactment of the Canons on

Clergy Subscription; the promulgation of Synodical Decrees on the Vatican Council of 1870; the appointment of a Committee for revising the authorized translation of the Scriptures; the revision of the Lectionary in the Prayer Book; the provision for Shortened Services [and it is encouraging to observe that the Act of Parliament for this purpose, 35 & 36 Vict. c. 35, amending the Act of Uniformity, recites, according to ancient and time-honoured practice, a reference to the Convocations in its preamble]; the revision of the Rubrics; the compilations of Forms of Prayer for Seamen, and of a Service for asking a Blessing on Missions; the compilation of a Manual of Family Prayer, and two Manuals of Private Prayer for English Church-people. One of these is intended for those who live by the honest and honourable labour of their hands, the other for those who are not engaged in bodily labour. Numerous reports, also of the highest interest, on Clergy Discipline and other cognate subjects, have been issued recommending measures which, if canonically enacted, would prove of incalculable benefit to the Church.

 Moreover at this time, 1885, the Lower House of Canterbury is engaged in providing a Manual of Private Prayer for devotion at the seven canonical hours. And it is to be hoped that in due time the Convocations will provide other Offices

Sovereign:
Q. Victoria.
1852–
1885.

<sub>Metropolitans:
Sumner,
Musgrave.</sub>

emphatically needed in this Church. Such are Offices for the Consecration of Churches and Cemeteries; for the Reception of Renegades; for the Confirmation of those who have been Baptized as Adults; for the Dedication of Bells; for the Appointment of Lay Deacons and Deaconesses, and for other like purposes. Such additions to our authorized formularies are much needed, and to supply them would be but to imitate the example of the Eastern Church [the mother of this Church], which supplies Offices in her " Eucholo-" gion" for the manifold contingencies of the Christian life. But the proceedings of these Convocations shall now be considered in fuller detail.

III.

CONVOCATIONS CONVENED 1852, DISSOLVED 1857.

<sub>Canterbury.

Private Collections, MSS., &c.</sub>

The Canterbury Convocation assembled at St. Paul's Cathedral on November 5, 1852. The President was Archbishop Sumner, and the preacher of the Latin sermon was Dr. Jeremie, Regius Professor of Divinity at Cambridge, who took for his text, "Tarry ye here and watch" [Mark xiv. 34]. Dr. Peacock, Dean of Ely, was elected Prolocutor of the Lower House, and a group of sessions was forthwith held, in which sundry heads of business were transacted, and matters placed in a train for future action. On the day first above mentioned, the revival of Synodical action in England was practically inaugurated.

Sovereign: Q. Victoria. 1852-7.

Groups of sessions of this Convocation were held in February, 1853; in February and July, 1854; in February and June, 1855; in February and April, 1856; and in February, 1857, in which year the Convocations were dissolved. During the whole of this time matters progressed favourably for the revival of Synodical action; for though there were some of the Bishops either lukewarm in the matter or absolutely adverse to it, and also a small and not very learned party in the Lower House who threw such impediments as they could invent in the way, yet this opposition was absolutely impotent, and the revival of the active functions of this Provincial Synod of the English Church became an accomplished fact.

There were also some uneasy spirits in both Houses of Parliament, who at the beginning of this Convocation endeavoured to create difficulties, but their ignorance of Constitutional Law, and of the whole subject into which they rambled, was so crass, that they completely missed their way as well as the object at which they aimed, and, to tell the truth, made themselves ridiculous.

The concurrent York Convocation met on November 5, 1852, the same day as that on which the Canterbury Convocation above recorded first assembled. The Metropolitan, Dr. Musgrave, again absented himself, having con-

York. Private Collections, MSS., &c.

stituted as his Commissioner to act vicariously the Rev. Canon Hawkins. There was a large attendance of members of the Lower House, but the Commissioner, acting, it must be presumed, on counsels from a higher quarter, not only fell again into the absurd error of supposing that a "Royal Licence" was required for entering on business, but also forbade any discussion, and that too in a manner the reverse of courteous. The next session was held on May 18, 1853, when the Metropolitan again appointed the Rev. Canon Dixon as his Commissioner to preside. This gentleman improved backwards on the example of the former Commissioner by declaring to the members present "that he would answer no question" and "listen to no argument;" and so he prorogued the assembly. A session was again held on Feb. 1, 1854, the Metropolitan, Dr. Musgrave, still absenting himself, having constituted on this occasion the Rev. Vernon Harcourt as his Commissioner, who again, labouring under the error, or at least seeming to do so, that a "Licence" was required before any practical business could be entered on, prorogued the assembly. The above course was repeated at York till 1857, when on Feb. 4 in that year Canon Vernon Harcourt again presided as Commissioner, and again repeated the process of prorogation before any useful business could be accomplished.

IV.

CONVOCATIONS CONVENED 1857, DISSOLVED 1859.

A new Canterbury Convocation, concurrently with a new Parliament, assembled on May 1, 1857, under the presidency of Archbishop Sumner, at St. Paul's Cathedral. After the Latin Litany had been read by the junior Bishop present, Dr. Jackson of Lincoln, the anthem "O pray for the peace of Jerusalem" was sung. Then followed the Latin sermon, preached by the Rev. W. Hayward Cox, Prebendary of Hereford, on the text, "And the servant of the Lord "must not strive," &c. [2 Tim. ii. 24, 25]. At the end of the sermon the "Gloria in Excelsis" was sung, and the Archbishop pronounced the Benediction. The Dean of Bristol, Dr. Gilbert Eliot, was elected Prolocutor of the Lower House, and throughout the sessions of this Convocation the time was mostly employed in getting matters into working order. Groups of sessions were held at Westminster in May and July, 1857; in February, 1858, and February, 1859; and on April 25, 1859, this Convocation was dissolved. *Sovereign: Q. Victoria. 1857-9.* *Canterbury.* *Chron. Conv. v. Vict. Reg. pp. 6 seq.*

This York Convocation was again forbidden by the Northern Metropolitan, Dr. Musgrave, to *York.*

Metropolitans: Sumner, Musgrave.

Private Collections, MSS., &c.

proceed to business. It was prorogued from time to time, on one occasion by the Dean of York, Dr. Cockburn, acting as Commissioner for the Metropolitan—the Dean not adopting the most courteous manner imaginable. In fact, nothing was practically done in this Northern Convocation, and nothing worthy of record occurred, except that again and again to the very last the old fanciful notion of the necessity of a "Royal Licence" for proceeding to business was paraded by the Commissioners and legal officials. Together with the last-mentioned Canterbury Synod, the York Convocation was dissolved in 1859.

V.

CONVOCATIONS CONVENED 1859, DISSOLVED 1865.

Canterbury.

Chron. Conv. vi. Vict. Reg. pp. 1 seq.

On June 1, 1859, a new Canterbury Convocation assembled at St. Paul's Cathedral. The President was Archbishop Sumner. The Litany in Latin having been said by the junior Bishop, the anthem, "O pray for the peace of Jerusalem," was sung. The usual Latin sermon was then preached by the Hon. and Rev. Samuel Waldegrave, M.A., the "Gloria in Excelsis" sung by the choir, and the Benediction in Latin pronounced by the Archbishop. Formal business having then been transacted in the Chapter House, the Clergy were desired to withdraw to the chapel at the north-west end of the Cathedral to elect their Prolocutor. This they did, and their choice fell again on the Very Rev. Gilbert Eliot, D.D., Dean of Bristol, who had filled the office during the last Convocation. This Convocation held groups of sessions at Westminster in June, 1859; January, February, and June, 1860; in February and March, 1861 [on which last occasion the Ven. E. Bickersteth, Archdeacon of Buckingham, was appointed Deputy Prolocutor to serve for Dr. Gilbert Eliot, Dean of Bristol]; in June and July, 1861; in February and May, 1862; in May and July, 1863; in February and April [on which occasion the Ven. Archdeacon Bickersteth was elected Prolocutor, on the resignation of the Dean of Bristol], and in June, 1864; in February, May, and June, 1865, in which year this Convocation was dissolved.

Sovereign: Q. Victoria. 1859–65.

In this Canterbury Convocation many matters were discussed and deliberated upon of great moment to the Church, and the proceedings, an account of which may be read in the " Chronicle "of Convocation," cannot fail to be instructive to those who take an interest in the Church's work and welfare. Such discussions and deliberations had reference, among other subjects, to Home and Foreign Missions, the Preparation of Occasional Services, Missionary Bishops, the Diaconate, Training for Holy Orders, Religious Sisterhoods, Increase of the Episcopate, the Burial Service, the

Metropolitans: Sumner, Longley.

Final Court of Ecclesiastical Appeal, Clerical Subscription, and the Revision of the 29th Canon, which relates to sponsors in Baptism.

There are, however, four Acts of this Convocation which demand special attention.

Harvest Thanksgiving Service.

The first of these Acts was the preparation of a Harvest Thanksgiving Service, which has proved a great boon to the Church, and it is to be hoped will be the forerunner of other Occasional Services and Liturgical Offices, much required as supplementary to the Prayer Book for special occasions.

Synodical condemnation of Dr. Colenso's volume.

The second of these Acts was the Synodical condemnation of a book entitled "The Penta-"teuch and Book of Joshua Critically Examined. "By the Right Rev. William Colenso, D.D., Bi-"shop of Natal. Parts I. and II." At the outset of his work this Prelate frankly confessed that he was brought up in the belief that not only every word but every letter in the English translation of the Bible was given us by inspiration, his attention, it would seem, not having been directed to variations in codices and translations. When this belief was shaken, as he informed his readers, the "loaded shell shot to the "fortress of his soul," which may well be believed. Being more of a mathematician than a theologian, and having been disturbed by the queries of an enquiring Zulu, this Bishop set himself to work out some very puzzling and intricate arithmetical calculations connected with Bible history. After having applied abstruse calculations, even calling logarithms to his aid, to a vast number of particular instances, and having supplemented his labours by application for help to some German writers, he came finally to the conclusion that the Bible history was untrue. Being satisfied in his own mind on this point, instead of resigning his Bishopric, he still retained his style, title, and income, and yet published to the Diocese of Natal, and indeed to the world at large, his book recording his convictions. Now, as Natal was a See in the Province of Capetown [or South Africa], and as that Province, if not in the Exarchate, is at least most intimately associated with the Province of Canterbury, it would have been a great omission in duty if the Synod of this last-named Province had not taken notice of a book of such tendency, and written by a Bishop holding such relations to this Church. Accordingly, the Upper House of Canterbury directed the Lower House to appoint a Committee for examination of the book. That Committee examined the book with great care, and reported to the Upper House. The Archbishop and Bishops there assembled passed this formal judgment: "That the said "book does in our judgment involve errors of "the gravest and most dangerous character, sub-"versive of faith in the Bible as the Word of "God." This judgment having been communi-

Sovereign: Q. Victoria. 1859-65.

Chron. Conv. vi. Vict. Reg. p. 1204.

cated to the Lower House, the Presbyters there resolved: That we "do hereby accept and concur in the 'judgment' of the Upper House." Thus was this mischievous book synodically condemned on May 20, 1863, the Synod exercising one of those functions proper to Provincial Synods, as before described. And it may be observed that the formal Synodical condemnation of a Bishop's writings had not taken place before this occasion since the Reformation.

<small>Metropolitans: Longley, Thomson.
Chron. Conv. vi. Vict. Reg. pp. 1237, 1285.
Supra, p. 32.</small>

The third Act of this Convocation specially worthy of record was the condemnation of a book entitled "Essays and Reviews." This was a volume consisting of seven essays. One of the writers was a former Head Master of Rugby, now a deservedly honoured, beloved, and devoted Bishop, whose contribution to the work has been entirely withdrawn, as announced in the Canterbury Synod, Feb. 9 and 11, 1870. The other six writers were, the Rev. Dr. Rowland Williams, Professor of Hebrew, St. David's College, Lampeter; Baden Powell, M.A., F.R.S., Savilian Professor of Geometry in the University of Oxford; the Rev. H. Bristow Wilson, Vicar of Great Staughton; C. W. Goodwyn, M.A.; the Rev. Mark Pattison, B.D.; and the Rev. Benjamin Jowett, M.A., Regius Professor of Greek in the University of Oxford. The book suggested numberless difficulties against a humble reception of the Christian faith. These diffi-

<small>Synodical condemnation of "Essays and Reviews."
Chron. Conv. viii. Vict. Reg. pp. 70–132.</small>

culties were, most of them, such as are familiar to any thoughtful mind. They had all been worn threadbare long ago by such writers as Blount, Bolingbroke, Chubb, Collins, Gibbon, Hobbes, Hume, Morgan, Paine, Toland, and Woolston. Moreover, in this book there was an imported contingent from foreign allies—one of the essays, at least, owing a considerable debt of gratitude for its contents to a treatise by Lessing.

The book, however stale its contents, yet in modern garb directly tended to suggest to half-educated and simple minds doubts and difficulties which, but for its appearance, never would have occurred to them, and so was calculated to work cruel mischief. Had not the great majority of contributors been Clergymen, no Synodical notice of the book would probably have been taken. But, that five Clergymen in the Province should unite in the publication of so mischievous a volume was rightly thought a sufficient reason for notice to be taken of it by the Canterbury Synod. Consequently, Committees both of the Upper and Lower Houses were appointed to examine the book. They severally reported; and on June 22, 1864, the Archbishop and Bishops resolved:
"That the Upper House of Convocation ....
" doth hereby synodically condemn the said
" volume, as containing teaching contrary to
" the doctrine received by the United Church

Sovereign:
Q. Victoria.
1859–65.

Chron.
Conv. vi.
Vict. Reg.
p. 1683.

Metropolitans: Longley, Thomson.

Chron. Conv. vi. Vict. Reg. p. 1830.

"of England and Ireland, in common with the whole Catholic Church of Christ." This condemnation of the book was transmitted to the Lower House, and the Presbyters there assembled resolved, on June 24, 1864, that "This House respectfully and heartily tenders its thanks to his Grace the President and the Bishops of the Upper House for their care in defence of the Faith, and that this House does thankfully accept and concur in the condemnation of the book by the Upper House, to which their concurrence has been invited by the Upper House." Thus the Synodical condemnation of this volume was in due form completed.

Clerical lawbreaking.

This volume, as will be seen hereafter, was also synodically condemned at York. And it is here observable that some of the English Clergy have lately, in very high quarters, been publicly denounced as "lawbreakers" because they declined to conform to some eccentric judgments of the Judicial Committee of Privy Council. However, if there was on this ground the slightest justification for such denunciation [which there is not], it is indisputably clear that Archiepiscopal and Episcopal authority had previously quite wilfully and very conspicuously commended to imitation an example of "lawbreaking." For as a volume was synodically condemned of which the most peccant parts had previously been judicially absolved by the Whitehall Tribunal, it is beyond all question certain, on the above theory of obedience, that those who joined in the condemnation, specially if ranking as Metropolitan or Bishop, very ostentatiously signalized themselves as marching in the first forefront of the most flagrant "lawbreakers."

[margin: Sovereign: Q. Victoria. 1859-65.]

The fourth Act of this Convocation worthy of special record was the alteration and re-enactment of sundry Canons, the 29th, 36th, 37th, 38th and 40th Canons of 1603-4. The oath which had been taken under the older Canons mentioned before ordination, and by the Clergy on appointment to Ecclesiastical offices, was now revised and remodelled, and cast in the form of the following declaration :—

[margin: New Canons enacted.]

> "I, A. B., do solemnly make the following
> "declaration: I assent to the Thirty-nine
> "Articles of Religion, and to the Book of
> "Common Prayer, and of Ordering Bishops,
> "Priests, and Deacons. I believe the doc-
> "trine of the United Church of England and
> "Ireland, as therein set forth, to be agreeable
> "to the Word of God; and in Public Prayer
> "and Administration of the Sacraments I
> "will use the form in the said Book pre-
> "scribed, and none other, except so far as
> "shall be ordered by lawful authority."

Also the oath against simony at institution into a benefice, as previously required by Canon 40, was changed into a declaration.

Metropolitans:
Longley,
Thomson.

Chron.
Conv. vi.
Vict. Reg.
pp. 2398
seq.

These new Canons were enacted in due Synodical form [before described in Part I., pp. 32, 33], in a chamber in Dean's Yard, Westminster, in presence of the Upper and Lower Houses, assembled in full Synod on June 29, 1865. It is to be observed, that during the process of enactment on that day, the Tower guns sent forth a salute which re-echoed through the Metropolis. It is not here meant to suggest that this salute was given in honour of the new Canons—it was, I believe, intended for another purpose. But it was a curious fact. Some may, perhaps, think it an ominous one that the ratification of the first Canons enacted in the Church of England, after an interval of 225 years, took place during the thunders of a Royal salute.

Excursion of the "Crown Office."

Chron.
Conv. vi.
Vict. Reg.
p. 2354.

It is moreover observable that the officers of the Crown Office who drew the Royal Licence for the enactment of these Canons missed their way to such a degree as to produce a document which was bad law and worse sense. Among other confusions, these learned persons provided in the Licence that the Canons, after being made, "promulged, and executed," should be set down in writing and exhibited for the approval of the Crown. Thus the whole order of things would be inverted. It was certainly a whimsical idea that the Canons should be first put into "execution" in the Ecclesiastical Courts, and, after having been there enforced, should then be submitted subsequently for the approval of the Crown. But the methods which the learned in the law adopt in Ecclesiastical proceedings are not always wholly intelligible. *[margin: Sovereign: Q. Victoria. 1859–1865.]*

In the York Convocation summoned in the year 1859, and concurrent with the Canterbury Convocation last recorded, so long as Dr. Musgrave occupied the See of York no active business was entered upon. The old hallucination respecting the necessity of a Royal Licence for entering on deliberations still bewildered the Northern Ecclesiastical authorities. But on the advancement of that most amiable and beloved Prelate, Dr. C. T. Longley, to the throne of York, whose confirmation as Metropolitan took place on July 1, 1860, matters in this respect underwent a complete change. *[margin: York. Private Collections. Accession of Dr. C. T. Longley.]*

On the 6th of February, 1861, the Provincial Synod of the Northern Province, after a suspension of Synodical action for 143 years, entered on active business. On that day Archdeacon Thorpe was elected as Prolocutor of the Lower House. On March 20, 1861, debates were carried on, and on the following day, March 21, the book entitled "Essays and Reviews" was synodically condemned, as was the case also in the Canterbury Synod. This book, therefore, having been synodically condemned in both Provinces, may be said to be under the ban of the English Exarchate. *[margin: Private Collections.]*

<small>Metropolitans: Longley, Thomson.</small>

<small>Private Collections.</small>

In June, 1865, a "Licence" was sent by the Crown to the Northern Synod for the enactment of the new Canons on Clergy Subscription. In July following the Synod assembled at York Cathedral, and on the 5th of that month the above-mentioned new Canons were decreed, six days after the same process had taken place in the Canterbury Synod, as above described.

VI.

CONVOCATIONS CONVENED 1866, DISSOLVED 1868.

<small>Canterbury.</small>

<small>Chron. Conv. vii. Vict. Reg. pp. 8 seq.</small>

The new Canterbury Convocation summoned to meet on February 2, 1866, assembled at St. Paul's Cathedral on that day, under the presidency of that amiable and revered Prelate, Dr. Charles Thomas Longley, worthily promoted from the See of York to that of Canterbury. The Latin Litany of Convocation was said by the Right Rev. Bishop of Salisbury, Dr. Walter Kerr Hamilton, after which the anthem, "O pray for "the peace of Jerusalem," was sung. The preacher of the Latin sermon, who took for his text, " And the apostles and elders came to- " gether for to consider of this matter " [Acts xv. 6], was the Rev. James Wayland Joyce, M.A., late Student of Christ Church, Oxford, and one of the Clergy Proctors for the Diocese of Hereford.

The Synod then adjourned to the Chapter House, and after the usual formalities had been there gone through, the Clergy returned to the chapel at the north-west end of the Cathedral, and then elected for a second time as Prolocutor the Venerable Edward Bickersteth, Archdeacon of Buckingham.

Sovereign: Q. Victoria. 1866–1868.

This Convocation held groups of sessions at Westminster in February, May, and June, 1866; in February and June, 1867; in February, June, and July, 1868; and was dissolved on Nov. 13 in the year last named.

The most important events connected with this Convocation were the debates on Ritualism, and on the questions then disturbing the Province of Capetown [or South Africa], arising out of the relations between Dr. Gray the Metropolitan of Capetown and Dr. Colenso of Natal. Dr. Colenso had been excommunicated on account of his book before mentioned, and deposed from his office as a Bishop by the South African Provincial Synod. And the question now arose whether Dr. Colenso or the South African Metropolitan and Bishops were to be considered in communion with the Church of England. This of course could only be answered in one way, that the Church of England was in communion with the South African Prelates; and it was so resolved by both Houses. The account may be seen of this Act in the "Chro-

Dr. Colenso not in communion with the Church of England.

Chron. Conv. vii. Vict. Reg. pp. 585–598, 604–632, 641–1565 seq.

Metropolitans:
Cant.
vacant.
Thomson.

Chron.
Conv. vii.
Vict. Reg.
pp. 692,
800, 1081
seq.

York.

Private
Collections.

"nicle of Convocation," June 29, 1866. Debates also took place on the question of a Synod of the Anglican Communion, which resulted afterwards in a Convention of a Pan-Anglican Synod at Lambeth.

On Feb. 2, 1866, the Convocation of York met at the Cathedral, under the presidency of the Metropolitan, Dr. William Thomson. After Divine Service in the Choir at 8 A.M. the members assembled in the Chapter House. The Lower House then retired to the Vestry for the election of their Prolocutor, and their choice fell unanimously on the Hon. and Very Rev. Dr. Duncombe, Dean of York, who had previously discharged the same office. This Convocation held sessions from time to time, but was of short duration, being dissolved in 1868, so that no business was transacted which need specially be recorded.

VII.

CONVOCATIONS CONVENED 1868, DISSOLVED 1874.

Canterbury.

Chron.
Conv. viii.
Vict. Reg.
pp. 7–12.

On Dec. 11, 1868, a new Convocation met at St. Paul's Cathedral. The See of Canterbury being now vacant on account of the lamented death of Archbishop Longley, the Bishop of London, Dr. Tait [Archbishop Designate of

Canterbury], presided, under a Commission from the Dean and Chapter of Canterbury, as guardians of the Spiritualties during a vacancy. The Latin Litany was said by Dr. William Connor Magee, Bishop of Peterborough, as being the junior Prelate present. The anthem, "O pray for the peace "of Jerusalem," was then sung, after which the Latin sermon was preached by Dr. James Amiraux Jeremie, Dean of Lincoln, upon the text, "Let us therefore follow after the things which "make for peace, and things wherewith one may "edify another" [Rom. xiv. 19]. At the end of the sermon, the "Gloria in Excelsis" was sung, and the Benediction pronounced by the President in Latin. After the usual formalities had been subsequently gone through in the Chapter House, the lower Clergy returned to the chapel at the north-west end of the Cathedral, and there, by a unanimous vote, under the presidency of Dr. Henry Longueville Mansel, the Dean, elected as their Prolocutor for the third time Dr. Edward Bickersteth, Archdeacon of Buckingham.

Sovereign:
Q. Victoria.
1868–
1874.

This Synod was then prorogued to February 2 following, and held groups of sessions in February and June, 1869; February, May, and July, 1870; in February and June, 1871; in February, March, April, May, and July, 1872; and in February, May, and July, 1873. After which group of sessions this Convocation was dissolved on January 29, 1874.

Metropolitans:
Tait,
Thomson.

Summary of Acts, Chron. Conv. viii. Vict. Reg. in loc.

In this Convocation matters of the deepest interest to the Church of England were discussed, and some concluded on. Among instructive debates were those on Clergy Discipline—Communication with the Eastern Church—the Athanasian Creed—Home Missions—Final Court of Appeal—Reform of Convocation—Re-marriage of Divorced Persons, and Increase in the Episcopate. But some matters besides the above require particular consideration. These are five in number.

Decrees on Vatican Council.

The first of these is the action taken with regard to the Vatican Council, which finally promulgated, with much pomp, at Rome, four Canons which it had decreed. The fourth of these Canons declared the personal infallibility of the Pope of Rome, and pronounced his definitions, without consent of the Church, to be "irreformable."

Chron. Conv. viii. Vict. Reg. pp. 513–14.

The question before this Convocation arose upon a "gravamen" presented by one of the Clergy Proctors for the Diocese of Hereford, and signed by twenty-seven members of the Lower House, setting forth that the Council assembled in the City of Rome, by assuming the name and claiming the authority of an Œcumenical Council, wholly ignored the due Canonical rights of all the Dioceses, Provinces, and Patriarchates of the Christian Church which do not submit to the Roman obedience. And as a "reformandum," it was prayed that His Grace the President and their Lordships the Bishops would take such measures as to them might seem fit for vindicating the independent position of the Church of England, and for addressing a remonstrance against the present assumption of the Roman Curia to other Churches of Christendom. Sovereign: Q.Victoria. 1868–1874.

When this document was presented to the Upper House, the late most learned and revered Bishop Wordsworth of Lincoln threw his whole heart into the matter. The Archbishop of Canterbury, having expressed a strong repugnance against proceeding in the matter, was from ill health absent from the first debate on the subject, which took place in the Upper House, when Bishop Wordsworth proposed that action should be taken in the matter. But Dr. Jackson, Bishop of London, who presided in his Grace's absence, and Dr. Ellicott, Bishop of Gloucester and Bristol, agreeing with the Archbishop, who had previously written a letter deprecating action, endeavoured to prevent any measures being taken. Their reasons were not altogether intelligible, nor did they carry any weight with the Upper House, as all the other Bishops present supported the Bishop of Lincoln. A joint Committee of both Houses was appointed to consider what should be done. When their report was presented, on June 16, 1871, the Archbishop and the two Bishops above mentioned had changed their minds, and Chron. Conv. viii. Vict. Reg. p. 509.

Ibid. pp. 600–622.

Ibid. p. 651.

Ibid. vol. iii. pp. 447–8.

Metropolitans:
Tait,
Thomson.
Chron.
Conv. iii.
Vict. Reg.
p. 450.

supported the recommendations of the Committee. The result was that the following Decrees were Synodically adopted by both Houses of the Canterbury Provincial Synod—

I.

Ibid.
p. 441.

"That the Vatican Council has no just "right to be termed an Œcumenical or "General Council, and that none of its "Decrees have any claim for acceptance as "Canons of a General Council."

II.

"That the Dogma of Papal infallibility "now set forth by the Vatican Council is con- "trary to Holy Scripture, and to the judg- "ment of the ancient Church Universal."

III.

"That the assumption of supremacy by "the Bishop of Rome in convening the late "Vatican Council contravenes Canons of the "Universal Church."

IV.

"That there is one true Catholic and "Apostolic Church, founded by our Lord "and Saviour Jesus Christ; that of this true

"Catholic and Apostolic Church the Church "of England and the Churches in com-"munion with her are living members; and "that the Church of England earnestly de-"sires to maintain firmly the Catholic faith "as set forth by the Œcumenical Councils "of the Universal Church, and to be united "upon those principles of doctrine and "discipline in the bonds of brotherly love "with all Churches in Christendom."

<small>Sovereign: Q. Victoria. 1868-1874.</small>

These four Decrees, with fitting superscriptions, were translated into Greek, according to the ancient manner of the Eastern Church, and into Latin, according to the ancient manner of the Western Church, by the present writer, with a view to their transmission to the Eastern Orthodox Churches and others. Copies were first sent, with an explanatory Latin letter, to the Archbishop of Utrecht, and to his Suffragans of the Trajectine Church in Holland. The Archbishop of Utrecht, Henry Loos, and the Bishop of Daventer, H. Heykamp, in whose Diocese Rotterdam is situated, replied with thanks in Latin epistles, the latter complaining in the bitterest terms of the treatment to which the Trajectine Church had been subjected by the imperiousness of the Vatican. This Prelate's letter was read in the Lower House of this Convocation on Feb. 13, 1872. The Canterbury Decrees were

<small>Canterbury Decrees on Vatican Council transmitted to other Churches. Vide Report Joint Com. on Vat. Counc. & Chron. Conv. Ann. 1871, pp.118-143.</small>

<small>Chron. Conv. viii. Vict. Reg. pp. 235-7.</small>

Metropolitans:
Tait,
Thomson.

eventually printed on large paper, with rubricated margins, in very splendid type and form, at the Cambridge University Press, and were forwarded to the Patriarchs of the Orthodox Eastern Church.

Revision of the authorized translation of Holy Scripture.

Chron. Conv. viii. Vict. Reg. pp. 74 seq. 202 seq. 328 seq.

The second important event connected with this Convocation was the appointment of a joint Committee for the Revision of the English translation of Holy Scripture. This was inaugurated by Dr. Samuel Wilberforce, Bishop of Winchester, on February 10, 1870. The joint Committee was eventually appointed, and power was given to the members to conjoin with themselves persons who they believed might assist the work. Two Companies thus composed were constituted, one for the revision of the Old Testament, the other for a revision of the New. Their work began on June 22, 1870. In consequence of a resolution passed by both Houses of this Convocation, scholars in America were invited to assist, and there also two Companies were formed to co-operate with those in England. The Revised New Testament was completed in 1880, and the book, printed at the Oxford and Cambridge University Presses, was published in 1881. The Revised Old Testament, there also printed, is now [1885] published.

Revised N. T. Pref. p. x.

The Revised Lectionary.

The third important event connected with this Convocation was the adoption of a "New "Lectionary" for the Book of Common Prayer. The principal alterations now made from the former book were: first [not to specify minor details], that an alternative First Lesson was appointed for Evensong on Sundays; secondly, that for the first half of each year the Second Lesson for the Morning should be taken from the Gospels, and the Second Lesson for the Evening from the rest of the New Testament; but that for the second half of each year the Second Lesson in the Morning should be taken from other parts of the New Testament, and the Second Lesson in the Evening from the Gospels. This Lectionary was recommended by the Third Report of the Royal Commission on Ritual. It was submitted to the Metropolitans and Bishops of England and Ireland, to the Deans of Cathedrals, and the Theological Professors in the Universities of Oxford, Cambridge, Durham, and Dublin. A joint Committee of the two Houses of the Canterbury Convocation was appointed to consider it, and that Committee recommended its adoption. Both Houses then agreed to an address to the Crown, requesting that measures necessary to give legal effect to the New Lectionary should be taken. Such measures were taken, and a Bill was brought into Parliament for the purpose. *Sovereign: Q. Victoria. 1868–1874. Chron. Conv. viii. Vict. Reg. pp. 2, 40, 196, 241, 278 seq. 399, 450, 471. Chron. Conv. May 3 and 4, 1870; June 16, 1871.*

And here an incident occurred well worthy of remark, and one which the reader may usefully bear in mind. The Bill for the Civil authorization of the New Lectionary was introduced *A Lord Chancellor's exposition of law.*

Metropolitans: Tait, Thomson.

first into the House of Commons as a Government measure. In the preamble was recited the previous approval of that Lectionary by Convocation. But in the House of Lords, an ex Lord Chancellor prevailed upon his hearers to have that recital excised. As his Lordship had held the most exalted legal office, the noble peers supposed that his statements of law were correct. In so supposing, however, they were sadly mistaken, as his statements were merely fictions of his own imagination, and fictions, too, exactly the contraries of truth. He told their listening and credulous Lordships, to use his own words, that—

> " Now, for the first time they had in that
> " Bill a recital of the approval of Convoca-
> " tion without any mention of the Licence
> " of the Crown to express that approval."

Now in the first place, his Lordship, as a lawyer, ought to have known [and in such a learned person of course one cannot suspect any looseness of expression] that a Licence from the Crown is not needed, and never ought to be issued but for one solitary purpose, namely, the enactment of Canons, a matter not now even contemplated. And, in the second place, his Lordship might have discovered by very cursory search, that in great Constitutional Statutes of the Realm,— such as 26 Hen. VIII. 1,—32 Hen. VIII. 25,— 5 & 6 Ed. VI. 12,—8 Eliz. 1,—13 Eliz. 12,—

the approval of the Convocations is recognized, while most certainly on no one of those occasions had any Licence of the Crown been granted. No doubt Writs for assembling those Convocations had been issued, just as the Writs had been issued for assembling the Convocations now in session, and of which his Lordship spoke. But most certainly Licences in none of those cases were issued, for in none of them was the enactment of Canons contemplated. However, the Church and the world are tolerably well accustomed to strange deliverances on the part of the learned profession when Ecclesiastical matters are concerned. Indeed, many very instructive and surprising instances in this respect may be derived from a perusal of the Ecclesiastical judgments of the Judicial Committee of Privy Council. Thus was the recital of the approval of Convocation excised from the Lectionary Bill on account of a statement wholly false. *Sovereign: Q. Victoria. 1868–1874.*

The fourth remarkable event connected with this Convocation was the authorization of some alterations and explanations made with regard to the Prayer Book. These were directed generally to effect the following results: (1) That the Morning Prayer, Litany, and Communion Office might be used as separate Services, and that without a sermon. (2) That Additional Services, approved by the Ordinary, might be introduced. (3) That Special Services, approved by the Or- *Shortened Services authorized. Chron. Conv. viii. Vict. Reg. pp. 28, 57, 107, 161, 174, 202, 226, 299, 301–2.*

dinary, might be used. (4) That sermons might be preached, without a previous Service. (5) That, except in Cathedral or Collegiate Churches, the Order for Morning and Evening Prayer might be shortened by certain specified omissions. These provisions had been recommended in the Fourth Report of the Ritual Commissioners, and a Royal Letter of Business to this Convocation was read in the Upper House, on Feb. 8, 1872, requesting the Synod to take the matters above mentioned into consideration.

Oddly enough, together with this Royal Letter of Business there was transmitted to the Convocation from the Crown Office a "Royal "Licence." This is a portentous instrument, fortified with a seal of imposing size larger than an ordinary plate. But the instrument was no way required; there was no question about enacting a Canon, nor any thought in anyone's mind of proposing such a proceeding. This Royal Licence was therefore a mere act of supererogation on the part of the Crown Office lawyers. But let this pass; 'tis only another specimen of the manner in which the learned profession, and those too in high place, perplex themselves in Ecclesiastical engagements.

The Royal Letter of Business having been received, the Synod took measures for considering the matters commended to its notice by the Crown. The subject having first been con-

[Marginal notes: Metropolitans: Tait, Thomson. Chron. Conv. viii. Vict. Reg. p. 36. Act of supererogation in Crown Office. Chron. Conv. viii. Vict. Reg. pp. 239–40.]

sidered separately in both Houses, the two united met in one body, on Feb. 13, 1872, and there by common voting agreed upon the measures desirable for the purpose in hand, as above recorded. Here Archbishop Tait, by assembling both Houses into one Synod for discussion and deliberation, shewed a wise discretion. On such a matter as that before this Convocation it was most desirable that the Presbyters should hear the arguments of the Bishops, and no less desirable that the Bishops should hear the arguments of the Presbyters, in accordance with the practice of Synods Œcumenical in the earlier ages, and in Synods Provincial in all ages of the Church.

<small>Sovereign: Q. Victoria. 1868–1874.</small>

<small>Chron. Conv. viii. Vict. Reg. pp. 237–8.</small>

Again, on Feb. 29, the two Houses sat together in Synod, and discussed the resolutions which had been come to in the Northern Convocation on the matters of the Shortened Services and the cognate subjects. Finally, on the 6th day of March, the two Houses, again united in Synod, canonically ratified the resolutions arrived at in both Provinces on these subjects, and those resolutions were duly signed as Decrees by the Archbishop, six Bishops, one Bishop by proxy, and by thirty-seven members of the Lower House, either under their own hands or by proxy. The management of this business by Archbishop Tait was such as to deserve the gratitude of succeeding generations in the Church

<small>Ibid. pp. 259 seq.</small>

<small>Ibid. pp. 301–2.</small>

Metropolitans:
Tait,
Thomson.

of England, as in this matter he re-established the wholesome practice of joint discussion between the two Houses of the Canterbury Synod, and was moreover careful that the Decrees arrived at should be properly and canonically confirmed. These resolutions were subsequently embodied in the Statute 35 & 36 Vict. 135, in the preamble of which the Convocational authority is recited in a manner as constitutional as can be imagined. And this, be it remembered, was the first occasion, since the ratification of the present Prayer Book in 1661, that any Synodical authority had been given for amending its order of Divine Service.

Revision of Rubrics.

The fifth event to be specially recorded as connected with this Convocation is as follows:—The Royal Letter of Business sent to the Archbishop not only had reference to the Shortened Services with the cognate matters, but to the contents of the Fourth Report of the Ritual Commissioners, which involved a revision of the whole of the Rubrics of the Prayer Book. Consequently, a Committee of the Lower House of this Convocation was appointed for such revision. Having the revision of the Commissioners before them, they prepared with great labour and research a report, which was printed in parallel columns with that of the Commissioners. This matter was long and earnestly discussed through many sessions of this Convocation. The compilation of an Additional Service at Evening Prayer was also begun, and a declaration agreed upon as fit to be appended to the Athanasian Creed.

The measures for a revision of the rubrics were now far advanced, in consequence of the Royal Letter of Business addressed to this Convocation, but were deferred for completion to the next Convocation, and have not as yet [1885] been carried into legal effect. This indeed could not be compassed without having recourse to an Act of Parliament directed to supersede the stringent provisions of the Act of Uniformity, 13 & 14 Car. II. 4. A Bill to inaugurate such an Act as that now required was drafted by a Committee of Convocation subsequently in 1878. But it could with no hope of success be introduced into Parliament except by the Government of the day. And here lies the difficulty, arising from the unhappy system in this country of government by party deeply ingrained into English political life, and, moreover, hopelessly ineradicable. Those who are in office are, on the one hand, so busily engaged in plans for keeping in, and so fearful of giving their adversaries a point of leverage for hoisting them out; and, on the other hand, those who are out are so deeply occupied with schemes for tripping up their opponents and getting into power, that there seems

Sovereign:
Q. Victoria.
1868–
1874.

Chron.
Conv. viii.
Vict. Reg.
Ann. 1873,
pp. 219–232.

Metropolitans: Tait, Thomson.

but little time left or opportunity allowed for any beneficial legislation whatever, much less for such as would be secured if the measures initiated by this Convocation and completed in the next were statutably adopted.

York.

Private Collections.

Concurrently with the last-mentioned Convocation of Canterbury the York Convocation was convened in 1868. Its sessions in March, 1871, require some special mention. The members of the Upper and Lower Houses assembled in Archbishop Zouch's Chapel in the Minster, under the presidency of their Metropolitan, Dr. William Thomson; the Hon. and Very Rev. Augustus Duncombe, Dean of York, being Prolocutor.

New Lectionary.

On this occasion the Prolocutor moved and the Rev. Canon Eden seconded a resolution that their Committee's report on the New Lectionary as proposed by the Ritual Commissioners should be adopted. This resolution was carried, and a rider was appended to it, moved by Canon Simmons and seconded by the Dean of Chester, which was also carried, that the Northern Convocation should address the Crown, praying Her Majesty that the use of the New Lectionary might be authorized by Act of Parliament. Thus the New Lectionary was approved by the York Synod, as was the case also in the Synod of Canterbury above mentioned, and so was sanctioned in both Provinces.

Supra, p. 291.

Rubrical revision.

This York Convocation was also engaged in

revising the rubrics, a work contemporaneously being carried on in the Canterbury Synod.

This Convocation refused to join the Canterbury Synod in its enterprize above mentioned [p. 290] for promoting a revision of the Authorized Version of the Scriptures. And as the English Company of Revisers of the New Testament have dealt with several passages in the volume in the same unhappy manner as they have dealt with Acts xv. 23, the members of the Northern Synod have some good reason now to congratulate themselves on their refusal.

As the mistranslation of Acts xv. 23 most vitally affects the whole subject dealt with in these pages, it is not out of place here to remark on the havoc made by the revisers with that verse. It contains the superscription of the Apostles and Presbyters to the Decrees of the Apostolic Council of Jerusalem, the first Council of the Church, the model and prototype of Church Councils in all subsequent ages of Christianity. This superscription in our authorized translation, no doubt, is generally acknowledged to be wrong. It is not warranted by the most trustworthy MSS. or by the best authorities, as will be specified hereafter in the concluding section of these pages. So our present translation wanted reforming. But the revisers have reformed backwards, and in place of mending it have made a far worse rent in the texture.

Sovereign:
Q. Victoria.
1868–1874.

Revised New Testament.

Acts xiv. 23; xx. 28.

Metropolitans:
Tait,
Thomson.

The authorized translation renders the passage thus: "The Apostles and elders and brethren "send greeting," &c. But the best authorities do not warrant the introduction of the word "*and*" between the words "elders" and "bre-"thren." According to the best scholars, such as Irenæus and Origen in early times, Bishop Wordsworth of Lincoln, Bishop Jacobson of Chester, and that master of exegesis Dean Alford

N. T.
Tauchnitz,
Leipsic,
1869.

in later times [Constantine Tischendorf approving the text they have adopted], the superscription to the Jerusalem Encyclical Letter runs thus: "*The Apostles and Elders, brethren, send greeting* "*unto the brethren,*" &c. But the late revisers, in opposition to the authorities above named,

Rev. N. T.
Pica 8vo.ed.
p. 599.

and in opposition to the recorded dissent of the American Company of Revisers, have rendered the superscription thus: "*The Apostles and the* "*elder brethren unto the brethren . . . . greeting.*" This method of translation is as mischievous as it is surprising, and that for manifold reasons.

(1) As regards scholarship. The word πρεσβύτερος has already occurred four times in this chapter [vv. 2, 4, 6, 23] as a substantive, and now on its fifth occurrence, and in the same connexion as before, it is changed into an adjective. And further, it rests with the revisers to produce an instance of the word πρεσβύτερος being used as an adjective *immediately antecedent* to its connected substantive in Hellenistic Greek. It may

suffice to say that between forty and fifty pas- **Sovereign:**
sages where the word occurs have been lately **Q. Victoria.**
referred to. But not one has been discovered to **1868–**
justify the reviser's method. **1874.**

(2) As regards common reason. According to this novel method of interpretation, though the mission from Antioch was sent to the Apostles and Presbyters only [ver. 2], and although the Apostles and Presbyters only met for deliberation [ver. 6], yet when the Decrees of the Council came to be authenticated the Presbyters are excluded from the superscription, and some other persons not before mentioned are substituted in their place.

(3) As regards example. In accordance with the translation hitherto adopted by scholars, the apposition of two nominatives at the beginning of an Epistle seems to have been the normal form in the Early Church. At least fifteen Epistles in the New Testament so begin; and this apposition of the very word in question, ἀδελφοί, actually occurs twice [vv. 7, 13] in the chapter before us. Moreover, this form of apposition is 1 Cor. xv. quite familiar to the humblest scholar both in 20. 23; Heb. xii. 9; Classical as well as in Hellenistic Greek. 1 John iv. 14.

(4) As regards correspondence of texts. And S. Clem. ad Cor. xiv., here more serious objections against the Revised XXXVII. XLIII. Version arise. In accordance with the trans- S. Ign. ad Rom. ix. lation hitherto adopted by scholars, the superscription of the Encyclical Letter corresponds

Metropolitans:
Tait,
Thomson.

exactly with the description of its contents when they were afterwards delivered by St. Paul, Timothy, and Silas, to the cities. But this is quite the reverse with the revisers' translation. For according to the translation hitherto adopted by approved scholars, the Apostles and Presbyters superscribed the letter; and its contents are afterwards described as the Decrees "ordained by the Apostles and Presby-"ters" [Acts xvi. 4]. But according to the translation of the English Company of Revisers two difficulties are introduced: (1) the Presbyters did not superscribe the letter, though the Presbyters afterwards are specially named as among those who decreed its contents; (2) and, on the other hand, the "elder brethren" did superscribe the letter, though no elder brethren afterwards appear in the description when its contents were delivered to the cities. And what is more strange still is this, that the revisers' rendering of this text, Acts xv. 23, excluding Presbyters, is diametrically contradicted by their own translation of Acts xxi. 25, where we are informed that the Presbyters were among those who "*wrote*" the judgment of the Apostolic Council of Jerusalem.

(5) And, lastly, as regards history. The revisers have here introduced "elder brethren," i.e. in plain English, Lay Elders as authoritative members of the Apostolic Council. But it is a grave question whether the revisers could

discover any precedent for such introduction in examples derived from Jerusalem, Alexandria, Antioch, Ephesus, the island of Crete, or indeed from any other part of the Early Church, whatever modern practice in this respect may be discovered by researches at Edinburgh or Glasgow. *[margin: Sovereign: Q. Victoria. 1865–1874.]*

It is satisfactory to reflect that the American Company of Revisers repudiate this excursion of the English Company, as may be seen recorded at p. 559 of the Revised New Testament. And the members of the York Convocation may at all events derive some consolation from the reflection that they certainly are free from any responsibility in this matter, as having declined to join with the Canterbury Synod in the original enterprize for a revision of the English translation of the Bible. At any rate, if Lay Elders were ever authoritative members of Church Councils, I fear that the main bulk of the contents of the volume now in the reader's hands must be condemned as misleading, and the principles maintained in it as wholly false.

VIII.

CONVOCATIONS CONVENED 1874, DISSOLVED 1880.

On March 6, 1874, the ninth Convocation of Queen Victoria's reign assembled at St. Paul's Cathedral, under the presidency of Archbishop *[margin: Canterbury. Chron. Conv. ix. Vict. Reg. pp. 14–25.]*

Metropolitans: Tait, Thomson.

Tait. The Latin Litany was said by Dr. James Russell Woodford, Bishop of Ely, the junior Bishop present. The anthem, "O pray for "the peace of Jerusalem," having been sung, the Dean of Ely, Dr. C. Merivale, preached the Latin sermon, on the text, "Then they that "feared the Lord spake often one to another" [Mal. iii. 16]. The "Gloria in Excelsis" having been sung at the end of the sermon, and the usual formalities in the Chapter House having been gone through, the Clergy, under the direction of the Very Rev. R. W. Church, Dean of St. Paul's, returned to the chapel at the north-west end of the Cathedral, and there unanimously elected for the fourth time as their Prolocutor the Venerable Edward Bickersteth, D.D., Archdeacon of Buckingham.

This Synod held groups of sessions in March, April, May, and July, 1874; in April, June, and July, 1875; in February, March, and July, 1876; in April and July, 1877; in February and May, 1878; in February, June, and July, 1879; and was dissolved on March 24, 1880.

Among the events of interest which occurred during this Convocation, the principal ones were as follows:—

Chron. Conv. ix. Vict. Reg. Ann. 1876, p. 3.

In 1876 the practice was first introduced of celebrating the Holy Communion in Westminster Abbey, on the first assembly of the members there for a group of sessions.

During this Convocation the Venerable Edward Bickersteth, Archdeacon of Buckingham, who had four times been elected Prolocutor, was promoted to the Deanery of Lichfield, an address of both Houses having been presented to the Crown requesting that his great services might receive some special acknowledgement. Had this Prolocutor's advancement been a still higher one it would have been well deserved by his diligent and useful labours in guiding for so long a time, and so successfully, the course of the Lower House of Convocation; but happily for its best interests it did not at this time lose from the helm the advantage of his skilful and experienced hands. *Sovereign: Q. Victoria. 1874–1880.*

In one of the earliest sessions, May 8, 1874, of this Convocation, a motion was made by one of the Clergy Proctors for the Diocese of Hereford, and seconded by the Archdeacon of Ely, which inaugurated an enterprize entailing much labour and research, but which, it may be hoped, will produce most beneficial results. This motion was—"That the President be requested to "direct the appointment of a Committee of this" [the Lower] "House, with instructions to prepare "a Manual of Private Prayers for members of the "Church of England," &c. The motion was carried unanimously. Consequently, the President directed the appointment of such a Committee, and the duty was committed to the "Committee *Manuals of Private Prayer.* *Chron. Conv. ix. Vict. Reg. p. 287.*

Metropolitans:
Tait,
Thomson.

"on the Third Service" of preparing such a Manual. This Committee has given long and diligent labour to the subject, and has enlarged on the original intention by compiling three Manuals for private devotion. The supply of such Manuals, should they hereafter be authorized by the Canterbury Synod, will, by God's blessing, prove a comfort and a help to many devoted sons and daughters of the Church of England. The results of the labours of this Committee shall be hereafter stated in their proper place.

A Form for a Third Service to be used at Evensong, Forms of Prayer for Seamen in Danger and of Thanksgiving after Dangers Past, and a Form of Service for Intercession on establishing Missions, were prepared in this Convocation.

Summary of Debates.

Many important debates took place on the reform of Convocation; on Ecclesiastical Appeals, so unfortunately decided by a tribunal unqualified for the purpose—the Judicial Committee of Privy Council; on a second forthcoming Pan-Anglican Synod; on the Laws of Burial, a subject then much discussed, as an Act of Parliament was passed at this time admitting Nonconformist ministrations into churchyards; and on Clergy Discipline. There were also most interesting discussions and reports presented on inter-communion with the Orthodox Church of the East, communications having been thence received, among which was a most kindly letter from the Patriarch of Constantinople to the Archbishop of Canterbury offering the use of cœmeteries for the interment of such of our countrymen as might die within the jurisdiction of himself or of the Bishops in his Patriarchate, and adding that all necessary ornaments and accessories needful for funerals should be supplied.

<small>Sovereign: Q. Victoria. 1874–1880.</small>

There was also in this Convocation much discussion on the Public Worship Regulation Bill, a measure most unhappily introduced into the House of Lords, and carried through Parliament, notwithstanding the most earnest and constant protests against it in the Lower House of Convocation, and also in the Upper House, eloquently urged by the late revered and learned Bishop Wordsworth of Lincoln. These protests were unavailing, notwithstanding their reasonableness. And it is certain that many of those who supported the measure in Parliament are now heartily ashamed of that performance, and are well satisfied that a more unwise and mischievous act of legislation has seldom been perpetrated.

<small>Public Worship Regulation Act.</small>

The intention of the Act was to repress excess of ritual; but it was so unwisely framed, without the least regard either to Constitutional or Ecclesiastical principles, that while seeking to obtain one object it produced results wholly different and most disastrous. By its heedless provisions, (1) the Crown was, under

Metropolitans:
Tait,
Thomson.

certain circumstances, empowered to appoint a single judge to preside in the Metropolitan Courts of both Provinces. But how a judge appointed by Secular authority was to adjudge and execute Spiritual penalties, such, for instance, as suspension from sacred offices, or excommunication, and the like, has never to this hour been explained, nor can it be. (2) This Act robbed each Metropolitan, under all circumstances, of half of his prerogative of appointing his own Provincial Judge, for both Metropolitans were compelled to appoint the same person, and neither could make such appointment without the other's consent. (3) This Act robbed every Diocesan Bishop in England of the right to have questions of ritual, arising within his Diocese, adjudicated in his own Consistory Court, unless both parties in the case assented. Thus was this solœcism in jurisprudence introduced, that the proper jurisdiction could be ousted at the will either of the accuser or the accused in a case. (4) Lastly, the whole Clergy of England were by this Act subordinated to a new jurisdiction, in the person of a single judge appointed under the Statute, who had never had the least experience in Ecclesiastical law, but only in a Court [the Divorce Court] established on principles directly opposed to the Word of God.

What made the matter worse was this:

Some years before, a joint Committee of both Houses of the Convocation of Canterbury had elaborated to the minutest details a scheme of Clergy discipline with a view to legislation. That Committee contained the late Dr. Henry Philpotts, Bishop of Exeter, the late Archdeacon James Randall, who was bred to the Bar and was a most acute and learned lawyer, the late Chancellor Massingberd, with some others quite capable of giving help in such an undertaking. This Committee reported, and twice their report was earnestly pressed on the Upper House by the Lower, with requests that measures might be taken for giving it effect. But all to no purpose. These requests were completely ignored, and a Bill wholly and diametrically opposed to the principles of the report was brought into the House of Lords, hurried with the most indecent haste through the Commons, and was enacted, having as its title The Public Worship Regulation Act. Its almost immediate effects were that three Clergymen of unblemished character were incarcerated within the walls respectively of Chester, Warwick, and Horsemonger-lane gaols. And should this Act be allowed to remain on the Statute Book even more disastrous results may be expected to ensue, not merely entailing sufferings on individuals, but calculated to sap the very foundations of all Church Government.

Sovereign:
Q. Victoria.
1874–
1880.

Metropolitans: Tait, Thomson.

A Crown Office excursion.

Chron. Conv. ix. Vict. Reg. pp. 298–30.

The business, however, which engrossed the largest amount of attention in this Convocation was the Revision of the Rubrics. Considerable progress in this work had been made in the last Convocation before its dissolution in 1874. But the work not having been completed, a fresh Royal Letter of Business was now sent to request that the rubrics, as recommended in the Fourth and final Report of the Ritual Commissioners, should be considered by the Synod. Again, as before, with this "Letter of Business" from the Crown came also a "Royal Licence." For what purpose it was sent no seer could divine, unless, perchance, some fees for drawing it may accrue in some quarters. If this be so, it can only be said that the money was very ill earned. For the Licence not only was not required, but even if required would have been most improperly drawn for any purpose whatsoever. There certainly does seem a Nemesis of fate which is ever dogging the steps of the learned profession, and misleading its members into error when they approach the Ecclesiastical region. To say nothing of the Ecclesiastical judgments of the Judicial Committee of Privy Council, here is the third labyrinth of error in which, within a very few years, the Crown Office has lost itself when approaching Convocation.

Revision of Rubrics.

However, the Royal Letter of Business having

been received, requesting a revision of the rubrics, this Synod set itself industriously to work on the matter. The labours of the last Convocation in the matter were most carefully revised, the assistance of the York Convocation was invoked, and by means of Committees of the Synods of both Provinces constant communications on the subject were kept up.

Sovereign: Q.Victoria. 1874–1880.

The two Houses of the Canterbury Convocation, in united Synod [July 19 and 20, 1876; and on July 1, 1879], discussed in common, and by common voting settled the rubrics for the Prayer Book; and finally the whole work being completed, the official return was made to the Crown, signed by the Archbishop and Prolocutor, July 1, 1879.

Chron. Conv. ix. Vict. Reg. An. 1876, pp.376–389, 406–419

If this revision of the rubrics, first drafted in the Fourth and final Report of the Ritual Commissioners, as subsequently reviewed and improved by the two Convocations, should be authorized by Statute, a great boon would be conferred on the Church of England. Authorization by Statute is needed, because as the Prayer Book itself is an integral part of the present Act of Uniformity [13 & 14 Car. II. 4], its rubrics cannot be constitutionally altered without a relaxation for this purpose of that Act. That a great boon would accrue by the adoption of these revised rubrics might be shewn by many instances where the old rubrics were either obscure or inconvenient, but have now been

Metropolitans: Tait, Thomson.

Important improvement of a rubric in the Communion Service.

either elucidated or rendered more suitable for the direction of public worship.

One instance alone shall here be specified. It touches the vital principles of Christian service, and may serve to shew how beneficial this revision might prove if the whole were ultimately carried out. By the present rubrics, when there is no Celebration it is ordered that the Communion Office shall end with the Prayer for the Church Militant, a Collect, and the Blessing. And so the congregation in many churches departs after the Prayer for the Church Militant. But when there is a Celebration, no particular point in the service is defined for the departure of those who do not intend to communicate. Consequently, following the practice to which they are accustomed when there is no Celebration, they abide in the church till after the Prayer for the Church Militant has been read, and then depart. But be it remembered, that the Elements are placed on the Altar before the Prayer for the Church Militant. And it is against the fundamental principles of Divine Service that any departure should take place after that part of the Office. This may be learnt from all the Ancient Liturgies, from St. James's, St. Mark's, the Clementine, St. Chrysostom's, and St. Basil's. There are two distinctly defined proceedings in the Old Liturgies, the "Little Entrance" and the "Great Entrance." The "Little Entrance" was when the Priest first went up with the books to the Altar; the "Great Entrance" when he subsequently placed the Elements there. Now between the "Little" and the "Great Entrance" pauses in all the Liturgies were prescribed for departure of such as were about to leave without participation, and the Deacon rose up and bid them depart. But in no case was there ever a departure after the "Great Entrance" had been accomplished. Indeed, over and above all ancient precedent, which looks but one way, there is much indecency involved in the bustle and noise of a departing congregation, after the most solemn part of the service has been begun. This matter was anxiously discussed both in Committee and in the Lower House, and a rubric was remodelled authorizing a pause for departure immediately after the Offertory Sentences and before the Oblation of the Elements, i.e. the "Great Entrance" of the Early Church. This is one instance, given merely as a specimen, in which the revised rubrics would secure a real advantage if adopted. <small>Sovereign: Q. Victoria. 1874–1880.</small>

Difficulties doubtless lie in the way of obtaining parliamentary sanction to a revision of rubrics. But in this Convocation a Bill was drafted by which it was thought that the end might be accomplished. The principles of that proposed measure are as follows: (1) That the Convocations of Canterbury and York should <small>Measure suggested for obtaining Ecclesiastical legislation in Parliament.</small>

Metropolitans: Tait, Thomson.

approve of proposed alterations; (2) that a scheme of those alterations should be laid before the Crown in Council, (3) and subsequently before Parliament; (4) that if no address in opposition to the scheme should be presented by either House of Parliament within forty days, then that an Order in Council should be made giving such scheme legal validity.

York.

The sessions of the York Convocation convened in 1874 and dissolved in 1880 were held under the presidency of the Metropolitan, Dr. William Thomson, the Honourable and Very Rev. Augustus Duncombe being again elected Prolocutor.

Private Collections.

This Convocation, being again invited by the Crown to revise the rubrics, appointed a Committee on the subject, and actively engaged in that work. The Northern Synod did not in this matter conclude on a joint report with the Southern Convocation, but made its own revision of rubrics, which was completed August 1, 1879, and made its separate report to the Crown on the 19th of November in that year; the Canterbury report on the same subject having been officially signed, as above said, by the Archbishop and Prolocutor, on July 1, 1879.

Supra, p. 310.

IX.

CONVOCATIONS CONVENED 1880.

Concurrently with a new Parliament a newly-elected Convocation of Canterbury assembled at St. Paul's Cathedral on April 30, 1880, under the presidency of Archbishop Tait. Dr. William Dalrymple Maclagan, Bishop of Lichfield, as junior Bishop [the Bishop of Salisbury, Precentor of the Province, being absent], said the Latin Litany in monotone, kneeling at a faldstool in the choir. After the Litany was ended, the choir sang the hymn—

" Veni Sancte Spiritus,
" Et emitte cœlitùs,
    "Lucis tuæ radium"—

as an anthem, in the place where it had previously been the practice to sing the anthem, " O pray " for the peace of Jerusalem." After which a most eloquent and polished Latin sermon was preached by the Ven. Edward Balston, D.D., formerly Head Master of Eton, now Archdeacon of Derby, who took for his text, " For where two or three are gathered together in My Name, there am I in the midst of them " [St. Matt. xviii. 20]. After the sermon the " Gloria in Excelsis," from a

Sovereign:
Q. Victoria.
1880–1885.

Canterbury.

Chron. Conv. x.
Vict. Reg.
in loc.

<small>Metropolitans:
Benson,
Thomson.</small>

Mass of Weber's, was sung by the choir, and the Archbishop then pronounced the Benediction. The usual formalities having subsequently been gone through in the Chapter House, the Lower Clergy assembled, under the presidency of the Very Rev. R. W. Church, Dean of St. Paul's, in the chapel at the north-west end of the Cathedral, for the election of a Prolocutor. The late Prolocutor, Dr. Edward Bickersteth, Dean of Lichfield, having declined to be again nominated, the choice of the Clergy unanimously fell on Lord Alwyne Compton, D.D., Dean of Worcester, who is eminently qualified for the office, both by his great abilities and by his intimate acquaintance with the antecedents of our Provincial Synods.

Groups of sessions of this Synod were held in June and July, 1880; in May and July, 1881; in February and May, 1882; in April and July, 1883; in February, May, and July, 1884.

<small>Accession of Dr. Benson to the See of Canterbury.</small>

During the existence of this Convocation the death of Archbishop Tait occurred. His successor in the See of Canterbury was Dr. Benson, first Bishop of Truro, who presided over the Canterbury Synod on April 10, 1883, for the first time,

<small>Chron. Conv. x. Vict. Reg. in loc.</small>

when his Grace was Celebrant at the Holy Communion in King Henry the VIIth's Chapel in Westminster Abbey.

The revision of the rubrics, which occupied the attention of the two last Convocations, having been now completed, and the result having been reported to the Crown, no Letter of Business was addressed to this Convocation, so that all matters discussed by it were inaugurated in the Synod itself. The most interesting and important discussions in this Convocation related to the following subjects: Intercommunion with the Eastern Orthodox Churches—Diocesan Conferences—Reform of Convocation—the Establishment of a Board of Missions—the Connexion of Church and State as affecting Ecclesiastical Judicature and Clergy Discipline—the Marriage Laws—the Contagious Diseases Acts—and to the proposition for establishing a Provincial House of Laymen to co-operate with the Canterbury Convocation. *[margin: Sovereign: Q. Victoria. 1880–1885.]*

An "Articulus Cleri" was also sent to the Upper House from the Lower, requesting their Lordships to take such steps as they might think fit for allaying the trouble which had been caused in some minds by an absurd judgment which had been lately delivered by the Judicial Committee of Privy Council, the Final Court of Ecclesiastical Appeal. That tribunal was so slenderly informed in matter of fact, and indulged itself in language so rambling, as to pronounce solemnly that judgments of Courts, including, of course, its own, were "STANDARDS "OF FAITH AND DOCTRINE ADOPTED BY THE "CHURCH OF ENGLAND." Such a preposterous *[margin: Amazing announcement made by the Judicial Committee of Privy Council.]* *[margin: Merriman v. Williams.]*

claim and such puerile self-assertion is rather calculated to excite ridicule than cause trouble to anyone. Still it was well that such hallucinations of brain, confusion of thought, and prostitution of language—especially as this language was adopted by exalted authorities in the learned profession—should not pass unrebuked.

Metropolitans: Benson, Thomson.

Most interesting discussions also took place upon the Report of the Royal Commissioners on Ecclesiastical Courts. The Lower House, though generally approving of that Report, demurred, as might be expected, to the following marvellous proposition—that the Final Court of Ecclesiastical Appeal should consist of five Lay Judges, but that they should not in a Spiritual case be bound to consult any Spiritual authority unless one of themselves desired it. This the Lower House thought no sufficient guarantee for such necessary instruction, and decided that they could not acquiesce in such a proposition. The Upper House resolved that it would be "desirable" that the Court should refer Spiritual questions for advice to the Bishops of the Province in which the cause arose, or to the Bishops of both Provinces. But the Lower House considered the word "desirable" too feeble a form of expression under the circumstances. And this decision of the Lower House was certainly reasonable enough.

Ecclesiastical Courts' Commissioners' Report.

Vid. Official Year-Book of the Church of England, 1883, p. 339.

Some important Acts of this Convocation have been the compilation by the Upper House of a

Manuals of Private Prayer.

"Manual of Family Prayer;" and by the Lower House of a "Form of Prayer for Rogation Days," and of a "Manual of Private Prayer for Working "Men," to be used twice daily. The Lower House has also sanctioned a second "Manual of Private "Prayer," to be used twice a-day, for those who do not live by the labour of their hands. And, further, for the more devout members of the English Church a "Manual of Private Prayer" is fully drafted for seven hours' devotions in the course of night and day: i.e. (1) In the night watches; (2) on rising up; (3) at the third hour; (4) at the sixth hour; (5) at the ninth hour; (6) at eventide; (7) on lying down to rest. By the Lower House this Manual has not yet [1885] been finally adopted, but is still under the consideration of the Committee charged with its completion. Much of the material of which it is constructed is derived from writers of the early ages of Christianity, and from the Liturgies of the Eastern Church, the spiritual mother of the Church of England. The original draft of this Manual has been printed in very splendid form on large paper at the Oxford University Press, and a copy in appropriate binding was, by the liberality of the publisher, presented to every member of the last Convocations of the two Provinces. It is as chaste a specimen of typography and binding as can be imagined.

Sovereign:
Q. Victoria.
1880–1885.

Metropolitans: Benson, Thomson. York.

The York Convocation convened concurrently with the last-mentioned Synod of Canterbury has continued to hold its sessions under the same President, the Most Rev. William Thomson, the Metropolitan, who has presided over its deliberations for sixteen years. But three Prolocutors have presided in the Lower House since the convention of this Convocation in 1880, viz. the Hon. and Very Rev. Augustus Duncombe, removed by death; the Very Rev. W. B. M. Cowie, formerly Dean of Manchester, now transferred to Exeter; and the Very Rev. Arthur Perceval Purey-Cust, Dean of York, who at present occupies the Prolocutor's chair.

Summary of proceedings.

Official Year-Book of the Church of England, 1883, pp. 352-355.

The subjects of chief interest which have occupied the attention of this Northern Synod have been—Marriage with a Deceased Wife's Sister, the Imprisonment of the Rev. S. F. Green, Rights of Patronage, Ecclesiastical Courts, Clergy Discipline and Episcopal Authority, and the wonderful proposition of the Ecclesiastical Courts' Commissioners, that in matters of faith and doctrine, as well as discipline, the whole of the Clergy of England, including Metropolitans and Bishops, should be all subordinated to the judgment of five Lay Judges taken in rotation from the Chancery and Common Law divisions of the High Court of Justice; and that too without any necessary reference on their part to any Spiritual authority whatsoever.

PART V.

PRESENT REGULATIONS AND METHODS OF PROCEEDING IN THE CONVOCATIONS OF CANTERBURY AND YORK, THE PROVINCIAL SYNODS OF THE CHURCH OF ENGLAND.

I.

CONVOCATIONS IN CONNEXION WITH THE CROWN.

THE Convocations are brought into connexion with the Crown by (1) a "Writ for Convention," (2) a "Letter of Business," (3) a "Licence" to enact Canons, (4) a Writ of Prorogation, (5) a "Writ of Dissolution."

(1) A "Writ for Convention" always issues from the Crown Office acourse with the Writs for assembling Parliament. This instrument is directed to each Metropolitan, "commanding and "entreating" him to convene the members of his Provincial Synod "to treat of, agree to, and "conclude upon" affairs concerning "Us" [the Sovereign], "the security and defence of the Church "of England, and the peace and tranquillity,

Royal Writ for Convention.

Append. A. I. II.

"public good and defence of Our kingdom." Before the year 1534, each Metropolitan could convene his Provincial Synod at any time he thought fit. The Sovereign sometimes requested him to do so, but only on occasion. Since that date, by the Statute 25 Hen. VIII. 19, such Writ is necessary; but it is always issued with the parliamentary Writs, and has become part of the customary law of England, and so long as Parliament sits the Metropolitans can convene their Convocations as often as they please.

<small>Letter of Business. Append. C. I. II. III.</small> (2) A "Letter of Business" is an instrument directed by the Sovereign to either Metropolitan, requesting him to direct the attention of his Synod to any particular subject. This is an instrument no way necessary for enabling the Convocation to proceed to business, and is only issued as occasion may arise.

<small>Licence to enact Canons. Append. D. II. IV.</small> (3) A "Licence" is only required for one particular purpose—to enable the Synod to "enact, promulge, and execute" a Canon. This instrument is only issued on occasion, and is no way necessary for any other purpose than as specified above.

<small>Writ of Prorogation. Append. E. I. II.</small> (4) A "Writ of Prorogation." This issues at the same time as the Writs for the prorogation of Parliament, and when Parliament is prorogued the Convocations are generally prorogued also; though not necessarily so, as was decided in Charles the First's time—a matter previously

recorded [pp. 167—169]. But it here must be observed that though Parliamentary Committees do not meet out of session, Committees of Convocations, who really do the work of those assemblies, by custom meet at any time, the respective Chairmen of those Committees convening them at any time of the year at their discretion.

(5) A "Writ of Dissolution," by which when any Parliament is dissolved the concurrent Convocations are dissolved also, and a new election of Proctors takes place. *Writ of Dissolution. Append. F. I. II.*

There is also another instrument, which seems to have been introduced without any warranty of law or reason—that is, one which intimates the Royal "Assent" after a Canon has been enacted—and therefore it is not included in the above list, as it seems not to agree with the Statute governing the case, and to have been only a gratuitous introduction of a useless proceeding invented by some legal ingenuity for adding a needless flourish of Secular authority, or for increasing official fees. The Sovereign, by the hypothesis, has already been made cognizant of all the contents of the Canon or Canons proposed, and has issued a "Licence" "to enact;" what possible need can there be then for subsequent assent to that which the Crown has previously sanctioned? This matter, however, has been explained more fully in former pages [pp. 146-7; and see Appendix D. II. ad fin.]. *25 Hen. VIII. 19.*

II.

PROCEEDINGS BEFORE ASSEMBLY.

<small>Append.
B. II.</small>

<small>Supra,
pp. 29-30.</small>

<small>Append.
B. III.</small>

<small>Append.
B. IV.</small>

<small>A peculiarity of English Provincial Synods.</small>

Upon the receipt of the Writ first above mentioned, each Metropolitan directs his mandate [in Canterbury through the Bishop of London, as Dean of the Province] to the several Bishops within his jurisdiction, warning them to attend with the Clergy of their Diocese, as formerly detailed, at a specified time and place. Each Bishop then cites the Dean and Archdeacons of his Diocese personally, and directs his Cathedral Chapter to elect one Proctor, and the Clergy of his Diocese [or of each Archdeaconry in the case of a York Diocese] to elect two Proctors to attend the Provincial Synod. The Chapter and the beneficed Clergy of the Diocese then respectively elect by suffrage their Proctors.

This method of appointing by election Presbyters as members of Provincial Synods is a practice which appears to be peculiar to England. In early times the Presbyters who attended Church Councils were appointed by their respective Bishops. Thus in the "Tractoriæ" or letter of summons directed to Chrestus, Bishop of Syracuse, and warning him to attend the

Council of Arles [A.D. 314], he is commanded to bring with him "two of the second throne," i.e. two Presbyters. And this appears to have been the ancient practice. But in England Proctors are elected by prescribed constituencies. When this practice first arose is a question not easy of solution. But at any rate such Clergy Proctors are mentioned in a mandate of Archbishop Kilwarby summoning his Provincial Synod in 1277; in a Canon, as quoted by Lyndwood, and attributed to the Council of Reading in 1279; and also in a mandate of Archbishop Peccham, which convened his Provincial Synod at the New Temple, London, in 1283. One thing, however, is clear—the right of Presbyters to have seats in Provincial Synods is certain, and may be proved from unquestionable evidence derived from all ages of the Church. The Fourth Canon of the Fourth Council of Toledo [above quoted at length, pp. 14–16] is conclusive on this point, and any pretences which have been made to deny them that right, even by a Lord Chancellor, are absolutely fallacious. In fact, the evidence on this point is overwhelming.

<small>Euseb. Eccl. Hist. Lib. x. c. 5. p. 392 D.</small>

<small>Reg. Giff. Vigorn. fol. 71. Synod. Prov. Pt. III. p. 25. Conc. M. B. ii. p. 93.</small>

As soon as the Proctors for the Clergy are elected, they enjoy in common with all the other members of the two Convocations the privilege of freedom from liability to arrest on civil process. The origin of this privilege is an illustration of the truth that considerable results

<small>Memorandum directed by Lord Selborne to Archb. Tait and Right Hon. W. E. Gladstone. Privilege of freedom from arrest pertaining to members of Convocation. Coke, Inst. iv. 323.</small>

sometimes follow from seemingly inconsiderable causes.

The privilege thus originated. In the fifth year of King Henry IV., Thomas Broke, Knight of the Shire for the County of Somerset, on going to Parliament took along with him Richard Chedder as an attendant. During the session of Parliament one John Salvage assaulted this Chedder, and this conduct seems to have been so distasteful to the members of our Legislature, being, one must think, somewhat jealous of their own dignity, that a Statute [5 Hen. IV. 6] was passed by which it was enacted that Salvage was to appear in the King's Bench, and if found guilty of the assault charged was to pay double damages, and make fine and ransom at the King's will. And further, that the same penalties might overtake any future offenders in like case, who should molest a member of the Legislature or his attendants during the session of Parliament, the Statute concludes with these words: "Moreover, it is accorded in the "same Parliament that likewise it be done in "time to come in like case." Upon this footstone was laid the parliamentary privilege of freedom from liability to arrest on civil process. This same privilege was subsequently extended to members of the two Convocations by the Statute 8 Hen. VI. 1, which provided that "all "the Clergy hereafter to be called to the Con-

"vocation by the King's Writ, and their servants and families, shall for ever hereafter fully use and enjoy such liberty or defence in coming, tarrying, and returning, as the great men and commonalty of the Realm of England, called or to be called to the King's Parliament, do enjoy and were wont to enjoy, or in time to come ought to enjoy." This matter is fully treated in "Coke's Inst." iv. 323.

This privilege has been frequently asserted, and on proper occasion never denied. During the sessions of the Canterbury Convocation in 1603–4, the Prolocutor, Dr. Ravis, was served with a subpœna by Harrington and Walker. On this breach of privilege by these two men, a warrant was issued against the former, and the latter was arrested by a Serjeant-at-Mace. Walker was brought before the Bishops, and sent down to beg pardon of the Prolocutor and the Lower House. As for Harrington, he was brought upon his knees for his offence before the Bishops themselves. During the sessions of the Canterbury Convocation begun Feb. 13, 1624, N.S., a subpœna was served on Mr. Murrell, Archdeacon of Lincoln; but this instrument was superseded by reason of Convocational privilege. In the York Convocation contemporaneous with the last-mentioned Synod, an application was made for the Convocational privilege in favour of Thomas Mellory, Dean

Syn. Ang. p. 61.

Conc. M. B. iv. 467.

of Chester, in order to stay some legal proceedings then pending against that gentleman. The privilege was granted, and an instrument for the purpose desired was executed, under the seal of the Metropolitan, Matthew Hutton. In 1628, the Under Sheriff of Hereford was ordered to attend, with Richard Colley, before the House of Lords, the said Colley having been illegally arrested, being the servant of a Clerk of Convocation, and so privilege having been breached. It was subsequently ordered that Dyos, the Under Sheriff, being brought up by the Serjeant-at-Arms, should submit himself to the Lower House of Convocation, and be discharged on paying his fine. During the sessions of the York Convocation which met Feb. 10, 1629, this privilege of freedom from arrest was obtained by no less than five of its members, viz. Richard Hunt, Dean of Durham; Gabriel Clerk and John Cosin, Archdeacons; W. James and Ferdinand Morecroft, Prebendaries. That this privilege was constitutionally recognized by Parliament in comparatively late times we have the evidence of a circumstance which occurred in 1702. On Nov. 18 in that year, the House of Commons addressed Queen Anne on the subject of some interference in a Worcester election, of which one Mr. Lloyd had been guilty, who was a member of Convocation. The address requested Her Majesty to order the

Attorney-General to prosecute Mr. Lloyd for his offence. But his Convocational privilege was acknowledged, inasmuch as the address specified particularly that the prosecution was to be begun after his "privilege as a member of the Lower "House of Convocation was out." On Nov. 20, the Lower House of Convocation, sensible of this proper acknowledgement, assured, through their Prolocutor and three Assessors, the Speaker of the House of Commons of the sense entertained for the regard which had been shewn to Convocational privilege. On this the Commons resolved—"That they would on all occasions "assert the just rights and privileges of the Lower "House of Convocation." Whether the same spirit has actuated every House of Commons since the date above given may be a query.

III.

PROCEEDINGS ON ASSEMBLY.

It will henceforth be sufficient to record the mode of proceeding in the Province of Canterbury, as the reader will thus gain a sufficient idea of the methods followed in the York Province, the only difference worth recording between the two being that the separation into two Houses has been the general rule in the Canterbury Synod, the exception in that of York.

The Canterbury Provincial Synod has been for many years summoned to meet first at St. Paul's Cathedral by the Archbishop's mandate. On their assembly the proceedings are as follows: The members, vested in their proper habiliments, pass from the Chapter House in formal procession to the choir of the Cathedral. A Latin Litany is said by the junior Bishop, and an anthem sung by the Choir. A Latin sermon is then delivered by a preacher appointed by the Archbishop. After the sermon the "Gloria in Excelsis" or a hymn is sung and the Benediction pronounced. The Synod then adjourns to the Chapter House, and after some formal business has been transacted the members of the Lower House retire to one of the side chapels for the election of a Prolocutor. This divine, on being presented to the Archbishop at a subsequent session, if approved of by him [and there is no instance, so far as the writer is aware, of disapproval], becomes Chairman of the Lower House. He not only there presides, but is the channel of communication between the two Houses, carrying messages from the Upper to the Lower, and reporting the proceedings of the Lower to the Upper. After the Clergy have retired for the election of their Prolocutor, the Synod is prorogued to some future, generally not distant, day.

IV.

PROCEEDINGS IN SESSION.

Through many ages the subsequent sessions were usually held at St. Paul's, until Oliver Cromwell's cavalry defaced the goodly Chapter House there, though sometimes at Westminster. Now the Synod is on the occasion of its first assembly at St. Paul's always prorogued to some future day at Westminster Abbey. Of late, on assembling there, Holy Communion has been administered to the members in Henry VII.'s Chapel, and at the conclusion of the service the whole Synod meets in the Jerusalem Chamber within the Abbey precincts. The Archbishop there admits the Prolocutor to his office, addresses the assembly on any subject which to him may seem expedient, and then retires with his Suffragans forming the Upper House to the Bounty Board Office in Dean's Yard, Westminster, where their sessions are held, leaving the members of the Lower House in the Jerusalem Chamber to hold their sessions either there or in the College Hall.

Separation into two Houses.

The separation of Provincial Synods respectively into two Houses does not date from any remote antiquity. It seems to have originated about the end of the fourteenth or the beginning of the fifteenth century. The practice was at first adopted only on special occasions, but in later times, at least in the Canterbury Province, has become the rule, not the exception. Indeed it is plain from the history of the earlier ages of the Church that while the "Corpus "Synodi" was in the Bishops, yet that those who were below the Episcopal order united with them in common deliberation, and on some occasions at least were on account of learning and eloquence the chief champions in debate. Striking examples of this may be found in the records of places and ages widely different. Thus at the Council of Antioch, in the third century, Malchion was chief speaker, and as Eusebius writes, " he "alone prevailed to detect the subtle-minded "man," when Paulus Samozatenus was delated for false teaching. At Nice, in the fourth century, Athanasius was chief champion of the orthodox faith. At our National Council of Whitby, in the seventh century, Wilfrid was chief speaker, and from the result appears to have been the most efficient advocate. But neither Malchion, Athanasius, or Wilfrid were Bishops on the occasions referred to.

Eccl. Hist. vii. 29.

Spelm. Conc. i. 150. Conc. M. B. i. 37.

To come much nearer to our own times, it

is to the learning and eloquence of a Presbyter in the Canterbury Synod that the Church of England is deeply indebted for the preservation of her Liturgy in its integrity. In King William the Third's reign, endeavours were made under Dutch influence, as has been before recorded, to Puritanize the English Prayer Book. It was the brilliant and touching address of Dr. Jane [then Prolocutor of the Lower House], which he wound up with the words, quoted from the Barons of old, "Nolumus leges Angliæ mu-"tari," that in great measure prevailed to sway the assembly and avert the catastrophe. *Supra, p. 247.*

When the two Houses have been thus constituted, as above mentioned, the deliberations and debates begin. It is not necessary to describe the methods of proceeding in the Upper House, as, the assembly being a small one, there is nothing very peculiar to record in their mode of conducting business. But the Lower House, constituting a much larger body, is necessarily subject to stringent rules of procedure. These are peculiar, having been traditionally handed down from earlier ages, and may thus be briefly summarized. *Proceedings in Upper House.*

At each of the sessions of the Lower House of Canterbury, which are held sometimes in the Jerusalem Chamber, sometimes in the Westminster College Hall, the Latin Litany is first read. The roll of the members is then called over— *Proceedings in Lower House.*

a process denominated "præconization"—when those present answer to their names. Except on the first day of a group of sessions, the proceedings of the previous day having been fairly transcribed are then read by the Actuary, i.e. the officer entrusted with the documents of the assembly, and by a vote of the House reduced to "Acts." But on the last day of a group of sessions this is done on the evening of the day itself. The Prolocutor then nominates some members, usually about six or eight, as his Assessors, who accompany him whenever he proceeds to the Upper House, and who are also consulted by him, if he so desires, should any doubtful question arise touching the proceedings of the assembly. Notices of motion are then given, and petitions and "gravamina" presented. As regards the presentation of a "gravamen"— a practice of the highest antiquity—it is the statement of any evil touching the Church to which the member presenting desires to call attention, and to it is usually appended a "re-"formandum," that is, a suggestion for the correction of the evil. Such a document may be dealt with in four different ways—(1) It may be signed only by the presenter, (2) or may receive the signatures of as many members as agree with it, and so in either case be carried by the Prolocutor to the Upper House; (3) or it may be referred by a vote of the House to either of the Committees who are sitting on the subject it involves; (4) or by such vote it may be discussed with a view to its being made an "Articulus Cleri," that is, an "Act" of the Lower House, and so be transmitted to the Upper. Then follow the debates arising either from messages sent from the Upper House, or upon motions after proper notice of individual members. But business sent from the Upper House always takes precedence. Each day's sitting is termed a separate session, and each day a prorogation of the whole Synod takes place in the Upper House and is formally communicated to the Lower. When the Convocation meets for several days consecutively, it is termed a group of sessions.

As regards the procedure in the York Synod there is nothing varying from the above methods which demands special notice, save that there the Houses have usually been united in session, at least of late years. And it may be a query whether Canterbury might not profitably imitate the York example in this respect by making the union of the two Houses the rule, not the exception. That the Bishops should hear the arguments of the Presbyters, and that the Presbyters should hear those of the Bishops, would seem highly desirable when common determinations have to be arrived at.

CONCLUSION.

Beyond all cavil or dispute, it may surely be affirmed, that this nation is indebted to the Convocations for the Synodical rejection of Papal Supremacy over this land; for the Synodical restoration of Communion in both kinds; for the Synodical abrogation of the cœlibacy of the Clergy; for the Article which defines the Canon of Scripture; for the Article which commends the three Creeds as the symbols of Christian faith; for the Canons which are the basis of the Code of Discipline for ministers of the Church; and for the compilation and Synodical authorization of the "Book of Common Prayer." This is the heritage which those Synods have handed down to us from of old. It is equally sure that the members of this Church are indebted to those Synods in our own times for the maintenance of the faith against false teaching; for the boon of Services for Public Prayer, and Manuals for Private Devotion provided; and also for keeping a watchful and constant supervision over all the interests of the Church of England. Such and such like are their proper duties and proper functions, and these by God's blessing we may hope and believe that they will, both now and in time to come faithfully and diligently discharge.

In conclusion, it is worthy of remark that the constitution of our Convocations or Provincial Synods, consisting of Bishops and Presbyters, without any admixture of laymen with voices decisive, is in accordance with the principle which has governed the constitution of Synods in all ages of the Church. That principle may be traced back even to Apostolic times.

The First Council of Jerusalem, recorded in the 15th chapter of the Acts of the Apostles, has always been considered in the Orthodox Church to be the true prototype and model for the constitution of such assemblies. The history, therefore, of that Apostolic Council is of the highest possible interest, and is closely applicable to the present subject.

A question had arisen in the Church at Antioch on a matter of disciplinary ritual—whether circumcision was necessary or not for Christians. For the settlement of doubts it was decided that SS. Paul and Barnabas, with others, should go up to Jerusalem "*unto* "*the Apostles and Elders*" about this question. "*The Apostles and Elders*" only assembled to consider of the matter. After discussion, St. James, Bishop of Jerusalem, and so chief of the assembly, delivered judgment. Messengers were then despatched from the whole Church of

Acts xv. 2.
Ibid. xv. 6.

Ibid. xv. 13.

Ibid. xv. 22.

Jerusalem to Antioch, bearing a letter thither containing the results of the deliberations. The superscription of the letter was that of *"the Apostles and Elders"* only, for the word *"and"* before the word *"Brethren,"* attached to the superscription in our Authorized Version, is not warranted by the most trustworthy authorities. This introduction of the word *"and"* is not supported by the Cod. Alexandrinus, Vaticanus, Ephraim Syri, Beza, or Sinaiticus: nor is it warranted by the Vulgate, nor by Irenæus "Adv. "Hær.," nor by Origen "Cont. Cels." The most reliable authorities give the superscription thus— " The Apostles and Elders, brethren, . . . send " greeting," &c., thus confining the superscription to the Apostles and Elders only. And it is further observable that when St. Paul and Silas subsequently journeyed through the cities, they delivered them "the decrees for to keep that " were ordained of *'the Apostles and Elders'* " which were at Jerusalem." Thus we see that in this Apostolic Council the question under discussion was submitted to the Apostles and Elders only, that they only came together to consider the matter, that they only signed the Encyclical Letter, and that to them only the Decrees of the Council are subsequently attributed.

As the Apostolic band was chosen by the Lord to constitute the first Order of the Ministry in His Church, so the second Order of Presbyters or Elders was inaugurated when "the Lord "appointed other seventy also and sent them "two and two before His face into every city "and place whither He Himself would come." Of these two Orders the first Apostolic Council of Jerusalem was composed; and in conformity with the example of that model Council, and in imitation of it as being the true prototype for all subsequent Synods, Church Councils have in all ages been convened consisting of the first and second Orders of the Ministry of Christ— Bishops and Presbyters. Such is the constitution of the two Convocations or Provincial Synods of the Church of England. They follow Apostolic precedent, and the example of the First Council of Jerusalem. So of this Church of England, as of Jerusalem of old, it may truly be said in the words of the Psalmist— "Her foundations are upon the holy hills." Her children may well be contented to abide by the prophetic exhortation : [St. Luke x. 1.] [Ps. lxxxvii. 1.]

> "Stand ye in the ways, and see, [Jer. vi. 16.]
> "and ask for the old paths,
> "where is the good
> "way, and walk
> "therein."

FINIS.

APPENDIX.

This Appendix contains copies of legal instruments, ancient and modern, employed in convening Convocations, in carrying on the business there transacted, in proroguing those assemblies, and in dissolving them; and also a copy of the "Submission of the Clergy," with the provisions of the Statute 25 Hen. VIII. 19 thereon founded. There is, moreover, inserted a copy of a Royal Writ of high antiquity and Constitutional interest, together with a copy of its successor, issued at the present time by the Crown, though undutifully now disregarded. Comments on some of the above instruments are added.

A.

THE ROYAL WRIT FOR CONVENING A CONVOCATION OR PROVINCIAL SYNOD.

Before the year 1534, when the Statute 25 Hen. VIII. 19 was enacted, the Provincial Synods or Convocations of the Church of England sometimes were convened at the sole motion and pleasure of the respective Metropolitans; and sometimes were convened by them after the reception of a Royal Writ, on those occasions when the Sovereign desired that some special Ecclesiastical business should be transacted.

But since the year 1534, each Metropolitan is statutably debarred from convening his Provincial Synod until he receives a Royal Writ requesting him to do so. The Metropolitan's authority for convention meanwhile is exercised in its entirety, and it is to his mandate that the returns of his suffragans are made and not to the Crown. Copies below are given of a Royal Writ preceding, and of two Writs succeeding the date above mentioned.

I.

Copy of a Royal Writ for Convention, issued by King Edward III. A.D. 1339.

["Conc. Mag. Brit." ii. 653, citing Rymer's "Fœd." v. 137.]

"Rex venerabili in Christo Patri J. eâdem gratiâ Archiepiscopo "Cantuar. totius Angliæ Primati, Salutem. Cum quædam alia et "urgentia negotia nos et statum regni nostri ac expeditionem "negotiorum nostrorum concernentia, etc. et nos in hiis vestris et "cæterorum Prælatorum et Cleri ejusdem regni consilio et auxilio "indigentes, nos de vestræ sinceritatis et benevolentiæ puritate "firmam fiduciam obtinentes, quòd tam pro defendendis et recupe- "randis coronæ nostræ regiæ juribus, quam dictæ Sanctæ Ecclesiæ "salvatione et tuitione nobis vigilantèr velitis assistere, et quantum "ad vos pertinet efficacitèr in opportunitatibus suffragari, vobis "mandamus rogantes, quatenus etc. totum Clerum vestræ Cantuar. "Provinciæ apud Londinium die Jovis proximo post festum Conver- "sionis Sancti Pauli proximè futurum Convocari faciatis. Teste "Custode Angliæ apud Langele Vicesimo Octavo die Novembris. "Per ipsum Regem et dictum Custodem."

II.

Copy of a Royal Writ for Convention, issued by King Henry VIII. A.D. 1545.

[Gibson's "Codex," App. p. 65.]

"Henricus, etc. Reverendissimo in Christo Patri Thomæ eâdem "gratiâ Cantuariensi Archiepiscopo, Totius Angliæ Primati et "Metropolitano, Salutem. Quibusdam arduis et urgentibus nego- "tiis nos securitatem et defensionem Ecclesiæ Anglicanæ ac pacem "tranquillitatem bonum publicum et defensionem Regni nostri et "subditorum nostrorum ejusdem concernen., Vobis in fide et di- "lectione, quibus nobis tenemini, rogando mandamus, quatenùs, "præmissis debito intuitu attentis et ponderatis, universos et singu- "los Episcopos Vestræ Provinciæ, necnon Archidiaconos Decanos "et omnes alias personas Ecclesiasticas cujuslibet Diœceseos ejus- "dem provinciæ ad comparend. coram Vobis in Ecclesiâ S. Pauli, "London: vel alibi prout melius expedire videritis, cum omni "celeritate accommodâ, modo debito, convocari faciatis ad tractand. "consentiend. et concludend. super præmissis, et aliis quæ sibi "clariùs exponentur tunc ibidem ex parte nostrâ. Et hoc, sicut "nos et statum Regni nostri ac honorem et utilitatem Ecclesiæ "prædictæ diligitis, nullatenùs omittatis. Teste me ipso apud "Westmonasterium Nono die Decembris Anno Regni nostri Tri- "cesimo Sexto."

III.

Copy of a Royal Writ for Convention, issued by Queen Victoria. A.D. 1847.

[Pearce, "Law Conv." p. 55.]

"Victoria, by the Grace of God of the United Kingdom of Great
"Britain and Ireland Queen, Defender of the Faith: To the Most
"Reverend Father in God, Our right trusty and well-beloved
"Councillor ——, by the same Grace Archbishop of Canterbury,
"Primate of all England, and Metropolitan, Greeting. By reason of
"certain difficult and urgent affairs concerning Us, the security and
"defence of the Church of England, and the peace and tranquillity,
"public good, and defence of Our Kingdom, and Our subjects of the
"same, We command you, entreating you by the faith and love
"which you owe to Us, that having in due manner considered and
"weighed the premisses, you call together with convenient speed, in
"lawful manner, all and singular the Bishops of your Province and
"Deans of your Cathedral Churches, and also the Archdeacons,
"Chapters, and Colleges, and the whole Clergy of every Diocese of
"the same Province, to appear before you in the Cathedral Church
"of S. Paul, London, on the —— day of —— next ensuing, or elsewhere,
"as it shall seem most expedient, to treat of, agree to, and conclude
"upon the premisses and other things which to them shall then at
"the same place be more clearly explained on Our behalf. And this,
"as you love Us, the state of Our Kingdom, and honour and good of
"Our aforesaid Church, by no means omit. Witness Ourself, at ——,
"the day of ——, in the —— Year of Our Reign."

A like Writ is transmitted to the Metropolitan of York.

B.

METROPOLITAN'S MANDATE, AND OTHER INSTRUMENTS FOR CONVENING A CONVOCATION OR PROVINCIAL SYNOD.

In the Province of Canterbury this Mandate is executed through the intervention of the Bishop of London, as Dean of the Province. In the Province of York the Metropolitan's Mandate is, "mutatis mutandis," sent directly to each comprovincial Bishop for execution.

I.

Copy of a Mandate for Convention, issued by Archbishop Robert Kilwarby. A.D. 1277.

[Vigorn. Reg. Giffard. Fol. 71.]

"Robertus Cantuariensis, Archiepiscopus: H. Londinensi Episcopo,
"Salutem. Meminimus in congregatione nostrâ communi dudùm

"habitâ Northamptoniæ negotia varia utilitatem pariter et honorem
"totius Ecclesiæ Anglicanæ tangentia in medio fuisse proposita, in
"quorum executione, licet viæ de communi consilio excogitatæ
"fuissent, et executores Viarum prædictarum varii deputati; quia
"tamen in quibusdam negotiis seu executionibus eorundem nobis
"adhuc exitus est incertus, quædam autem penitùs inconsummata
"existunt; emerserunt autem quædam nova, quæ ad aversionem
"nostrorum jurium, consuetudinum libertatum et grave periculum
"Ecclesiæ Anglicanæ redundant; Fraternitati vestræ per præsentia
"Scripta Mandamus, quatenus omnes fratres et coepiscopos seu
"Suffraganeos nostros auctoritate nostrâ faciatis peremptoriè per
"vestras literas evocari; quatenùs nobiscum in civit. London in
"Crastino B. Hylarii in propriis personis conveniant, unâ cum
"aliquibus personis majoribus de suis Capitulis, et locorum Archi-
"diaconis, et Procuratoribus totius Cleri Diocæsium singularum,
"nobiscum super negotiis memoratis, tum prædictis quam instan-
"tibus efficaciùs tractaturi; ut eisdem, eorundem communi mediante
"consilio, finis imponatur laudabilis, et ut itâ incerta certitudinem
"et inconsummata consummationem et emergentia nova consilium
"debitum sortiantur. Qualitèr autèm hoc nostrum mandatum
"fueritis executi nos per vestras literas patentes harum seriem
"continentes certificare curetis die et loco prædictis.

"Datum apud Mechlindon XVI. Kal. Decembris,
A. D. MCCLXXVII."

II.

Copy of a Mandate for Convention, issued by Archbishop Howley. A.D. 1847.

[Pearce, "Law of Convocation," p. 59.]

"William, by Divine Providence Archbishop of Canterbury,
"Primate of all England, and Metropolitan: To our Brother, the
"Right Reverend Father in God, Charles James, by the same
"Providence Lord Bishop of London, Health and brotherly love in
"the Lord. We have lately humbly received, with that reverence,
"obedience, and submission which became us, the Writ of Her Most
"Gracious Majesty our Sovereign Lady." [The Royal Writ given above, A. III., is here recited in full.] "Wherefore we recommend
"to and require you, our said Brother, that you peremptorily cite all
"and singular the Bishops Suffragans of our Cathedral Church of
"Christ, Canterbury, constituted within the Province of Canterbury;
"and will that by them you peremptorily cite and monish the Deans
"of the Cathedral and Collegiate Churches, and their several
"Chapters, and the Archdeacons and other Dignitaries of Churches,
"exempt and not exempt, personally, and each Chapter of the
"Cathedral and Collegiate Churches by one, and the Clergy of

"every Diocese within our Province aforesaid by two sufficient
" Proctors, to appear before us, or our substitute or Commissary in
"this behalf, if we should happen to be hindered, in the Chapter
" House of the Cathedral Church of Saint Paul, London, on
" Wednesday the Twenty-second day of September next ensuing the
" date of these presents, with continuations and prorogations of days
" then following, and places, if it be necessary, to be done herein;
" to treat upon arduous and weighty affairs which shall concern the
" state and welfare, public good and defence of this Kingdom and
" the subjects thereof, to be then and there seriously laid before
"them, and to give them their good counsel and assistance in the
" said affairs, and to consent to such things as shall appear to be
" wholesomely ordered and appointed by their common advisement
" for the honour of God and the good of the Church, and further,
" to do and receive what shall be lawful, and the nature and quality
" of this affair demand and require of them; but that you, our Right
" Reverend Brother, cause the said Mandate to be executed in all
" things as far as it concerns you and the Chapter of your Cathedral
" Church and the City and Diocese of London, and that you obey
" the same in all things with effect. Moreover, we do cite you by
" these presents to appear on the said day and place before us, or
" one or more of our Substitutes or Commissaries in this behalf,
" together with others, our Right Reverend Brethren, Bishops of our
" said Province of Canterbury, to treat upon the said affairs before
" mentioned, and also to do and receive what shall be lawful and
" shall concern your Lordship, as above is contained. We will and
" require you, moreover, to intimate and publish, or cause to be inti-
" mated and published, to the Bishops, Deans, Archdeacons, and
" others, the before-mentioned Dignitaries of the Churches, that
" you will not and do not intend to excuse them at this time from
" appearing in this affair of Convocation and Congregation, to be
" held, by God's help, the day and place aforesaid, unless for some
" necessary cause to be then and there alleged and propounded, and
" by us to be approved, but will canonically punish the contumacies
" of such as shall be absent: And furthermore, we do enjoin
" and require you as before, that you will enjoin or cause to be
" enjoined all and singular the Bishops Suffragans of our Province
" of Canterbury, that each of them do, under their Seal of what they
" shall do, as far as it concerns them from the day of the reception
" of these presents, certify us, or one or more of our substitutes or
" Commissaries, the said day and place, by their Letters Patent
"containing the names and surnames of all and singular the
" persons by them respectively cited: And what you shall do in the
"premisses, you shall take care duly to certify us, or our substitute
" or Commissary, on the same day and place, by your Letters Patent
" containing the tenour of these presents, together with the names of
" all and singular the Bishops of our Province of Canterbury, the
" Deans, Archdeacons, and other the Dignitaries of your Diocese

"in a separate Schedule to be annexed to your Return. In Witness
"whereof we have caused our Archiepiscopal Seal to be hereunto
"affixed. Given at Lambeth Palace, the Thirteenth day of August,
"in the Year of our Lord 1847, and in the Nineteenth Year of our
"Translation."

III.

Copy of Citation to a Provincial Synod, directed by the Bishop of London, as Provincial Dean, to the Suffragan Bishops of the Province of Canterbury.

[Pearce, "Law of Convocation," p. 62.]

"Charles James, by Divine Providence Bishop of London: To
" our brother the Right Reverend Father in God ——, by the same
" permission Bishop of ——, Health and brotherly love in the Lord.
" By virtue and authority of certain Letters of the Most Reverend
" Father in God John Bird, by Divine Providence Archbishop of
" Canterbury, Primate and Metropolitan of all England, lately re-
" ceived by us with all due reverence, of the tenour following, to
" wit."

[Here follows the Archbishop's Mandate, supra No. II. verbatim.]

"We, by the tenour of these presents, cite and peremptorily ad-
" monish you, the said Right Reverend Father, and by entreating
" do require you peremptorily to cite and admonish, or cause to be
" cited and admonished, the Dean and Chapter and the Archdeacons
" of your Cathedral Church, and other the Dignitaries of Churches
" exempt and not exempt, and the Clergy of your Diocese aforesaid,
" that you and they appear before the said Most Reverend Father or
" his Substitute or Commissary [if he should happen to be hindered],
" in the Chapter House of the Cathedral Church of Saint Paul,
" London, on —— the —— day of —— instant, with continuation and
" prorogation of days then next following, and places if it be neces-
" sary to be done herein, to treat according to the force, form, and
" effect above written, and tenour of such Letters of the said Most
" Reverend Father, and to give your and their good counsel and
" assistance upon the said affairs, and further to do and receive what
" the said Letters of the said Most Reverend Father do denote and
" require. We will and require you, moreover, that you take care
" duly to certify the said Most Reverend Father, or his Substitute
" or Commissary, what you shall do in the premisses on the said day
" and place by your Letters Patent and sealed with your Seal con-
" taining the tenour of these presents, together also with a schedule
" thereto annexed, containing the names of all and singular the
" persons cited and admonished by you or your authority. Dated at
" London, the —— day of ——, in the Year of our Lord One
" thousand eight hundred and forty-eight."

IV.

Copy of Citation to a Convocation or Provincial Synod, directed by a Diocesan Bishop to a Dean and Chapter, commanding the attendance of the Dean and one Chapter Proctor.

[Pearce, "Law of Convocation," p. 71.]

" A. B., by Divine permission Bishop of ——: To our beloved in
" Christ the Dean and Chapter of our Cathedral Church of ——,
" Health, grace, and benediction. By virtue and authority of certain
" Mandatory Letters of the Most Reverend Father in God ——, by
" Divine Providence Archbishop of Canterbury, Primate of all Eng-
" land, and Metropolitan, bearing date the —— day of ——; also of
" a certain Writ or Mandate therein contained of our Most Gracious
" Sovereign ——, by the Grace of God of the United Kingdom of
" Great Britain and Ireland ——, Defender of the Faith, and so forth,
" dated at Westminister the —— day of —— last, and in the —— Year
" of our Reign, issued out and directed to us for holding and cele-
" brating a sacred Synod and general Convocation of the Prelates
" and Clergy of the whole Province of Canterbury: We do perempto-
" rily cite and admonish you, the Dean and Chapter aforesaid, that
" you the Dean personally, and the said Chapter by one sufficient
" Proctor lawfully and sufficiently empowered by their Chapter, do
" appear before the said Most Reverend Father in God the Arch-
" bishop of Canterbury, or his Substitute or Commissary, in the
" Chapter House of the Cathedral Church of Saint Paul, London, on
" ——, the —— day of —— instant. Moreover, we command you as
" above, that you duly certify to us or to our Vicar-General by your
" Letters Patent, containing the name of the Procurator chosen and
" empowered in manner aforesaid by the said Dean and Chapter, on
" or before the —— day of —— instant, and without further delay.
" Dated at ——, the —— day of ——, in the Year of our Lord ——,
" and in the —— Year of our Translation."

V.

Copy of Citation to a Convocation or Provincial Synod, directed by a Diocesan Bishop to Archdeacons, commanding their personal attendance and the attendance of two Clergy Proctors for the Diocesan Clergy.

[Pearce, "Law of Convocation," p. 74.]

" Charles James, by Divine Providence Bishop of London: To our
" beloved in Christ the Archdeacon of the Archdeaconry of London,
" or his Official, Greeting. By virtue and authority of certain
" Mandatory Letters of the Most Reverend Father in God, John

"Bird, by Divine Providence Archbishop of Canterbury, Primate
"of all England, and Metropolitan, bearing date the Second day of
"May instant, also of a certain Writ or Mandate therein con-
"tained of our Most Gracious Sovereign Lady Victoria, by the grace
"of God of the United Kingdom of Great Britain and Ireland
"Queen, Defender of the Faith, and so forth, dated at Westminster,
"the Fifteenth day of April last, in the Eleventh Year of her Reign,
"issued out and directed to us for holding and celebrating a sacred
"Synod and general Convocation of the Prelates and Clergy of the
"whole Province of Canterbury: We do peremptorily cite and
"admonish you, the Archdeacon aforesaid, that you cause all and
"singular the Rectors, Vicars, and others, as well exempt as not
"exempt, having and obtaining Benefices and Ecclesiastical Promo-
"tions within the Archdeaconry of London; and also we command
"you and them that you the Archdeacon personally, and the Clergy
"of your said * Archdeaconry, by two and sufficient Procurators
"lawfully and sufficiently empowered, do appear before the said
"Most Reverend the Archbishop of Canterbury, or his Substitute or
"Commissary, in the Chapter House of the Cathedral Church of
"Saint Paul, London, on —— the —— day of —— instant. More-
"over, we command you as above that you duly certify to us,
"or our Vicar-General, by your Letters Patent containing
"the tenour of these presents, sealed with your Seal, the names
"of all and singular the persons cited or admonished in this
"behalf; also the names of the Procurators chosen for the Clergy
"aforesaid, and everything else you shall do in and about the
"premisses, on or before the Sixteenth day of May instant, without
"further delay. Dated at London, the Fifth day of May, in the Year
"of our Lord One thousand eight hundred and forty-eight, and in the
"Twentieth Year of our Translation."

The like Writ is sent to each Archdeacon.

VI.

Copy of a Citation directed by an Archdeacon to the Clergy to elect Diocesan Proctors.

[Pearce, "Law of Convocation," p. 79.]

"John Sinclair, Clerk, Master of Arts, Archdeacon of the Arch-
"deaconry of Middlesex, lawfully constituted: To all and singular
"Clerks and literate persons whomsoever and wheresoever in and
"throughout the whole Archdeaconry of Middlesex, Greeting.

* There appears to be some inaccuracy of drafting here; in the Province of Canterbury the Clergy of each Diocese, not of each Archdeaconry, appearing by two Proctors. In York, two Proctors for each Archdeaconry are cited.

"Whereas we have with all due reverence received Mandatory
" Letters from the Right Honourable and Right Reverend Father
" in God, Charles James, by Divine Providence Lord Bishop of
" London, of the following tenour, to wit."

[Here follows the Bishop's Citation, suprà No. V. verbatim.]

" We therefore, according to the tenour and effect of the said
" Mandate, charge and firmly enjoin you that you cite or cause to be
" cited peremptorily all and singular Rectors, Vicars, and all others,
" as well exempt as not exempt, having and obtaining Benefices and
" Ecclesiastical Promotions within our Archdeaconry, that they
" and every one of them appear before us or our Official or his
" Surrogate, in the Vestry Room of the Parish Church of
" Saint Paul, Covent Garden, in the County of Middlesex, on
" ——, the —— day of —— next ensuing, at Two o'clock in the
" afternoon, then and there to nominate and elect two sufficient
" Procurators to appear for them on the day and place mentioned
" in the said Royal Writ, according to the force, form, tenour, and
" effect thereof and of the said Mandatory Letters of the said
" Lord Bishop, to consent to those things which shall then and
" there happen, by God's help, to be ordained by their common
" advisement for the honour of the said Kingdom and good of the
" Church. And what you shall do in these premisses you shall
" duly certify to us, our official, or some other competent judge in
" this behalf, together with these presents. Dated the Thirty-first
" day of August, in the Year of our Lord One thousand eight hundred
" and forty-seven."

[Here follow the names of the Clergy and of their Parishes.]

VII.

Copy of a Citation sent by the Archdeacon's Apparitor to each Beneficed Clergyman to attend for the Election of Proctors.

[Pearce, " Law of Convocation," p. 80.]

" Reverend Sir,

" By virtue of a Process under Seal you are cited to appear before
" the Venerable John Sinclair, Clerk, A.M., Archdeacon of the
" Archdeaconry of Middlesex, or his Official or Surrogate, at the
" Vestry Room of the Parish Church of Saint Paul, Covent
" Garden, in the County of Middlesex, on ——, the —— day
" of ——, at Two o'clock of the same day, then and there to
" nominate and elect two fit and sufficient Procurators to appear
" before the Most Reverend Father in God, William, by Divine
" Providence Lord Archbishop of Canterbury, Primate of all
" England, and Metropolitan, or his Substitute or Commissary, in
" the Chapter House of the Cathedral Church of Saint Paul,
" London, on the —— day of ——, to treat, confer, and conclude

"of and upon those things which then and there by mature
"deliberation shall be agreed upon for the honour of God and the
"good of the Church.

"———, Apparitor."

VIII.

Copy of the Return of the Bishop of London, as Dean of the Province of Canterbury, to the Metropolitan's Mandate.

[Pearce, "Law of Conv.," p. 65. Gibson's "Syn. Ang.," p. 336.]

"To the Most Reverend Father in God ———, by Divine Provi-
"dence Lord Archbishop of Canterbury, Primate of all England and
"Metropolitan, or your Substitute or Commissary in this behalf;
"we, ———, by Divine permission Bishop of London, send Greeting,
"with all due reverence and obedience. Whereas we have lately
"humbly received your Mandatory and Citatory Letters to be put
"in execution, sealed with your Seal and directed to us in the words
"or of the tenour following, to wit."

[Here follows the Archbishop's Mandate, supra No. II. verbatim.]

"And by virtue and authority of which Letters we, ———, Bishop of
"London, have caused respectively all and singular our brethren
"the Suffragan Bishops of your Province of Canterbury constituted
"within your said Province to be peremptorily cited and admonished,
"and through them the Deans of the Cathedral and Collegiate
"Churches and every Chapter thereof, and the Archdeacons and
"Dignitaries of Churches exempt and not exempt, and the Clergy
"of every Diocese of your Province aforesaid, by two sufficient
"Proctors to appear before you, our said Most Reverend Father,
"or your Substitute or Commissary or Commissaries, on the day and
"place more fully specified and declared in your said Mandatory
"and Citatory Letters, with continuation and prorogation of days
"and places, if it be necessary to be done in that behalf, to treat
"upon arduous and weighty affairs which shall concern the state
"and welfare, public good and defence, of this Kingdom and the
"subjects thereof, to be then and there more seriously laid before
"them, and thereupon to give their good counsel and assistance, and
"to consent to those things which shall happen to be wholesomely
"ordered and appointed by their common advisement for the honour
"of God and the good of the Church; and further to do and receive
"what the nature and quality of this affair do demand and require
"of them; and further, by the authority of and by the receipt of
"your Mandatory and Citatory Letters, we, ———, Bishop of London
"aforesaid, do acknowledge ourself to be cited peremptorily to
"appear before you, or your Substitute or Commissary or Commis-
"saries, on the day and place above recited, to treat upon the affairs
"above mentioned; and we will obey your said Letters according
"to the force, form, tenour, and effect thereof. Moreover, we have
"intimated and declared, and caused to be intimated and declared, to

APPENDIX. 351

"the Bishops, Deans, and Archdeacons, and Dignitaries of Churches
"aforesaid of your Province of Canterbury, that you do not intend
"to excuse them at that time from a personal appearance in this
"business of Convocation and Congregation, to be celebrated by
"God's help on the day and place aforesaid, unless for some neces-
"sary cause then and there to be alleged and by you to be ap-
"proved, but will canonically punish the contumacies of such as
"shall be absent. Also, moreover, by virtue and authority of your
"said Letters, we have enjoined all and singular our brethren, the
"Bishops aforesaid, that each of them do distinctly and plainly
"certify to you, or your Substitute or Commissary or Commissaries,
"on the said day and place, by their Letters Patent containing the
"names and surnames of all and singular the persons by them
"respectively cited, of what they have severally done so far as
"relates to themselves. And, moreover, by virtue of the authority
"as aforesaid, we have caused to be peremptorily cited the Dean
"and Chapter of our Cathedral Church of Saint Paul, London, and
"all the Archdeacons and other Dignitaries of Churches, exempt
"and not exempt, and the whole Clergy of the City and Diocese
"of London, that they appear before you, the said Most Reverend
"Father, or your Substitute or Commissary or Commissaries, on the
"day and place above specified, according to the form and tenour
"of your aforesaid Letters and the effect thereof above mentioned.
"And we have so executed your said Letters as far as relates to us
"and is in our power, and the names of all and singular the Right
"Reverend Fathers our brethren in your said Province of Canter-
"bury, and of others above named being in our said Diocese of
"London, cited and admonished in this behalf, together with the
"names as well of the Dean as the Proctor of the Chapter of our
"Cathedral Church of Saint Paul, London, as of the Archdeacons
"and Clergy of our whole Diocese of London, respectively nomi-
"nated, elected, and constituted, are here underwritten and set
"down. In testimony whereof we have caused our Episcopal Seal
"to be affixed to these presents. Dated the —— day of ——, in the
"Year of our Lord One thousand eight hundred and forty-seven,
"and in the Twentieth of our Translation.
"——, Registrar."

[Here follow the names of the Bishops of the Province of Canterbury, the names of the Deans and Archdeacons cited, and also the names of the Proctors elected within the Diocese of London.]

IX.

Copy of the Return of a Suffragan Bishop to the Metropolitan's Mandate for Convening a Provincial Synod.

[Pearce, "Law of Convocation," p. 68.]

" To the Most Reverend Father in God ——, by Divine Providence,
"&c., and Metropolitan; ——, by Divine permission Lord Bishop of

"——, sendeth Greeting and brotherly love in the Lord. Whereas "with all due honour and reverence we lately received your Letters "Mandatory hereto annexed, we do acknowledge that we have been "cited by force and virtue of the same, and according to the tenour "and effect of the said Letters, and by virtue thereof we caused "peremptorily to be cited the Dean and Chapter of the Cathedral "Church of ——, and the Archdeacon[s] and all the Clergy of the "Archdeaconry[ies] within our Diocese, and all and singular others "to be cited to appear before you or your representative on the day, "hour, and at the place and to the effect mentioned in your said "Letters; and everything else which your said Letters demand and "require we have diligently done and executed; and the names of "the persons cited, and of their Proctors rightly elected, are as "below described. In testimony whereof we have caused the Seal "of our Consistory Court to be put to these presents, this —— day "of ——, in the Year of our Lord One thousand eight hundred and "forty-seven, and of our Translation the Twentieth."

[Here follow the names of the persons cited and elected to appear as above.]

X.

Copy of the Return of a Dean and Chapter to the Metropolitan's Mandate for Convening a Provincial Synod.

[Pearce, "Law of Convocation," p. 73.]

"To the Honourable and Most Reverend Father in God ——, by "Divine permission, &c., and Metropolitan ——; we, the Dean and "Chapter of the Cathedral Church of ——, send Greeting with all "humility and reverence, and do hereby acknowledge that we have "with all due honour and obedience received your Letters Man- "datory hereunto annexed, and have elected and lawfully constituted "the Reverend ——, Clerk, &c. ——, Proctor for the Chapter of "the Cathedral Church of ——. In witness whereof we have caused "our Chapter Seal to be hereunto affixed, this —— day of ——, in "the Year of our Lord One thousand eight hundred and forty- "seven."

XI.

Copy of an Archdeacon's Return, certifying the Election of Proctors by the Clergy.

[Pearce, "Law of Convocation," p. 83.]

"John Sinclair, Clerk, Master of Arts, Archdeacon of the Arch- "deaconry of Middlesex, in the Diocese of London, lawfully con- "stituted: Whereas we have received certain Mandatory Letters of "the Right Reverend Father in God, Charles James, by Divine

" permission Lord Bishop of London, to us directed, in the words or
" to the effect following, to wit."

[Here follows the Bishop's Citation, suprà No. V. verbatim.]

" In obedience to which Mandate, we, the Archdeacon aforesaid,
" as by these Letters Patent sealed with our Seal, certify to the said
" Right Reverend Father in God, Charles James, Lord Bishop of
" London, or his Commissary, Vicar-General, or other competent
" judge, that we have caused to be cited and admonished all and
" singular the Rectors, Vicars, and others, as well exempt as not
" exempt, having and obtaining Benefices and Ecclesiastical Pro-
" motions within the Archdeaconry of Middlesex, whose names are
" herein underwritten :—"

[Here follow the names of the Clergy, and their Parishes.]

" to appear before us or our Official, his Surrogate, or other competent
" judge, on ——, the —— day of —— instant, at the hour of
" Two o'clock in the afternoon, in the Vestry Room of the
" Parish Church of Saint Paul, Covent Garden, within the Arch-
" deaconry aforesaid, for the purposes in the said Mandate men-
" tioned and specified : And we, the Archdeacon aforesaid, do further
" certify the Reverend John Hume Spry, Doctor in Divinity,
" Rector of Saint Marylebone, in the County of Middlesex, and the
" Reverend Thomas Randolph, Rector of Much Hadham, in the
" County of Herts, to be Procurators for the Clergy of the Arch-
" deaconry of Middlesex aforesaid ; and the said John Hume Spry
" and Thomas Randolph were thereupon nominated and declared to
" be Procurators for the Clergy of the Archdeaconry aforesaid, and
" that they should be admonished to appear at the time and place
" and to the effect in the said Mandate mentioned and specified.
" Given under the Seal which we use in this behalf, the —— day
" of ——, in the Year of our Lord One thousand eight hundred and
" forty-seven."

By the execution of the foregoing instruments the Provincial Synods or Convocations are constituted and convened, and are then in a condition to proceed to active business. The above proceedings before assembly in the Province of Canterbury are virtually the same as those adopted in the Province of York, with two exceptions, viz. : (1) in York the Metropolitan's Mandate is directed personally to each Bishop, and not through intervention of a Provincial Dean ; (2) and two Proctors are cited and elected for each Archdeaconry, and not for each Diocese.

The Constitution of such assemblies dates from times far beyond legal memory, and the most important instruments connected with their convention, as above set down, will be seen on comparison to be derived from very high antiquity. That Constitution is conformable to the ancient practice of the Primitive Church; but from the loss of authentic records before the Saxon invasion in the fifth century, students of history will vainly seek for accurate information respecting its first inauguration in Britain. A good deal has been said in late years about the reform of Convocation, and some marvellous suggestions invoking Parliamentary assistance for the purpose have been made by several members of the learned profession very high in office. Indeed, among other official documents, a memorandum on this question was addressed not long since to an Archbishop and a Prime Minister by a Lord Chancellor. This remarkable instrument has been considered by a Committee of the Canterbury Convocation in the present year 1885, and a report concluded on by which his lordship's historical researches appear to have been the reverse of successful or exhaustive. This report may be purchased at the National Society's Office, price sixpence, and is highly instructive. It is somewhat earnestly commended to the reader's notice as illustrating the methods employed by the learned profession in dealing with Ecclesiastical records and Church history. For the noble writer of the memorandum above mentioned, having laid an insecure foundation on two false suppositions and seven false assertions, piled up a huge edifice of error crowned with a grotesque conclusion which the first breath of historical truth has swept into heaps of ruin. Or to view the matter in another aspect, his lordship made a false start, took a wrong direction, then missed his way, and so finally lost himself hopelessly in a trackless wilderness of mistakes.

A considerable number of high legal authorities, however, in conformity with his lordship's view, have from time to time, in answer to official enquiries, given of late years formal opinions that the authority of Parliament would be required for any reform in the Constitution of a Convocation. But whence these learned persons derived their Constitutional lore is a mystery insoluble. To say nothing here of other Christian countries, whose history all looks the same way, if the records of our own land, at least such as remain from the times of the Druids and the worship of mistletoe down to this year of grace 1885, were ransacked to the last syllable, no instance could be found of the interference of Parliament or any like body with the Constitution of the Church's Synods. And anyone labours under serious error who imagines that she will ever submit to the inauguration of such a profane solœcism in these later days. This fantastic parliamentary vision, however, is but one of those strange chimæras to which some learned persons in their Ecclesiastical excursions on occasion fall a helpless prey. Their disastrous miscarriages, occurring from time to time, recall to mind the luckless lot of those Athenian innocents who became periodically devoted victims to the monstrous progeny of the unnatural Cretan Queen.

C.

ROYAL LETTER OF BUSINESS.

On some occasions when the Sovereign desires that any particular matter should become the subject of deliberation, a "Letter of Business" is directed to a Convocation from the Crown. But this is not very frequently issued, nor is it in any way required as antecedent to Synodical deliberations.

I.

Copy of a Letter of Business of King Edward I. A.D. 1283.

[Wake's " State," App. No. xxvii. p. 17.]

" Edwardus, Dei Gratiâ Rex Angliæ, Dominus Hyberniæ et Dux
" Aquitaniæ : Venerabilibus in Christo Patribus J. eâdem gratiâ
" Cant. Archiepiscopo totius Angliæ Primati, Episcopis, Abbatibus,
" Prioribus, et aliis Domorum Religiosarum Præfectis, Decanis,
" Capitulis Ecclesiarum Cathedralium et Collegiatarum, de Pro-
" vinciâ Cant. et eorum procuratoribus apud Northampton in
" instantibus octavis S. Hilarii Conventuris, Salutem.
" Cum mittamus ad vos dilectum consanguineum et fidelem
" nostrum Edmundum Comitem Cornubiæ, et dilectum nobis in
" Christo Abbatem Westmonasterii Thesaurarium nostrum, et Jo. de
" Kyrkeby Archidiaconum Covent. ad quædam ardua et specialia
" negotia nos et vos et totum Regnum nostrum tangentia vobis

"nomine nostro exponenda, dilectiones vestras affectuosè requirimus
"et rogamus, quatenùs eidem Comiti, Abbati, et Johanni vel duobus
"eorum, quos præsentes esse contigerit, firmam fidem adhibentes ea,
"quæ ipsi omnes vel eorum [duo] vobis nomine nostro dicent, efficacitèr
"explere et expedire curetis amore nostri, prout vobis scire faciant
"ex parte nostrâ. Teste me ipso apud Rothelan V⁰ die Januarii
"Anno Regni nostri XI⁰."

II.

Copy of a Letter of Business of King William III. A.D. 1689.

[Card. "Confer." p. 443.]

"William R.

"His Majesty has summoned this Convocation, not only because
"'tis usual upon holding of a Parliament, but out of a pious zeal to do
"everything that may tend to the best establishment of the Church
"of England, which is so eminent a part of the Reformation,
"and is certainly the best united to the Constitution of this Govern-
"ment, and therefore does most signally deserve and always shall
"have both his favour and protection; and he doubts not but that
"you will assist him in promoting the welfare of it, so that no
"prejudices with which some men may have laboured to possess
"you shall disappoint his good intentions or deprive the Church
"of any benefit from your consultations. His Majesty therefore
"expects that the things that shall be proposed shall be calmly and
"impartially considered by you, and assures you that he will offer
"nothing to you but what shall be for the honour, peace, and
"advantage both of the Protestant Religion in general and par-
"ticularly of the Church of England."

What was offered was the scheme for a "Comprehension" Liturgy; for which see above, pp. 243–50.

III.

Copy of a Letter of Business of Queen Victoria. 1872.

[Chron. Conv. Lower House Cant., Feb. 13, 1872, p. 240.]

"Victoria Reg.

"Victoria, by the Grace of God of the United Kingdom of Great
"Britain and Ireland Queen, Defender of the Faith: To the Most
"Rev. Father in God our right trusty and well-beloved Coun-
"cillor, Archibald Campbell, by the Grace of God Archbishop of
"Canterbury, Primate of all England, and Metropolitan, Greeting.
"Whereas, by Our Royal Licence to the present Convocation of the
"Province of Canterbury, We have amongst other things empowered
"and authorised them to confer, treat, debate, consider, consult,

"and agree of and upon such points, matters, and things as We
"from time to time should deliver to you in writing under Our Sign
"Manual or Privy Signet to be debated, considered, consulted, and
"agreed upon; And whereas our Commissioners for inquiring into
"the differences of practice which have arisen from varying inter-
"pretations put upon the Rubrics, Orders, and Directions for
"regulating the course and conduct of Public Worship, the
"Administration of the Sacraments, and the other Services con
"tained in the Book of Common Prayer, according to the use of the
"United Church of England and Ireland, and more especially with
"regard to the Ornaments used in the churches and chapels of the
"said United Church, and the Vestments worn by the Ministers
"thereof at the time of their ministration, with a view of explaining
"or amending the said Rubrics, Orders, and Directions, so as to
"secure general uniformity of practice in such matters as may be
"deemed essential, have submitted to Us their Fourth and final
"Report:

"Our pleasure therefore is, and We do hereby authorise you, the
"said Most Reverend Father in God, the said Archbishop of
"Canterbury, President of the said Convocation, and the Bishops of
"your said Province, and the Deans of the Cathedral Churches, and
"also the Archdeacons, Chapters, and Colleges, and the whole Clergy
"of every Diocese of your said Province, to debate, consider, con-
"sult, and agree upon the point, matters, and things contained in
"the said Fourth and final Report of Our said Commissioners; and
"after mature debate, consideration, consultation, and agreement, to
"present to Us a Report or Reports thereon in writing. And for so
"doing this shall be your Warrant.

"Given at our Court, St. James's, the Seventh day of February,
"1872, in the Thirty-fifth Year of Our Reign.

"By Her Majesty's command,

"H. A. BRUCE."

For a similar "Letter of Business" see Chron. Conv., July 7, 1874, p. 299.

The reader will observe that the "Letter of Business" proper is contained in the second of the paragraphs above printed.

As regards the first paragraph, the legal officials in the Crown Office who drafted this instrument, and the law officers of the Crown, if they were consulted in the matter, instead of following the wholesome examples of such Letters of Business as have been above set down, involved themselves in some embarrassing confusions about a "Licence." [See Chron. Conv., Feb. 9, 1872, pp. 103–4. Report signed, Feb.

13, 1873. Chron. Conv., July 8, 1874, p. 374]. For the purposes specified in this "Letter of Business" no "Licence" was required, as it was by no one contemplated that any Canon should be "enacted, promulged, or executed." And therefore the issue of any such instrument as a "Licence" was on this occasion wholly superfluous, and the recital of it altogether surprising and misleading. By the original Royal Writ [see A. III.] for convening this Convocation the assembly had already, through its President, been required by the Sovereign to "treat of, agree to, and conclude upon . . . . "affairs concerning Us, the security and defence of the "Church of England, and the peace and tranquillity, public "good and defence of our Kingdom." The proper object of a "Letter of Business," therefore, on this occasion, was merely to specify some particular matters which should be discussed and reported on touching such "security," "defence," "tranquillity," and "public good."

These excursions, consequently, of the Crown Office officials and their learned advisers, if they were consulted, both in the matter first of issuing a needless "Licence," and secondly in the needless recital of it, were flagrant instances of that pernicious practice denounced by the late Lord Westbury as a bad professional habit, and fitly described by his lordship as "writing by the yard." No doubt this practice of "writ-"ing by the yard" is on all occasions when indulged in to be deplored as a waste of official time, whatever the value of that may be. But in this instance it was far more deeply to be deprecated, as being also very misleading, and indeed worse than misleading. It was here exceedingly mischievous; for it leads simple people by its verbiage to suppose that the Convocations after their assembling are not in a condition to "confer, treat, debate, consider, consult, and "agree," on matters touching the security and defence of the Church of England without the receipt of such instruments as those now in question from the Crown. And that is a supposition which is wholly unconstitutional, the reverse of the truth, and quite contradictory to all experience and to matter of fact. The conclusion of the Lower House of the Convocation of Canterbury on this subject was emphatically expressed on April 28 and 29, 1874, when unanimously it refused in an address to the Crown [very incautiously worded by the Upper House] to take notice of a superfluous Royal Licence, needlessly issued from the Crown Office in error. [See Chron. Conv. Lower House Cant., in loco pp. 67, 98].

D.

THE ROYAL ASSENT AND LICENCE TO ENACT, PROMULGE, AND EXECUTE CANONS.

The reader should understand distinctly that a "Royal "Licence," so far as it regards new Canons, is legally issued for one threefold purpose, and for that purpose only—that is, for the "enacting," "promulging," and "executing" them. It is an instrument rendered necessary by the provisions of the Statute 25 Hen. VIII. 19; and the terms "enact," "pro-"mulge," "execute," have three distinct and well-defined legal meanings, which the gentlemen of the long robe in high official quarters have in our day hopelessly misunderstood, and indeed barbarously mangled, as will be seen below in No. IV. of this Section. (1) The process of "en-"acting" a Canon has been previously fully described in this volume at pp. 32-33. (2) To "promulge" a Canon is to make it public and transmit it to the Provincial and Consistory Courts for the information and guidance of the respective Ecclesiastical Judges. (3) To "execute" a Canon is to enforce its provisions in an Ecclesiastical Tribunal. For the above threefold purpose, and for that only as regards new Canons, a Royal Licence is required. Such an instrument has not very often been needed, and consequently not been very frequently issued. Instances have occurred in the years 1587 N.S., 1603, 1606, 1640, 1661, 1689, 1710, 1713, 1716, 1861, 1865; and, by an odd misapprehension of the legal advisers of the Crown, instruments purporting to be "Licences" were issued in 1872 and in 1874, when the enactment of Canons was not even contemplated by anybody whatsoever. These instruments, however, being improperly drafted, were not merely superfluous, but even if required would have been worthless for any proper purpose.

I.

Copy of a Synodical Request to Queen Elizabeth for Royal Assent and Licence. A.D. 1586, O.S.

[Extract. è Regist. Prov. Sed. Archiep. Cantuar. Copies also in York Records, Paper Office, and Registers of the Church of Exeter. Atterb. "Rights," p. 638; Card. "Syn." p. 566.]

"Most Excellent and Most Gracious Sovereign Lady. We, the "Prelates and Clergy of the Province of Canterbury, now gathered "together in a Convocation or Synod, calling to our minds and "considering with al thankful remembrance the manifold and great "benefits that every member of this Realm generally hath and doth "daily receive, by the blessing of Almighty God, under Your "Majesty's most happy and peaceable government: and we our- "selves especially, by Your gracious and princely care over us, "whereby we do not only enjoy our lives and livings in happy "peace, but also the free exercise of our ministry and function, the "true preaching of the Word of God, and the sincere administering "of the Holy Sacraments, to us far more dear than our lives and "livings: And further, seeing the infinite occasions that, through "the execrable malice of the enemies of the Gospel of Christ, do "daily arise whereby Your Highness is driven to many extraordinary "and inestimable expences for the necessary defence of the Gospel "and Your Highness' dominions; in token of our dutiful and "thankful hearts to Your Majesty's most royal person, have with "one joint consent and hearty good wil, over and above one subsidy "of six shillings in the pound already granted to Your Highness, "Your heirs and successors, in this our Convocation or Synod, "yielded to give, and by these presents do give and grant to Your "Highness' person a benevolence or contribution of three shillings "of every full pound of al Ecclesiastical and Spiritual Promotions "within the said Province of Canterbury, &c., &c., &c.

"And we, your said Prelates and Clergy, most humbly beseech "Your Majesty to take in good part our loving minds and good wil, "and not only to accept this smal gift of ours, tho' it be nothing "answerable to our desires, but also, by Your Majesty's Letters "Patent under Your Great Seal, TO ASSENT thereunto and TO LICENSE "and authorize us, in this our Convocation and Synod, TO DEVISE, "MAKE, AND ORDAIN SUCH ORDERS, DECREES, AND CONSTITUTIONS, "PROVINCIAL AND SYNODAL, as we shall think most expedient for the "more speedy and sure levying and payment of the same benevolence "or contribution; AND THEREBY ALSO TO GIVE AND TESTIFY YOUR "MAJESTY'S ROYAL ASSENT TO SUCH ORDERS, DECREES, AND CONSTI- "TUTIONS as in this our Synod or Convocation we shal make, "decree, or ordain, for the speedy and sure levying and payment "thereof to such persons as Your Majesty shal appoint for the receipt "thereof, as is aforesaid."

APPENDIX. 361

This request for a "Licence" was sealed with the Seal of the Archbishop [John Whitgift] of Canterbury, in the presence of the Bishops and representative Clergy of that Province, in St. Peter's Church, Westminster, on the 4th of March, 1586, O.S.

The above request was in conformity with the Statute 25 Hen. VIII. 19 governing the case, and was drawn by the hand of a person knowing what he was about.

To the above request answer was made by the issue of a "Royal Assent and Licence" to enact, drawn likewise in conformity with the Statute and by the hand also of a person knowing what he was about, which certainly has not been the case in our days under like circumstances. The following was the Assent and Licence issued.

II.

Copy of Royal Assent and Licence of Queen Elizabeth's Reign. A. D. 1586, O. S.

[Atterb. "Rights," &c., Add. pp. 642-3.]

"Regina, etc. Omnibus ad quos, etc. Salutem.
"Cum Prælati et Clerus Cantuar. Provinciæ nostra auctoritate in
"Synodo suâ seu Convocatione congregati ex intimâ ex propensâ
"animorum suorum affectione, quam erga nos gerunt, ultra et præter
"subsidium sex solidorum singularum librarum annuarum, etiam
"quandam benevolam contributionem trium solidorum pro singulis
"libris annuis omnium et singulorum beneficiorum suorum Ec-
"clesiasticorum et promotionum spiritualium quorumcunque ac
"omnium possessionum et reventionum eisdem annexarum seu
"quovis modo spectantium et pertinentium, dederint et concesserint,
"prout per quoddam scriptum seu instrumentum publicum sigillo
"prædilecti et fidelis consiliarii nostri Johannis, Arch. Cant.
"munitum et nobis exhibitum gerens datum 4 die Martii, A.D. juxta
"comp. Eccl. Angl. 1586, planius liquet, et apparet—SCIATIS IGITUR
"QUOD NOS, ad humilem petitionem Prælatorum nostrorum et Cleri
"antedicti præfatæ benevolæ contributionis concessionem appro-
"bamus et eandem confirmamus, ratificamus, et stabilimus, ac ei-
"dem omnibusque et singulis clausulis, sententiis, provisionibus,
"et exceptionibus in dicto instrumento contentis et specificatis
"REGIUM NOSTRUM ASSENSUM ex certâ scientiâ et mero motu nostris
"PRÆBEMUS PER PRESENTES. AC INSUPER SCIATIS QUOD, ex gratiâ
"nostra speciali ac certâ scientiâ et mero motu nostris LICENTIAM
"facultatem et authoritatem PRÆLATIS NOSTRIS ET CLERO PRÆDICT.
"IN HÂC PRÆSENTI SYNODO CONGREGATIS DECERNENDI ORDINANDI
"ET CONSTITUENDI QUÆCUMQUE DECRETA ORDINATIONES ET CONSTI-

A A A

"TUTIONES SYNODALES, AC EADEM SIC PER IPSOS DECRETA, ORDINATA, ET
"CONSTITUTA EXECUTIONI MANDANDI, et cum effectu exequendi quæ
"sibi commoda et opportuna videbuntur pro meliori, vera, ac justâ
"collectione et solutione dict. benevolæ contributionis et cujuslibet
"inde parcellæ, DEDIMUS CONCESSIMUS ET CONFIRMAVIMUS AC ETIAM
"DAMUS CONCEDIMUS ET CONFIRMAMUS per presentes. In cujus
"rei," etc.

As the above "Assent and Licence" is not conveyed in the most polished Ciceronian Latin imaginable, the words which really are needful for arriving at its purport are printed in capitals to save the reader trouble. The words so printed are quite sufficient to shew that the Royal "Assent and "Licence" was one proceeding, as intended by the Statute which governs the case, 25 Hen. VIII. 19. [See supra, pp. 146-7.] And it may here be observed that this was the first "Licence" issued [at least the first of which there is any record] after the passing of the Statute requiring such an instrument, and therefore, being comparatively so nearly contemporaneous with the Statute, it may be supposed that the matter was then well understood by all concerned. At any rate, as this is a document of the highest Constitutional importance, it shall have the benefit of a translation here, so far as is requisite for present purposes.

"The Queen, &c. To all to whom, &c. Greeting.
"Since the Prelates and Clergy of the Province of Canterbury...
"over and above a subsidy of six shillings in the pound ... have
"granted a benevolence of three shillings in the pound, as more
"fully appears by a certain writing or public instrument, sealed with
"the Seal of Our well-beloved and faithful Councillor, John, Arch-
"bishop of Canterbury, and exhibited to Us, bearing date the Fourth
"day of March, in the Year of our Lord 1586, according to the
"computation of the Church of England: Now know all men that
"We, according to the humble petition of Our Prelates and Clergy
"aforesaid, accept, approve, CONFIRM, RATIFY, AND ESTABLISH THE
"GRANT OF THE BEFORESAID BENEVOLENCE; and of Our certain know-
"ledge and mere motion WE GIVE OUR ROYAL ASSENT BY THESE
"PRESENTS to that instrument and to all and singular the clauses,
"sentences, provisions, and exceptions in the aforesaid instrument
"contained and specified. And moreover, know all men that of
"Our special favour and certain knowledge and mere motion We
"have given, granted, and confirmed, and also do give, grant, and
"confirm by these presents, to Our Prelates and Clergy aforesaid,
"assembled in this present Synod, LICENCE, POWER, AND AUTHORITY

" TO DECREE, ORDAIN, AND CONSTITUTE CERTAIN DECREES, ORDINANCES,
" AND SYNODICAL CONSTITUTIONS, AND TO PUT INTO EXECUTION AND
" CARRY OUT WITH EFFECT THE THINGS SO BY THEMSELVES DECREED,
" ORDAINED, AND CONSTITUTED, as shall seem convenient and oppor-
" tune for the better, true, and just collection and payment of the
" said benevolent contribution and of each part thereof."

The reader will observe that the Clergy (1) consulted, conferred together, and treated; (2) decided on the contents of the proposed Canons; (3) applied for "Assent and Licence," in accordance with the Statute governing the case; (4) received "Assent and Licence" as one instrument. But this has been in subsequent times improved upon backwards by some ingenious people of the learned profession, and later instruments have been dichotomized without any legal warranty in more recent issues, and the unstatutable novelty has been introduced of granting "Licence" before enactment, "Assent" after. And thus the words "Assent and Licence" in the first place have been reversed in order of words, and in the second place one instrument has been converted into two. So on the anvil of the learned profession, without the least warranty of law, another link has been ingeniously forged for Ecclesiastical fetters.

Meanwhile, it must be reasonably supposed that at the date of the proceedings first above recorded [1586], i.e. only fifty-two years after the enactment of the Statute, its provisions were rightly understood. And those definite provisions were manifestly accurately then complied with, both by the Convocation and by the Sovereign, as must be plain to anyone of common capacity who will take the trouble to compare the several documents. Further, should any reader [which is hardly possible] fail to be convinced of this after such comparison, he may set all doubt at rest by perusing an elucidation of this subject to be found in Atterbury's "Rights," &c., pp. 99 seq.

However, in the year 1611 [Trin. Term, 8 Jac. I.] a surprising resolution was announced by the Judges, that "as a " Convocation cannot assemble without the assent of the King, " so after their assembling they cannot confer to constitute " any new Canons without 'Licence del Roy'" [Coke's "Rep." xii. 70]. This certainly was a marvellous affirmation wholly unwarranted by the terms of the Statute governing the case, in no line of which does the word "confer" appear, nor as regards new Canons does that Statute lay any restraint whatever on the Convocations, save in respect of "enacting, promulging, and executing." And, still further, this judicial excursion was contradictory to the practice which had been adopted from the date of the enactment of the Statute through many subsequent years. The reader is here requested very exactly to remark, and very carefully to remember, that this was an impotent struggle on the part of the learned in the law unstatutably to disable the Convocations in their deliberative capacity by a judicial resolution, to the same extent as they were restrained in their legislative capacity by an Act of Parliament [25 Henry VIII. 19]; and that was nothing short of an attempted outrage on the Constitution of the country and on the rights and liberties of the Church. If public rights could be trampled out by judicial resolutions I am afraid the vaunted liberties of England would on occasion fare very poorly indeed.

This aggressive resolution, however, of the Judges in 1611 was delivered at a time when the learned profession seem to have been banded together, at least if we may credit history, to magnify Royal prerogative beyond all Constitutional limits, and that most sensibly if ever the rights and liberties of the Church came into question. Still, notwithstanding the palpable exaggeration and unstatutable aggression of this judicial resolution, it produced subsequent effects; and Licences from the Crown Office, ingeniously contrived and drafted by the learned officials there, have on occasion been since issued, giving permission not only to "enact, promulge, and execute" Canons, but also to "confer, "treat, debate, consider, consult, and agree" upon them. Thus the official draftsmen of "Licences" have taken leave to improve backwards, to the disadvantage of the Church, on the judicial resolution in 1611 above quoted at an alarming rate; and without the least Constitutional warranty whatever, while "writing by the yard," have contrived to exaggerate and swell to a romantic bulk that indefensible announcement. When assaulting Olympus aforetime the assailants contented themselves merely with a double accumulation. Pelion only was mounted on Ossa. But our modern legal giants have contrived a fivefold agglomeration for their enterprizes, having heaped no less than five accretions—"treat," "debate," "consider," "consult," and "agree"—on the aggressive base "confer," unstatutably and illegally laid by the Jacobæan Judges in Trinity Term, 1611.

However, a joint Committee, consisting of six Bishops and six members of the Lower House, presented a Report on Feb. 13, 1863 [Vide Chron. Conv. in loco, pp. 1119—20], to the Upper House of the Canterbury Convocation, setting this matter in its true light. That Report, "On the Sta-"tutable Mode of Enacting a Canon," shews that it is a notorious fact and an unanswerable proposition that, as regards new Canons, the Royal Licence is legally required only for the purpose of enactment, promulgation, and execution, and that meanwhile conference, debate, and agreement upon them should precede their presentation to the Sovereign, who is requested to grant a Licence for their enactment. Indeed, not only is the law clear, but the reason of the thing is manifest.

Consequently, when in this generation requests by the Canterbury Convocation for Licences have been made to the Crown, the method of proceeding warranted by Statute and reason has been closely adhered to, as will be seen by an inspection of the copy of a Synodical request below recorded. Indeed, not only has that method been adhered to, but it will be seen that in drafting the document very special care was taken to declare emphatically that the Convocation had already done the very thing which the Jacobæan Judges had resolved could not be done—a resolution which more modern legal officials have, as above said, outrun with nothing less than gigantic strides of aggression. And this course was taken in Convocation, to my certain knowledge, with deliberate and settled purpose to contravene and set at nought and repudiate the tyrannical and unconstitutional restrictions which those learned persons had endeavoured to impose on the Provincial Synods, and to denounce those backward improvements to the disadvantage of the Church which have been illegally superadded by the learned in the law.

And here a very earnest hope is added, that in future years the Convocations, if either of them should request a Licence, will be equally careful in the terms of their application. For most assuredly, if they make a slip in this matter there are those who have skill and ingenuity enough, and the will too, to turn it afterwards to the Church's disadvantage. The reader will now see, if he should take the trouble to peruse the following document, what careful precautions have been taken by the Canterbury Convocation in this generation on this subject.

III.

Copy of a Synodical Request to Queen Victoria for a Royal Licence. A.D. 1861.

[Chron. Conv. Upper House Cant., Feb. 26, 1861, pp. 326—7.]

" We, Your Majesty's faithful subjects, the Archbishops, Bishops, "and Clergy of the Province of Canterbury, in Convocation assem- "bled, humbly represent to Your Majesty, that in obedience to Your "Majesty's Royal Writ, WE HAVE CONFERRED TOGETHER AND CON- "SIDERED of divers urgent matters concerning Your Majesty, the " security and defence of the Church of England, and the peace and " tranquillity public good and defence of Your Majesty's kingdom " and subjects: And particularly WE HAVE CONFERRED TOGETHER AND " CONSIDERED the Twenty-ninth Canon of 1603 of the said Church: " and we are desirous that the said Canon should be altered, or " amended, or repealed and a new Canon substituted in the place " thereof: and We humbly pray that your Majesty will be graciously " pleased to grant to us Your Majesty's Royal Licence, to make, " promulge, and execute such altered and amended Canon, or such "new Canon accordingly.

"(Signed.)

"(A true copy.)

" J. B. CANTUAR., President.

" H. WADDINGTON.

" Whitehall, Feb. 19, 1861."

In reply to this request the following Licence was issued.

IV.

Copy of a Royal Licence of Queen Victoria's reign. A.D. 1861.

[Chron. Conv. Upper House Cant., Feb. 26, 1861, p. 327.]

"Victoria, by the Grace of God of the United Kingdom of Great
" Britain and Ireland Queen, Defender of the Faith, and so forth:
" To all to whom these presents shall come, Greeting.

"Whereas in and by one Act of Parliament made at Westminster
" in the Five-and-twentieth Year of King Henry the Eighth, reciting
" that wherever the King's humble and obedient subjects, the
" Clergy of the Realm of England, had not only acknowledged
" according to the truth that the Convocations of the same Clergy
" were always, had been, and ought to be assembled only by the
" King's Writ, but also, submitting themselves unto the King's
" Majesty, had promised in verbo sacerdotii that they would never
" from thenceforth presume to attempt, allege, claim, or put in ure,
" or exact, promulge, or execute any new Canons, Constitutions,
" Ordinances, Provincial or other, or by whatsoever other name they
" should be called, in the Convocation, unless the said King's most
" Royal Assent and Licence might to them be had, to make,
" promulge, and execute the same; and that the said King did give
" His most Royal Assent and authority in that behalf; it was
" therefore enacted by the authority of the said Parliament, accord-
" ing to the said submission and petition of the said Clergy, amongst
" other things, that they, ne any of them, from thenceforth should
" enact, promulge, or execute any such Canons, Constitutions, or
" Ordinances Provincial, by whatsoever name or names they might be
" called, in their Convocations in time coming, which always should be
" assembled by authority of the King's Writ, unless the same Clergy
" might have the King's most Royal Assent and Licence to make,
" promulge, and execute such Canons, Constitutions, and Ordinances,
" Provincial or Synodal, upon pain of every one of the said Clergy
" doing contrary to the said Act, and being therefore convict, to suffer
" imprisonment and make fine at the King's will; and further, by
" the said Act it is provided that no Canons, Constitutions, or
" Ordinances should be made or put in execution within this Realm,
" by authority of the Convocation of the Clergy, which shall be
" contrariant or repugnant to the King's Prerogative Royal, or the
" Customs, Laws, or Statutes of this Realm, anything in the said Act
" to the contrary thereof notwithstanding; and lastly, it is also
" provided by the said Act, that such Canons, Constitutions,
" Ordinances, and Synodals Provincial which then were already
" made, and which were not contrary or repugnant to the Laws,
" Statutes, and Customs of this Realm, nor to the damage or hurt
" of the King's Prerogative Royal, should then still be used and
" executed as they were afore the making of the said Act, till such

"time as they should be viewed, searched, or otherwise ordered and
"determined by the persons mentioned in the said Act, or the more
"part of them, according to the tenour or form and effect of the said
"Act, as by the said Act, amongst divers other things, more fully
"and at large doth and may appear: And whereas We have lately
"received a humble representation and petition from the Arch-
"bishop, Bishops, and Clergy of the Province of Canterbury in
"Convocation, of the tenour following, to wit:—'We, Your Majesty's
"'faithful subjects, the Archbishop, Bishops, and Clergy of the
"'Province of Canterbury in Convocation assembled, humbly repre-
"'sent to Your Majesty that, in OBEDIENCE TO YOUR MAJESTY'S ROYAL
"'WRIT, WE HAVE CONFERRED TOGETHER AND CONSIDERED of divers
"'urgent matters concerning Your Majesty, the security and
"'defence of the Church of England, and the peace and tran-
"'quillity public good and defence of Your Majesty's kingdom and
"'subjects: And particularly WE HAVE CONFERRED TOGETHER AND
"'CONSIDERED THE TWENTY-NINTH CANON OF 1603 of the said
"'Church, and we are desirous that the said Canon should be
"'altered and amended, or repealed and a new Canon substituted
"'in the place thereof. And we humbly pray that Your Majesty
"'will be graciously pleased to grant to us Your Majesty's Royal
"'Licence to make, promulge, and execute such altered and
"'amended Canon, or such new Canon accordingly.' Know ye
"that We, for divers urgent and weighty causes and considerations
"Us thereunto especially moving, of Our special grace, by virtue of
"Our Prerogative Royal and supreme authority in causes Ecclesias-
"tical, have given and granted, and by these presents DO GIVE AND
"GRANT, FULL, FREE, AND LAWFUL LIBERTY, LICENCE, POWER, AND
"AUTHORITY unto the Most Reverend Father in God, Our right trusty
"and well-beloved Counsellor, John Bird, Archbishop of Canter-
"bury, President of this present Convocation of the Clergy of the
"Province of Canterbury for this present Parliament now assembled,
"and to the rest of the Bishops of the same Province, and to all
"the Deans of Cathedral Churches, Archdeacons, Chapters, and
"Colleges, and the whole of the Clergy of every Diocese within the
"said Province, that they the said Archbishop of Canterbury,
"President of the said Convocation, and the rest of the Bishops of
"the said Province, or the greater number of them, whereof the
"said President of the said Convocation to be one, and the rest of the
"Clergy of this present Convocation, within the said Province of
"Canterbury, or the greater part of them, SHALL AND MAY, from
"time to time during the present Parliament, CONFER, TREAT, DEBATE,
"CONSIDER, CONSULT, AND AGREE OF AND UPON and concerning the
"altering, amending, or repealing the said Twenty-ninth Canon of
"1603, of the said Church of England, all or any part of the same.
"And We do GIVE and grant full, free, and lawful liberty, LICENCE,
"power, and authority to them to substitute a new Canon in the
"place thereof, and TO MAKE, PROMULGE, AND EXECUTE such altered

"and amended Canon or such new Canon accordingly, as they the
"said President and the Bishops, or the greater part of them, and
"the Clergy of the said Province, or the greater part of them, shall
"think necessary, fit, and convenient for the honour and service of
"Almighty God, the good and quiet of the Church and better
"government thereof, to be, when allowed, approved, and con-
"firmed by Us, from time to time observed, performed, fulfilled, and
"kept, as well by the Archbishop of Canterbury, the Bishops and
"their successors, and the rest of the whole Clergy of the said
"Province of Canterbury, in their several callings, offices, functions,
"ministries, degrees, and administrations, as also by all and every
"Dean of the Arches and other Judge of the said Archbishop's
"Courts, Guardians of Spiritualities, Chancellors, Deans and Chap-
"ters, Archdeacons, Commissaries, Officials, Registers [? Registrars],
"and all and every other Ecclesiastical Officers and their inferior
"Ministers whatsoever, of the same Province of Canterbury, in
"their and every of their District Courts, and in the order, manner,
"and form of their and every of their proceedings, and by all other
"persons within this Realm as far as lawfully being members of the
"Church it may concern them. And WE DO ALSO BY THESE PRESENTS
"GIVE AND GRANT unto the said Archbishop of Canterbury, President
"of the said Convocation, and to the rest of the Bishops of the
"Province of Canterbury, and unto all Deans of Cathedral Churches,
"Archdeacons, Chapters, and Colleges, and the whole Clergy of Our
"several Dioceses within the said Province, FULL, FREE, AND LAWFUL
"LIBERTY, LICENCE, POWER, AND AUTHORITY, that they the said Arch-
"bishop of Canterbury, President of the said Convocation, and the
"rest of the said Bishops of the same Province, or the greater
"number of them, the said Canon, all or any part thereof, so altered,
"amended, or repealed, or a NEW CANON MADE, PROMULGED, AND
"EXECUTED, altered, amended, or substituted in place thereof, so by
"them from time to time conferred, treated, debated, considered,
"consulted, and agreed upon, shall and MAY SET DOWN IN WRITING,
"IN SUCH FORM as heretofore hath been accustomed, and THE SAME
"SO SET DOWN IN WRITING TO EXHIBIT and deliver, or cause to be
"exhibited and delivered unto Us, to the end that We, upon mature
"consideration by Us to be taken thereupon, MAY ALLOW, APPROVE,
"CONFIRM, AND RATIFY, OR OTHERWISE DISALLOW, ANNIHILATE, AND
"MAKE VOID THE WHOLE OR ANY PART OF THE SAID CANON, so to be
"by force of these presents altered or amended, considered, con-
"sulted, MADE, PROMULGED, EXECUTED, and agreed upon, as We shall
"think fit and requisite and convenient. Provided always that the
"said Canon so to be altered or amended, considered, consulted,
"made, promulged, executed, and agreed upon, as aforesaid, be not
"contrary or repugnant to the doctrines, orders, and ceremonies of
"the Church of England already established. Provided also, and
"Our express will, pleasure, and command is, that the said Canon,
"or any part thereof, so to be by the force of these presents altered

"or amended, considered, consulted, made, promulged, executed,
"and agreed upon, shall not be of any force, effect, or validity in
"law, but only so much thereof as after such time as We by Our
"Letters Patent under Our Great Seal shall allow, approve, and
"confirm the same, anything before in these presents contained
"to the contrary thereof on any wise notwithstanding. In witness,
"&c. Witness, &c., the Twenty-seventh day of June.

"By Her Majesty's Command,

"EDMUNDS."

A similar Licence [Chron. Conv. Upper House Cant., June 28, 1865, pp. 2353–5] was issued in the year 1865. And the reader's special attention is requested to the contents of the above-recited Licence, as such an instrument is of high Constitutional importance and very deep significance. It must also be remembered that these documents, constructed in the Crown Office, have the advantage of being drawn under the direction of the Attorney and Solicitor-Generals, and moreover pass under the inspection of the Home Secretary, an official who, by the way, at least of late years, has been also himself a member of the learned profession. So that very high legal authority is in such cases accumulated.

Now it would be to impose too severe a strain on the patience and perseverance of any reader to request him to wade through the torrent of words and encounter the hurricane of verbiage which pervades the above-recorded instrument. In capital letters, therefore, those passages are printed which his eye may catch at a glance, and which will impart to him the information necessary for knowing what are the contents of the document, though no amount of perseverance and no application of the most improved capacity could possibly enable him to reconcile the self-contradictions contained in it. By surveying, then, the passages printed in capitals, the reader will learn as follows:

(1) That the Convocation, in obedience to the original Royal Writ for Convention, had already "conferred together "and considered" of the proposed new Canon, a truth to which the Crown Office instrument bears testimony by the recital

of the recorded fact "verbatim." But this notwithstanding, the instrument proceeds to grant "liberty, licence, power, and "authority," to "confer, treat, debate, consider, consult, and "agree of and upon" the Canon in question. This certainly was an odd imagination, to give licence to do that which had already previously been done, and, having recited a past performance, to grant prospective liberty of a future approach towards acts already consummated. Nor was it indeed altogether respectful to the Crown for its own officials to draft an instrument giving leave to the Convocation to do that which the Crown had previously by the Royal Writ for convention required that assembly to do; that is, to "treat of, "agree to, and conclude upon" "urgent affairs concerning "Us, the security and defence of the Church of England". [Vid. supra, Royal Writ, Append. A. III.].

(2) The reader will also learn, from an inspection of the passages printed in capitals, that Licence was granted to "make, promulge, and execute" the new Canon, and that after the new Canon was "made, promulged, and executed," it should be "set down in writing," in its enacted form. And further, the reader will learn that Licence was granted to the Convocation "to exhibit and deliver" the Canon, "made," "promulged," and "executed," to the Sovereign, to the end that the Crown might "allow, approve, confirm, and ratify, "or otherwise disallow, annihilate, and make void, the whole "or any part of the said Canon."

These were beyond question curious methods of inversion, as it is directed that the new Canon should be first "made," that is "enacted," in due Synodical form, as described above, p. 33; secondly, "promulged," that is transmitted to the several Ecclesiastical tribunals throughout the land for the guidance of the Judges there; thirdly, "executed," that is enforced and carried into effect in the cases of litigants; and then subsequently should be "set down in writing" and exhibited to the Crown for "allowance, approval, confirma- "tion, and ratification," or for "disallowance, annihilation, and avoidance." After these ingenious problems of inversion carefully worked out, and these odd retrograde excursions of a Cabinet Minister and of members of the learned profession when engaged on Ecclesiastical matters of high Constitutional importance,

> "Quis neget arduis
> "Pronos relabi posse rivos
> "Montibus, et Tiberim reverti?"

The truth is, giving these learned persons the credit for originally understanding the subject they dealt with, it is plain that they subsequently lost themselves hopelessly in their own mazes of verbiage, for they certainly contrived to construct a labyrinth of circumlocution transcending the skill of Dædalus, and defying human intelligence to discover either means of ingress or of egress. But if, on the other hand, they did not at the outset understand the subject they dealt with, and if the same intellectual incapacity should afflict the Crown Office officials and their legal advisers when the next Licence is required, it would be no less than desirable that they should seek some external aid for the proper performance of their special duties.

It may here be added by way of sequel that two "Letters "of Business" and four "Licences" have been issued from the Crown Office since the year 1861 inclusive, but in no one of the six cases was the instrument rightly and constitutionally constructed. To be specific on this head. The two "Letters of Business" were overloaded with matter wholly irrelevant, altogether misleading, and very mischievous, as above shewn, Append. C. III. The two Licences just above mentioned were self-contradictory by the methods of inversion applied, as we have seen. And the other two Licences were noway required, and if required would have been utterly worthless for any purpose whatsoever, as they contained no "Assent and Licence" to "enact," "promulge," or "execute" [Chron. Conv. Lower House Cant., Feb. 13, 1872, p. 239; Upper House, July 7, 1874, p. 298.] Beyond all question, the Cyclopean blows delivered by the legal artificers in their labours to forge disabilities for the Church have recoiled ruthlessly on their own heads, to the serious injury of their intellectual organs—

> .... "Nec lex est justior ulla,
> "Quàm necis artifices arte perire suâ."

APPENDIX. 373

These accumulated facts corroborate the truth of an assertion made at page 212 of this volume, to the effect that the Ecclesiastical atmosphere is uncongenial to the healthy exercise of the legal brain; and this is a truth in support of which considerable evidence has been already produced in pages 203-212 above inclusive.

There is an instrument to be mentioned in passing, by which the Crown has on occasion given "Assent" to Canons after "Enactment." But as this appears to be an unstatutable document, as before said [Supra, 146-7, and Append. D. II.], being involved in the issue of the "Licence" as intended by the Statute governing the case [25 Hen. VIII. 19], it is not needful here to insert a copy. Any curious enquirer, however, may find examples of such an instrument in Atterbury's "Rights," &c., pp. 601-2; Gibson's "Codex," pp. 993-4; and Sparrow's "Collections," pp. 337-73.

The sum of the whole matter seems to be this. The original Royal Writ for Convention [Supra, A. III.] is (1) not only the permission but the "command" to "treat of, agree to, and conclude upon" "difficult and urgent affairs concerning . . . . "the security and defence of the Church of England;" (2) the "Assent and Licence" [Supra, D. II.] is one instrument, giving permission to "enact, promulgate, and execute" Canons; (3) the subsequent "Letters Patent," or new invention of "Assent" following enactment, are an unnecessary appendage, and an unstatutable flourish of addition contrived in times since the enactment of the Statute governing the case, and never intended by its provisions nor warranted by them.

E.

ROYAL WRIT AND METROPOLITAN'S MANDATE FOR PROROGATION.

I.

Copy of a Writ of Queen Victoria for Proroguing a Convocation.

[Pearce, "Law of Convocation," p. 108, and note, p. 109.]

" Victoria, by the Grace of God of the United Kingdom of Great " Britain and Ireland Queen, Defender of the Faith: To the Most " Reverend Father in God, Our right trusty and well beloved

"Councillor, ——, by the same Grace Archbishop of —— &c., and
"Metropolitan, Greeting. Whereas We have lately, by Our Writ
"issued at Our command, ordered that the Convocation of the
"Clergy of your Province of ——, at the Cathedral Church of ——,
"or elsewhere, as it should seem expedient, should be begun and
"be holden on the Twenty-second day of September now next
"ensuing: Nevertheless, for certain urgent causes and considerations
"Us especially moving, We have thought fit that the said Convo-
"cation be prorogued until Wednesday, the Thirteenth day of
"October next, so that neither you Our Archbishop, nor the
"Bishops, Deans, Archdeacons, nor any other Ecclesiastical persons
"of your Province of ——, whom it concerns in this behalf, may
"by any means appear on the said Twenty-second day of September
"next, at the Cathedral Church of —— aforesaid, or elsewhere, as it
"should seem most convenient: We will also that you, the afore-
"said Archbishop, and all and singular the Bishops, Deans, Arch-
"deacons, and all other Ecclesiastical persons of your Province of
" ——, whom it does or shall concern in this behalf, be therefrom to
"Us wholly Discharged, commanding, and by the tenour of these
"presents firmly enjoining and requiring you, the aforesaid Arch-
"bishop, and all and singular the Bishops, Deans, Archdeacons,
"and all other Ecclesiastical persons whatsoever of your aforesaid
"Province of ——, whom it does or shall concern in this behalf, that
"on the said Thirteenth day of October next, at the aforesaid
"Cathedral Church of ——, or elsewhere, as it shall seem most
"expedient, you and every one of you personally appear and be
"present, and that in doing, executing, and performing all and
"singular the premisses, you be intent, advising, helping, and also
"obedient, as it behoves you. Witness Ourself, at Westminster, the
"Tenth day of August, in the Eleventh Year of Our Reign."

Convocations are by ancient custom prorogued by Royal Writ to the day following that to which Parliaments are prorogued.

II.

Copy of a Metropolitan's Mandate for Proroguing a Convocation.

[Private Collections.]

"We, John Bird, by Divine Providence Archbishop of Canter-
"bury, Primate of all England, and Metropolitan, President of the
"present Provincial Synod or Convocation of the Bishops and
"Clergy of the Province of Canterbury, do by this present writing
"continue and prorogue the said sacred Provincial Synod or
"Convocation, and continue and prorogue all and singular the
"certificates or returns already made and delivered, and all others
"which have not yet been made and delivered in the same state in
"which they are now, until Thursday, the Nineteenth day of August

"next ensuing, to a certain Upper Chamber, commonly called the
"Jerusalem Chamber, situate in the Deanery belonging to the
"Collegiate Church of St. Peter, Westminster, with further
"continuation and prorogation of days then following and places,
"if it shall be necessary to be done in this behalf.
"J. B. CANTUAR."

Each day's assembly of a Convocation is termed a Session; and on each day the Convocation is prorogued to some future day at the Metropolitan's discretion by the foregoing instrument.

F.

ROYAL WRIT FOR DISSOLUTION.

I.

Copy of a Writ of King Henry VIII. for Dissolving a Convocation. A.D. 1544.

[Pearce, "Law of Convocation," p. 109.]

" Henricus, etc.: Reverendissimo in Christo Patri Thomæ eâdem
"gratiâ Cantuariensi Archiepiscopo, totius Angliæ Primati, et
"Metropolitano, Salutem. Cum præsens Convocatio Cleri vestræ
"Cantuariensis Provinciæ apud Sanctum Paulum, London, de
"mandato nostro per breve nostrum jam modo tent. et instans exstitit;
"certis tamen urgentibus causis et considerationibus nos specialitèr
"moventibus de advisamento concilii nostri, ipsam præsentem
"Convocationem hac instante die Lunæ, duximus dissolvendam.
"Et ideò Vobis mandamus quod eandem præsentem Convocationem
"hac instante die Lunæ apud Sanctum Paulum prædictum debito
"modo, absque dilatione dissolvatis dissolvive faciatis, prout con-
"venit, significantes ex parte nostrâ universis et singulis Episcopis
"necnon Archidiaconis, Decanis, et omnibus aliis personis Eccle-
"siasticis quibuscunque dictæ vestræ Cantuariensis Provinciæ,
"quorum interest aut interesse poterit in hâc parte, quòd ipsi et
"eorum quilibet huic mandato nostro exequend. intendentes sint et
"obedientes prout decet. Teste Meipso apud Westmonasterium
"Tricessimo primo die Martii, Anno Regni Nostri Tricessimo
"quinto."

II.

Copy of a Writ of Queen Victoria for Dissolving a Convocation. A.D. 1874.

[Chron. Conv. Jan. 29, 1874, p. 2.]

" Victoria, by the Grace of God of the United Kingdom of Great
" Britain and Ireland Queen, Defender of the Faith: To the Most
" Reverend Father in God, Our right trusty and well-beloved Coun-

"cillor, Archibald Campbell, by the same Grace Archbishop of
"Canterbury, Primate of all England, and Metropolitan, Greeting.
"Whereas, by the advice of Our Council, We have thought fit that
"the present Convocation of the Clergy of your Province of Canter-
"bury be this day dissolved, We therefore command you that this
"present Convocation, at the Cathedral Church of St. Paul, London,
"or otherwise, as it should seem most convenient, in lawful man-
"ner, without delay, you dissolve, or cause to be dissolved, as is
"most convenient, signifying on our part to all and singular Bishops,
"and also Deans, Archdeacons, and all other Ecclesiastical persons
"whatsoever of your said Province of Canterbury, whom it does or
"shall concern in their behalf, that they and every of them be
"intent and obedient in the performance of this command, as it
"behoves them. Witness Ourself, at Westminster, the Twenty-
"sixth day of January, in the Thirty-seventh Year of Our Reign.
"E. ROMILLY."

On the receipt of the above Writ by the Metropolitan, a Commission under his Seal is sent to the Vicar-General of the Province, who, at its accustomed place of meeting, duly dissolves the Convocation in conformity with ancient practice.

G.

"SUBMISSION OF THE CLERGY," AND EXTRACTS FROM "CLERGY SUBMISSION ACT."

To the above documents shall be added here the "Submis-
"sion of the Clergy," and those parts of the "Submission
"Act" [25 Hen. VIII. 19] which govern the relations be-
tween the Convocations and the Crown, in order that the reader may convince himself on perusal that the contents of that Act have been rightly above interpreted.

The Submission of the Clergy, and those parts of 25 Hen. VIII. 19 which, as confirmed in Queen Elizabeth's reign, alone Statutably govern the relations between the Convocations and the Crown.

[From a Copy in Lord Longueville's Library, Conc. M. B. iii. 749.]

"We .... Do offer and promise, in verbo sacerdotii, here unto Your
"Highness, submitting ourselves most humbly to the same, that
"we will never from henceforth *enact, put in ure, promulge, or
"execute any NEW Canons or Constitution Provincial, or any new NEW
"Ordinance* Provincial or Synodal, in our Convocation or Synod in
"time coming [which Convocation is always, hath been, and must
"be, assembled only by Your high Commandment or Writ], unless

"Your Highness, by Your Royal Assent, shall license us to assemble our Convocation, and to *make, promulge, and execute* such Constitutions and Ordinances as shall be made in the same, and thereto give Your Royal Assent and authority. Secondarily, that whereas divers of the Constitutions, Ordinances, and Canons Provincial or Synodal which HATH BIN HERETOFORE ENACTED be thought to be not only much prejudicial to Your Prerogative Royal, but also over much onerous to Your Highness' subjects, Your Clergy aforesaid is contented, if it may stand with Your Highness' pleasure, that it be committed to the examination and judgment of Your Grace and of thirty-two persons, whereof sixteen to be of the Upper and Nether House of the Temporalty, and other sixteen of the Clergy, all to be appointed and chosen by Your Most Noble Grace. So that finally, whichsoever of the said Constitutions, Ordinances, or Canons, Provincial or Synodal, shall be thought and determined by Your Grace, and by the most part of the said thirty-two persons, not to stand with God's laws and the laws of your Realm, the same to be abrogated and taken away by Your Grace and the Clergy, and such of them as shall be seen by Your Grace, and by the most part of the said thirty-two persons, to stand with God's laws and the laws of Your Realm, to stand in full strength and power; Your Grace's most Royal Assent and authority once impetrate and fully given to the same."

This then was the Convocational "Submission of the Clergy" carried up to King Henry VIII., and accepted by that Sovereign on Thursday, May 16, 1532. The promises contained in it amount briefly to this, that they would not enact any NEW Canons without Royal *Assent and Licence*, and that the OLD Canons should be reviewed by the King and a body of Thirty-two Commissioners, with a view to a reform of the laws Ecclesiastical. This was the footstone of the "Clergy Submission Act," 25 Hen. VIII. 19, which two years afterwards embodying these promises, inaugurated that instrument, "*the Royal Licence*," which has been above considered [Appendix D].

In 1534, N. S., in consequence of a representation of the House of Commons to King Henry VIII., and as a sequel to the Synodical deliberations and conclusions above recounted, the Statute 25 Hen. VIII. 19 was enacted. And of course its provisions must be read in the light of those preceding events. So much of the Act 25 Hen. VIII. 19 as is pertinent to the present purpose is here given from an authentic source.

EXTRACTS FROM THE "CLERGY SUBMISSION ACT,"
25 HEN. VIII. 19.

[Conc. M. B. iii. 770.]

"A ceste bille avec une provision annexé les seigneurs sont
"assentuz."

"Where the Kyngis humble and obedient subjects, &c.

[Preamble.]

. . . .

. . . .

"Be yt therefore nowe enacted by auctoritie of this present
"Parliament, according to the said submission and peticion of the
"said Cleregy, that they, ne enny of them, from hencefurth shall
"presume *to attempt, alege, clayme, or put in ure* any Constitucions or
"Ordinanncys Provinciall or Sinodalys, or any other Canons, nor
"shall *enact, promulge, or execute* any suche Canons, Constitucions,
"or Ordinannce Provinciall, by whatsoever name or names they
"may be called, in their Convocacions in tyme commyng, whiche
"alway shal be assembled by auctorite of the Kyngis Wrytt, oneles
"the same Cleregy may have the Kingis moste ROIALL ASSENT
"AND LICENCE to make, promulge, and execute suche Canons,
"Constitucions, and Ordinanncys Provinciall or Sinodall, upon pain
"of every one of the said Cleregy doyng contrary to this Act and
"being thereof convicte, to suffer empresonament and make fyne
"at the King's will."

[*Direction for Review of Ecclesiastical Laws by thirty-two Commissioners.*]

. . . .

. . . .

[*Saving Clause for Royal Prerogative, Customs, Laws, and Statutes of the Realm.*]

. . . .

. . . .

"Provided also that suche Canons, Constitucions, Ordynannces
"Provincyall and Synodalls, *beyng allredy made*, which be not con-
"trariannt nor repugnant to the Lawes, Statutes, and Customes of this
"Realme, nor to the damage or hurte of the King's Prerogative
"Royall, shall now still be used and executyd as thei were affore
"the makeing of this Act, tyll suche tyme as they be vewed,
"serched, or otherwise ordered and determined by the said xxxii.
"persons, or the more part of them, according to the tenour,
"fourme, and effect of this present Act.

"Soit baillé aux communes. A cest provision les communes sont
"assentez."

On a perusal of the "Submission" and the Statute above quoted, when compared, it is manifestly plain that under the terms of this Act, the "Royal Assent and Licence" is statutably necessary only (1) for "attempting, alledging, claiming, or "putting in ure," i.e. enforcing in the Spiritual Courts, OLD Canons [with provisos as to their remaining "in viridi "observantiâ" until reviewed]; (2) for "enacting, promulging, "and executing" NEW Canons. But that under the terms of this Statute the "Royal Assent and Licence" is not required for any other purposes whatsoever than for those defined in the Act; inasmuch as this is a highly penal Statute, entailing penalties no less than fine and imprisonment at the Sovereign's will, and therefore must be construed strictly within the terms of the letter. And that this limitation of requirement has always been held to exist in past ages, is manifest from the fact that on no occasion previous to the years 1872 and 1874 was a Royal Licence ever issued save for purposes of Canonical legislation. And on those two recent occasions its issue was merely the outcome of official blundering, and of a total misapprehension of Constitutional Law by the authorities in the Crown Office, by the Law Officers of the Crown, and by the respective Cabinets of the day.

H.

ROYAL WRIT CONTAINING THE "PRÆMUNIENTES" CLAUSE FOR SUMMONING SPECIFIED CLERGY TO THE BRITISH PARLIAMENT.

Here an instrument is appended which is noway connected with Convocations, being a Writ for summoning Parliament, but which is added here for two reasons: (1) Because it has been ignorantly confused and identified with Convocational history; and (2) because it is a Constitutional curiosity, being still at this time continually issued by the Crown, but as continually disobeyed by those to whom it is directed.

The following Writ, whenever a new Parliament is summoned, is directed to the two Metropolitans personally, and to each Bishop personally who has a seat in Parliament, citing each severally as a Peer of the Realm, to attend there.

It contains a Royal command, denominated the "Præmuni-"entes" Clause [Vide supra, pp. 26-28]. And by it the Sovereign directs that each Prelate should provide that some specified Clergy and three elected Proctors should give their attendance in Parliament. The reader is requested to bear in mind that this instrument is in no way connected with the Convocations, but is only inserted here because it has been confusedly mixed up ignorantly with their history.

I.

Copy of a Writ summoning certain Clergy to Parliament, as issued by King Edward I. A.D. 1295.

[Conc. M. B. ii. 215. Wake's "Auth. Christ. Prin." 363-5.]
" Breve regium Archiepiscopo Cantuar., directum de Parliamento
" tenendo apud Westmonasterium cum clausulâ 'Præmunientes.'"
—Ex Rot. Claus. 23 Ed. I. M. 3, dorso.

" Rex venerabili in Christo patri R. eâdem gratiâ Cant. Archiepis-
" copo totius Angliæ Primati, Salutem. Sicut lex justissima providâ
" circumspectione sacrorum principum stabilita hortatur et statuit,
" ut quod omnes tangit ab omnibus approbetur; sic et innuit
" evidentèr, ut communibus periculis per remedia provisa communiter
" obvietur. Sanè satis nosti, et jam est, ut credimus, per universa
" mundi climata divulgatum, qualitèr Rex Franciæ de terrâ nostrâ
" Vasconiæ nos fraudulentèr et cautelosè decepit eam nobis nequitèr
" detinendo : nunc verò prædictis fraude et nequitiâ non contentus,
" ad expugnationem regni nostri classe maximâ et bellatorum
" copiosâ multitudine congregatis, cum quibus regnum nostrum et
" regni ejusdem incolas hostilitèr jam invasit, linguam Anglicanam,
" si conceptæ iniquitatis proposito detestabili potestas correspondeat
" [quod Deus avertat] omninò de terrâ delere proponit. Quia igitur
" prævisa jacula minùs lædunt, et res vestra maximè sicut cæterorum
" regni ejusdem concivium agitur in hâc parte ; Vobis mandamus in
" fide et dilectione, quibus nobis tenemini, firmitèr injungentes quòd
" die dominicâ proximè post festum Sancti Martini in hyeme proximè
" futurum apùd Westminster personalitèr intersitis; 'Præmunientes'
" priorem et Capitulum Ecclesiæ vestræ, Archidiaconum, totumque
" Clerum vestræ Diœceseos ; facientes quòd iidem Prior et Archi-
" diaconus in propriis personis suis, et dictum Capitulum per unum,
" idemque Clerus per duos Procuratores idoneos plenam et suffi-
" cientem potestatem ab ipsis Capitulo et Clero habentes unà
" vobiscum intersint, modis omnibus tunc ibidem ad tractandum
" ordinandum et faciendum nobiscum, et cum cæteris Prælatis
" proceribus et aliis incolis regni nostri, qualiter hujusmodi periculis
" et excogitatis malitiis obviandum.

" Teste Rege apùd Wengeham, 30 die Septembris."

Like Writs, from the year 1295 down to the year 1880, when the present Parliament was convened, have been continuously issued, save during the time of the Great Rebellion. Copies of such instruments, of various dates, are in existence. One of the year 1537, issued by King Henry VIII., may be seen in Wake's "State," &c., Append. 225. One of the year 1571, issued by Queen Elizabeth, is given in Wake's "Authority of Christian Princes," p. 365. Of one issued by King William III. in 1702 I possess a copy, contained in a bound volume of pamphlets of that time. And a copy of one issued by Queen Victoria, and transcribed from a House of Lords' official copy, is below given. They all are virtually identical.

II.

Copy of a Writ summoning certain Clergy to Parliament, as issued by Queen Victoria. A.D. 1866.

[House of Lords' Official Copy, in my possession.]

"Victoria, by the Grace of God of the United Kingdom of Great
"Britain and Ireland Queen, Defender of the Faith: To the Right
"Reverend Father in God, John, Bishop of Lichfield, Greeting.
"Whereas, by the advice and assent of Our Council, for certain arduous
"and urgent affairs concerning Us, the state and defence of Our said
"United Kingdom and the Church, We have ordered a certain
"Parliament to be holden at Our City of Westminster, on the
"Fifteenth day of August next ensuing, and there to treat and have
"conference with the Prelates, Great Men, and Peers of Our Realm:
"We, strictly enjoining, command you, by the faith and love by
"which you are bound to Us, that the weightiness of the said affairs
"and imminent perils considered [waiving all excuses], you be, at
"the said day and place, personally present with Us and with the
"said Prelates, Great Men, and Peers, to treat and give your
"counsel upon the affairs aforesaid, and this as you regard Us and
"Our honour and the safety and defence of the said United Kingdom and Church, and dispatch of the said affairs in no wise do
"you omit; Forewarning the Dean and Chapter of your Church of
"Lichfield, and the Archdeacons and all the Clergy of your Diocese,
"that they the said Dean and Archdeacons in their proper persons,
"and the said Chapter by one, and the said Clergy by two meet
"Proctors, severally having full and sufficient authority from them
"the said Chapter and Clergy, at the said day and place be
"personally present, to consent to those things which then and there
"by the Common Counsel of Our said United Kingdom [by the

"favour of the Divine clemency] shall happen to be ordained.
"Witness Ourselves, at Westminster, the Sixth day of July, in the
"Twenty-ninth Year of Our Reign."

This Writ, containing the "Præmunientes" clause, though now neglected by those to whom it is directed, was aforetime respectfully obeyed. In the issue of this Writ the Sovereign makes no distinction as regards Provinces. It is directed separately to each Metropolitan, and to every Bishop in England and Wales having a seat in Parliament. From the time of its first inauguration in 1295, the archives of the different Episcopal Sees contain records of its constant execution [See Atterb. "Rights," &c., pp. 248 seq., and 566 seq.]. Indeed, so instructive are these records that in some instances they hand down to this day the very names of the men who were elected as Parliamentary Proctors. Thus we find, in various Dioceses, John de Theneto holding that office in 1296, J. de Harrington in 1323, John Menys in 1503, Henry de Pynkenee in 1535; and the author above quoted asserts that in Riley's "Placita" more than a hundred of these records, of later date, may be found; in many such instances the names being recorded of the Parliamentary Proctors elected. Records subsequent to the dates above given of these Parliamentary Proctors may also be found in many Diocesan Registries. Such are records of the years 1536, 1539–1541, and 1542. In the latter year, George Carew and Thomas Brerewood were elected in the Exeter Diocese; and proceeding onwards, in 1676 Richard Cumberland and John Dobson were chosen as the Parliamentary Proctors for the Diocese of Peterborough.

It appears that, at the discretion of the electors, the same persons were elected as Proctors for Convocation and for Parliament; but this practice was clearly not universal, as is plain from the York Register, which shews that in 1539 one set of Proctors was elected for attendance in Convocation, and another set for Parliament [Atterb. "Rights," p. 617].

That this Royal Writ, so continuously issued through many ages of English history, dating from the thirteenth century to the year 1880, should now be obstinately disobeyed is surely a Constitutional solœcism. One whole batch of Writs for the assembly of the British Parliament is absolutely ignored. And it is a reasonable enquiry, and no fair mind can deny it, whether in the presence of such neglect the Parliament at this day existing is fully and duly constituted. If the whole batch of Writs directed by the Crown to Sheriffs of Counties, or the whole batch directed to Mayors of Boroughs, was neglected, and no returns made, there is but little doubt what reply would be made to such a query. And as this parallel case is patently present, it would be beyond measure instructive, to some people at least, to hear this question fairly argued, with the interest which might be added to it by the aid of all the ingenuity, research, and learning, at least in secular respects, which abound in the neighbourhood of the Temple and Lincoln's Inn.

One of the acutest men of the last century, and one as deeply versed in Constitutional history as ever held a pen, thus wrote: "Not only has the King a right of thus calling "the Clergy to attend, but the Clergy also have a right to "attend, and the Lords and Commons have a right of being "attended by them." And subsequently this author makes a humble request to their Lordships the Bishops, that "they "would please to consider of how great moment it is towards "preserving the Constitution, and the rights of their Clergy, "to preserve the regular execution of their Writs of Summons "for the Parliament, and a remembrance of it in the records "of their Sees."

Printed at the University Press, Oxford
By HORACE HART, *Printer to the University*

By the same Author.

ENGLAND'S SACRED SYNODS: a Constitutional History of the Convocations of the Clergy, from the Earliest Records of Christianity in Britain to the date of the Promulgation of the present Book of Common Prayer. With a list of all Councils held in England. (1855.)
London: RIVINGTONS.

THE DUTY OF THE CIVIL POWER TO PROMOTE THE FAITH OF THE NATIONAL CHURCH: an Assize Sermon, preached at Shrewsbury, March 23, 1857.
London: RIVINGTONS.

THE NATIONAL CHURCH: an Answer to an Essay on "The National Church" in Essays and Reviews. (1861.)
Loudon: SAUNDERS, OTLEY, & Co.

ECCLESIA VINDICATA: a Treatise on Appeals in Matters Spiritual. Dedicated, by permission, to the Earl of Derby, K.G., Chancellor of the University of Oxford. (1862.)
London: SAUNDERS, OTLEY, & Co.

CONCIO AD CLERUM: the Latin Sermon preached in St. Paul's Cathedral, London, February 2, 1866, at the opening of the Convocation of Canterbury. Printed by command of the Archbishop.
London: RIVINGTONS.

THE KINGDOM NOT OF THIS WORLD: some Remarks on passages touching Church Government in the Charge of the Bishop of St. David's. (1866.)
London: RIVINGTONS.

THE SWORD AND THE KEYS—THE CIVIL POWER IN ITS RELATION TO THE CHURCH; with Appendix containing the Statutes which give final Ecclesiastical Appeal to the Judicial Committee of Privy Council, and also all Judgments delivered by that tribunal since 1865. (1869.) Second Edition, published by E. C. Union, 1881.
London: RIVINGTONS.

THE CRISIS IN THE CHURCH OF IRELAND: a Letter to the Bishop of Derry, on the Constitution of Diocesan and Provincial Synods. (1869.)
London: RIVINGTONS.

ON THE INTRODUCTION OF LAITY INTO SYNODS: a Letter to Lord Alwyne Compton, Prolocutor of the Canterbury Convocation. (1880.)
Oxford and London: PARKER & Co.

ON THE COURT OF FINAL APPEAL, AS PROPOSED BY THE COMMISSIONERS ON ECCLESIASTICAL COURTS. (1884.)
Oxford and London: PARKER & Co.

MR. WHITAKER'S PUBLICATIONS.

THE BOOK OF PRIVATE PRAYER: Short Forms of Daily Prayer. Cloth, 6d.; or neatly bound, with gilt edges, price 1s. 6d.

THE BOOK OF PRIVATE PRAYER: Forms of Prayer for Use Twice Daily. Cloth, 2s.; neatly bound, with gilt edges, 3s. 6d.

THE BOOK OF PRIVATE PRAYER: Arranged for Use Seven Times a Day. *A New Edition in preparation.*

*** Copies of the First Edition of the "Seven Times a Day" Book of Private Prayer may still be obtained. Cloth, 1s.; or neatly bound, with gilt edges, price 2s. 6d.

The above are issued by Direction of the Lower House of Convocation of the Province of Canterbury.

THE RULE OF PRAYER: An Easy Explanation of the Lord's Prayer. Chiefly intended for the Use of Young Persons. 32mo, cloth, 1s.; or neatly bound in Turkey roan, with gilt edges, 2s.

DEVOTIONAL READINGS FOR FAMILY PRAYER Adapted to the Course of the Christian Year. With a Form of Responsive Devotions for the Household for Every Day in the Week. By the Rev. J. J. DILLON, M.A., Rector of Aghade, in Diocese of Leighlin. Vol. I. MORNING. Vol. II. EVENING. Two Volumes, imperial 32mo, cloth, 6s.; Turkey roan, gilt edges, 9s.

Post 8vo, cloth limp, each 2s.

BIBLE READINGS FOR FAMILY PRAYERS. By the Rev. W. H. RIDLEY, M.A., Author of "Holy Communion."

GENESIS AND EXODUS. | ST. LUKE AND ST. JOHN.
ST. MATTHEW AND ST. MARK. | THE ACTS OF THE APOSTLES.

Also by the same Author.

ON PRAYING: The Necessity and Advantage of Diligent Prayer. 18mo, cloth, red edges, 9d.

THE PATH OF DUTY: A few Plain Directions for more worthily performing—I. OUR DUTY TOWARDS GOD; II. OUR DUTY TOWARDS OUR NEIGHBOUR. 18mo, cloth, 1s.

NEW WORKS AND NEW EDITIONS.

A NEW EDITION, with Additions, revised by the Author.
RIDLEY ON THE HOLY COMMUNION. Printed on fine thick paper, cloth, red edges, 1s.; Turkey roan, gilt edges, 2s.

REVISED EDITION, in very large type and strongly bound in limp cloth, price 7d.
THE HOLY COMMUNION. PART I. ITS NATURE AND BENEFITS. With a Notice of some common Objections to receiving it. PART II. AN EXPLANATION OF WHAT IS REQUIRED OF THOSE WHO COME TO THE LORD'S SUPPER. In plain Language. By the late Rev. W. H. RIDLEY, M.A., Rector of Hambleden, Bucks; Hon. Canon of Christ's Church, Oxford.

Canon Ridley's "Holy Communion" has now been many years in use in thousands of parishes: no other work has been found so generally acceptable. The plain, forcible language in which it is written and the sound practical advice it contains combine to render the book a great favourite, especially among the poorer classes.

CONFIRMATION AND FIRST COMMUNION. PART I. THE NATURE, ORIGIN AND BENEFITS OF CONFIRMATION. With Aids to Meditation for Young Persons preparing for that Holy Rite. PART II. PREPARATION FOR CONFIRMATION. PART III. PREPARATION FOR FIRST COMMUNION. Uniform in size and type with "Ridley on the Holy Communion." Cloth, 9d.; Turkey roan, gilt edges, 2s.

THE NARROW WAY. A Complete Manual of Devotion. With a Guide to Confirmation and Holy Communion. Two Hundred and Forty-fifth Thousand. Price, cloth, 6d.; or neatly bound in Turkey roan, with gilt edges, 1s. 6d.

THE NARROW WAY. Printed in large type, upon good paper, cloth, 1s.; Turkey roan, gilt edges, 2s.

"The two new editions of *The Narrow Way* will, no doubt, make this deservedly popular manual of doctrine and devotion more popular than ever. Both are admirably printed and tastefully bound. The book is too well known to need description or praise. Intended specially for the use of the young, and written in clear, simple language, it is suited for persons of any age. There is, perhaps, no book of the size and price which is so complete a guide in doctrine and duty. It is valuable as a gift to confirmation candidates or young communicants. The sick find it all they need to help them in gaining knowledge of the truth, and to guide them in self-examination and prayer."—*Gospeller.*

"I must thank you for the new editions of *The Narrow Way.* I have used the book for years, finding no book so useful for all purposes in parish work. It has so much in it, and not too much upon any one subject; and all is so well and clearly stated that it suits all ages and all needs. Most works have to be supplemented by some other book; but *The Narrow Way* goes over the ground of Christian faith and duty with great completeness. I give it to confirmation candidates, and to persons preparing for Communion; to enquirers who wish to learn what to believe and do, and how to pray. And I find it a most helpful companion to the sick and troubled. The Introductions and Devotions are taken from the best sources; and there is a good index which can be marked according to the needs of those who use the book. The great drawback hitherto, has been the rough binding and the poor printing. Now, the new books are made attractive, and the clearness of the type leaves nothing to be desired. I am glad to hear of the number of thousands that have been sold, and am sure that the sale must go on increasing."—*From a* CLERGYMAN.

THE BOOK OF COMMON PRAYER and THE NARROW WAY. Bound in One neat Volume, price in Turkey roan, gilt edges, 2s. With gilt cross stamped on side same price.

THE RULE OF FAITH. Being an Easy Exposition of the Apostles' Creed. Chiefly based upon the Work of Bishop PEARSON. 32mo, cloth, 6d.

THE RULE OF LIFE. Being an Easy Exposition of the Ten Commandments. 32mo, cloth, 6d.

NEW WORKS AND NEW EDITIONS.

THE DAILY ROUND
MEDITATION, PRAISE AND PRAYER,
Adapted to the Course of the Christian Year.

Ten Editions of this Work are now ready:

1. Demy 48mo, Cloth, 3s.; Morocco, 5s.
2. Demy 48mo, with Red Border lines and Red Initials, Cloth, 3s. 6d.; Morocco, 5s. 6d.
3. Demy 32mo, Cloth, 3s.; Turkey Roan, gilt edges, 4s.; Morocco, 5s. 6d.
4. Demy 32mo, with Red Border lines and Red Initials, Cloth, 3s. 6d.; Turkey roan, gilt edges, 4s. 6d.; Morocco, 6s.
5. *Imperial 32mo, Cloth, red edges, 3s.; Turkey Roan, gilt edges, 4s. 6d.; Morocco, 6s.
6. Royal 24mo, Cloth, 3s. 6d.; Turkey Roan, gilt edges, 5s.; Morocco, 6s. 6d.
7. Royal 24mo, with Red Border lines and Red Initials, Cloth, 4s. 6d.; Turkey Roan, gilt edges, 6s.; Morocco, 7s. 6d.
8. *Foolscap 8vo, Cloth, red edges, 4s. 6d.; Turkey Roan, gilt edges, 6s.; Morocco, 9s.
9. Crown 8vo, Rubricated; a beautiful PRESENTATION VOLUME, Cloth, 7s. 6d.; Turkey Roan, gilt edges, 10s.; Morocco, 14s.
10. Demy 8vo, Large Type, a most acceptable Present to Aged Persons, Cloth, 10s. 6d.; Morocco, 18s.

* *The Editions thus marked are ordinarily kept in stock by every Bookseller.*

The late BISHOP OF MANCHESTER in writing of the work says:—"I have examined and tested 'The Daily Round' rather carefully, and find it to be a book after my own heart, calm, sober, well-proportioned, and with an eminently healthy and firm grasp of Christian truth. It appears to me to be framed according to that 'sound rule of faith' and that 'sober standard of feeling' than which the saintly author of the 'Christian Year' says 'there is nothing of so much consequence in matters of practical religion,' and which are in such entire harmony with the spirit of the Church of England. It is a book likely to be of much service to many souls, and I wish for it a circulation proportionate to its usefulness."

The late ARCHBISHOP OF CANTERBURY:—"I have examined the book with great interest, and I am glad to be able to testify that those portions of it which I have read seem to me well suited for the purpose for which they have been compiled. I wish the volume all success, and trust that by God's blessing it may be found serviceable to many."

The "Daily Round" *is also recommended by the present Archbishop of Canterbury.*

The late BISHOP OF LONDON:—"When I wrote before I was able only to thank you for sending 'The Daily Round.' Having now used the book from time to time, I can from my own experience recommend it to those who find it helpful to have a note struck to lead their meditations and prayer at leisure moments."

The "Daily Round" *is also recommended by the present Bishop of London.*

"Nearly every Bishop of all Schools of the Church of England has expressed approval of 'The Daily Round.' To each day of the Church's year is devoted a single page, not of a sermon nor of a prayer, but of meditation; and each page has five parts—some words of Scripture, a statement of what those words mean, some thoughts and reflections on practical points, three or four lines of a short and well-conceived collect, and a verse of a hymn. Even a slow reader need not devote more than five minutes per diem to each page; and we shall not be surprised to find 'The Daily Round' growing into a companion to the Prayer Book, as dearly loved in our times as 'The Whole Duty of Man' was esteemed in the days of our great grandfathers."—*Examiner.*

"Those who feel the need for a manual of meditation, prayer and praise for daily use will prize this work. Under the conviction that religion is for the whole life, and for every hour of life, and not for its close or stray hours, the author has striven to help the reader to do his daily duty in the spirit of the Word of God. The plan followed is that suggested by the Church Calendar, so that a systematic consideration of Divine things is ensured."—*The Christian.*

"This work is aptly described as consisting of meditation, prayer and praise, adapted to the course of the Christian year, and contains a passage of Scripture, with a brief comment or meditation, and a verse for each day in the year. It has been well received, and may fairly be ranked amongst the best works of the class to which it belongs. Issued as it is in elegant binding, it forms a most suitable present for a Christian friend."—*Rock.*

DAILY LIFE
ITS TRIALS, DUTIES AND DIFFICULTIES.

SHORT PRACTICAL ESSAYS. By the Author of "The Daily Round." Fcap. 8vo, cloth, 4s. 6d.

NEW WORKS AND NEW EDITIONS.

THE UNCANONICAL AND APOCRYPHAL SCRIPTURES

Being the Additions to the Old Testament Canon which were included in the Ancient Greek and Latin Versions; the English Text of the Authorised Version; together with the Additional Matter found in the Vulgate and other Ancient Versions, Introductions to the several Books and Fragments, Marginal Notes and References, and a General Introduction to the Apocrypha. By the Rev. W. R. CHURTON, B.D., Fellow of King's College, Cambridge; Canon of the Cathedral of St. Albans, and Examining Chaplain to the Bishop. Crown 8vo, pp. 607, price 7s. 6d.; morocco, gilt edges, 14s.

"We strongly recommend to the notice of our readers the scholarlike and most beautifully printed edition of the Apocrypha which Canon Churton has provided for us."—*Church Quarterly.*

"The books of the Apocrypha were part of the Canon of the Alexandrian Jews, and are found in the Septuagint, not in a place by themselves, as if they were there merely on sufferance, but freely interspersed among the other books. Whether in this form they were made use of by the writers of the New Testament, as it is not improbable they would be, has been disputed; but the Epistle to the Hebrews at least seems to echo the ideas, and even the very words, of the Book of the Wisdom of Solomon. . . . In Scotland, it may be presumed that, except to students, these writings are scarcely known: but many will remember that, some years ago, the selection of a text from the Apocrypha, under the sanction of royalty itself, for the monument to the Prince Consort at Balmoral, called forth a storm of clerical indignation, and was strongly resented as an insult to 'Bible-loving Scotland.' . . . To each book there is an introduction, telling all that is known, or can be reasonably conjectured, as to its date and authorship; while there is also an admirable introduction to the entire collection, containing in a small compass much useful information. . . . In every way the work seems complete: and it is well printed and got up. The English reader could not desire a better edition of the Old Testament Apocrypha."—*Scotsman.*

THE GOSPEL STORY: A Plain Commentary on the Four

Holy Gospels. Containing the Narrative of our Blessed Lord's Life and Ministry, in simple Language. By the Rev. W. MICHELL, M.A. Two Volumes, fcap. 8vo, cloth, with Map of Palestine, 6s.

"Everyone who knows *The Gospel Story* will welcome the new edition. It is revised: it is improved in type and in binding: and it is sold at a lower price. The modest title of the book fails to give an idea of the great store of information and of sound theology that can be found in it. One of the foremost authorities in the English Church has declared it to be the best commentary on the Gospels we have. There are 907 pages in the two volumes, which contain 463 chapters. Hardly a question which would occur to an ordinary reader of the Gospels does not find clear, full treatment. The way in which deep matters of theology are dealt with so as to set forth the truth in plain form is something to thank God for. Those who use one book of religious reading can choose no better. Sunday School teachers will find it a help in trying to bring home to the young the lessons of our Lord's life and words. It is suited to the unlearned and the learned alike. It is so simple that no one can fail to understand it, and it is so full of matter so freshly and forcibly put that no one can fail to learn from it. There is a growing feeling of the value of the words that Christ spoke, and the works that He did which show Him to us. Those who wish for a trustworthy guide through the pages of the Gospels cannot do better than buy *The Gospel Story.*"—*The Gospeller.*

LIVES OF THE SAINTS. By Rev. S. BARING-GOULD, M.A.

Mr. WHITAKER *having purchased the Copyright of this popular Work, with the stock, is now preparing an entirely New Edition, with about Five Hundred beautiful Illustrations.*

The New Edition will form Seventeen Volumes, large crown 8vo, and will be issued in a handsome cloth binding. Each Volume contains the complete list of Saints for the month, except July, October, and November, which are in Two Volumes. Of Vol. XVI. (the Index) some copies will be printed on paper in tone and size uniform with the first edition, so that persons wishing to complete their sets may do so.

EMBLEMS OF SAINTS, by which they are distinguished in

Works of Art. By the late Very Rev. F. C. HUSENBETH, V. G. Provost of Northampton. Edited by the Rev. AUGUSTUS JESSOP. With numerous additions. (*Forming Vol. XVII. or Supplement to* BARING-GOULD.)

www.ingramcontent.com/pod-product-compliance
Lightning Source LLC
Chambersburg PA
CBHW022110290426
44112CB00008B/620